PRETENDING TO...

*Memories of my F... ... ... as on
Entertainer, Improv Comic, Actor,
Broadcaster, and Tour Guide*

By Christopher David Linnell

PRETENDING TO MAKE A LIVING

*Memories of my Four Decades as an
Entertainer, Improv Comic, Actor,
Broadcaster, and Tour Guide*

By Christopher David Linnell

ChristopherLinnell@HireAStar.net

www.*PretendingToMakeALiving*.com

© 2013 by Christopher David Linnell
Second Edition. All rights reserved.

ISBN-13: 978-1484951385
ISBN-10: 1484951387

Printed in the United States of America.

ACKNOWLEDGEMENTS

I would like to thank my parents, Dave and Marilyn Linnell, for their love and support, and for what they gave me, by way of example. My dad is an affable clown and the king of slapstick humor, with a gregarious personality that everyone loves. My mom has the quick wit, artistic eye, and attention to detail. They both supported me in my career as child and teen, and I love them dearly.

I also thank maternal grandmother, Elsa Ottilie Lieder-Hansen. After my Papa Fred died she became my best friend. We didn't agree on politics or religion, or much else for that matter, except for The Golden Rule. But she listened to me and I listened to her, and she was available to me 24/7 more than anyone else whenever I needed her. I loved her dearly and miss her terribly.

I'd also like to thank my long-suffering sister, Tammy, and both of my ex-wives, Carrie and Svetlana. It may seem strange to lump the three of them together, but each of them in turn served as my assistant and helped me with my many shows, and all three of them stood by (Carrie for eleven years) and loved me while I got all the attention. I haven't seen any of the three of them in years, but I love them all.

I must thank my long-suffering husband, Juan, who is truly the most talented artist in our home, and has survived a full decade of my escapades. Granted, I haven't been working as an entertainer as much in the past decade as I did in the first three, as I turned more to tours than to entertaining to make my living. But he's had one job for thirteen years, and I've had at least thirteen. On his job he's considered the best and is the most beloved. On my jobs I've only been the most memorable...for better or worse.

In particular, Juan sat alone in the house day and night for five months in the summer and fall of 2010 as I wrote my screenplay out on the patio in a cloud of cigar smoke, often from dawn to midnight, as I moved from the desk in my office to my desk in the garage to the table on the patio, depending on the weather. This manuscript entailed the same ordeal from January and into June of

2013. He wasn't happy about it, but we survived it. We've survived a lot together, and we've done a lot. Together Juan and I have worn more costumes to more events just for fun than I used in the whole thirty years of entertaining prior. He and I are Ying & Yang, each complementing the other's shortcomings.

I would also like to thank Victoria Webb (www.VictoriasWebb.com) for the headshot on page 141, and Ed Peoples (author of *The ZORN Conspiracy* and *The Searching*) for the 1989 picture of Crisco the Clown on page 29, as well as some of the early 1980s pictures of me as my celebrities beginning on page 294; most of the rest are self-portraits, including all those displayed on page 5. I also thank my proofreaders, Marilyn Linnell and Peggy Hanley. Russ and Michael worked on it, too, but Mom and Peg actually finished in time for publication.

My parents and grandmother all encouraged me to become a writer, as did my sixth grade teacher on Guam, Mr. Roy D. Hay, when I submitted to him a meticulously-researched thirty-two page term paper about the Great Depression. Mr. Hay gave me an A+ for that paper, as did my junior high, high school, and college history teachers. I got a lot of use out of that paper. Also encouraging me to become a writer was my high school English teacher, Larry Kenneth Potts, whose snarky critiques on my papers were priceless. The two of us have come full-circle now, as I am an author and he is a performing artist. He is a folk musician and recording artist; visit: www.LarryPottsMusic.com.

And I offer big thanks to my late, great buddy, Bill Soberanes, and his beautiful bride, Jane. They demonstrated that money is not the gauge of success; love and happiness is. I love and miss you, Bill & Jane.

TABLE OF CONTENTS

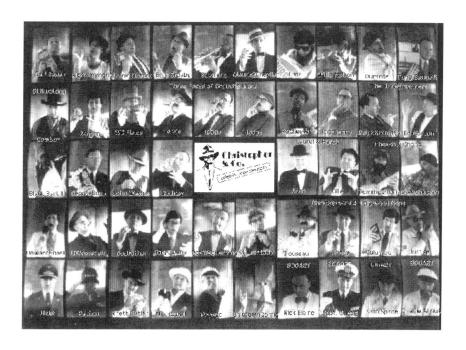

INTRODUCTION

Don't be fooled by the title. I have managed to make a living on and off for forty years as a performing artist (though not a particularly lucrative nor steady living). But I've always contended that acting in general, and doing celebrity impersonations specifically, is basically just about pretending to be someone else. Reporter Andrew Jowers used a similar expression in the April 29, 1992, edition of the *Santa Rosa Press Democrat* in the title of an article about my business, and I thought it appropriate here.

That word "memoir" sounds so stuffy; but that's what this amounts to. *Pretending to Make a Living* is a collection of my memories from six decades: A) working as an entertainer, performing as an improv comic, clown and puppeteer, singer, and doing stand-up and walk-around comedy and celebrity impersonations in private parties, promotions, fairs, festivals, and in corporate comedy; B) working in radio as an air personality, news writer and anouncer, and commercial writer, producer, and voice artist; C) working as a model, and as an actor in commercials, television, and movies; and D) working as a tour guide.

Because the chapters are arranged by subject rather than chronology, this book starts with a short biography to give you a timeline frame of reference. In that chapter I touch upon stories on which I expand later. Thereafter each chapter tells the story of a specific sort of professional activity. Therefore I jump back in time frequently to the roots of each separate pursuit.

Let me make it clear that I wrote these stories mostly from memory, researching such facts as names and dates as best I could from my files and the Internet. But my descriptions of events and the people involved in them is drawn from my memory and opinions. I have changed a few names, but the stories are true to the best of my recollection. I've loved my life, my relatives, my spouses, and my career, including most of my clients, colleagues, competitors, co-workers, and bosses; so this is not a memoir that trashes everyone, although I do tell the truth.

I must say that I am a bit ashamed to be talking so much about myself. Not that talking about myself has ever been tough for me, of course (wink, wink, nudge, nudge, knowing glance, saynomore), but, as a writer and reporter, it feels unnatural to consistently speak in the first person. But this *is* a memoir, and that is the task. So forgive me for sounding so full of myself. It's just that this is the book that I thought would be the most marketable at this point in my fledgling career as an author.

This is actually my second book...sort of. In 2010 I wrote a movie screenplay, which I published as a paperback book in March of 2013, and which is available for purchase at: www.*HellinHeavenTheScreenplay*.com; it's also available as an original spec screenplay for producers. I began working on this book in January of 2013. I had begun several other screenplays, books, and plays over the years, but with the advent of fast and inexpensive on-demand printing, and the ease of marketing and sales on the Internet, self-publishing has become easily feasible for first-time writers, and I began to think it was time to actually finish a book.

As far as timing is concerned, several times in my life I said to myself that if I kept working for someone else, I'd never do what I wanted to do. At some point you have to take the risk of working for yourself in your preferred field, no matter how tough it may seem at first. Actress Anne Hathaway as Selina Kyle in the 2012 movie *The Dark Knight Rises* said, "I started out doing what I had to. Once you've done what you have to, they never let you do what you want to."

Although I have had many ideas for books over the years, I figured that for an unknown author, the most important aspect of the success of a book is the promotion it receives, and I figured that I would be most interesting to the media and the public as a professional comedian and celebrity impersonator. My celebrity voices have no bearing on a murder mystery, or a suspense novel, or a fictional biography. But if my first book is a collection of my memories of forty years of entertaining, I hope that radio and television hosts and the attendees at book signings and service club speaking engagements will be interested in meeting a guy who does two hundred voices. Besides, with no kids of my own, how else could I pass on what I've learned in life?

After all, my paternal grandfather was a brick mason who could point to thousands of homes and chimneys and stone and brick walls, and say with pride, "I built that." My maternal grandfather was an electrician who could point to hydroelectric dams in Washington and Korea and say, "I wired those." My father is a technician and locksmith who can point to typewriters, adding machines, vault doors, and ATMs and say, "I worked on those." And my mother is an artist who lives in a home filled with beauty that she painted.

But I've spent my life making people laugh. You can't point to that, you can't stand on that, you can't manipulate that, or hang that on a wall. Sure, there are pictures, and audio and video recordings, and newspaper and magazine articles; but they don't convey the same feeling of accomplishment that an abrupt belly-laugh conveys when it's wrenched out of a room full of people, or the soothing reciprocity of a round of sincere applause. The only way to preserve my story, the *whole* story, is to write about it in my own words, by my own hand. Not through the eyes of other writers, but from my own head.

If I die tomorrow, they won't say, "He was a comic who never made it big." I hope they'll say, "He was an entertainer and writer who loved almost every minute of his life." This book verifies that my life wasn't wasted.

1 - Biography

I was born in Berkeley in 1961. My father, Dave, was a technician for Bank of America, and my mother, Marilyn, was educated and credentialed as a primary school teacher, but worked full-time as a mom and homemaker until my sister, Tammy, and I entered high school.   I was an entertainer almost from birth. According to my mother's meticulous notes, at age one I would run down the hall from my bedroom when I heard the television in the living room spouting commercials, and I would mimic the actors and sounds. Tammy was born in June of 1963, and my parents tell me that by that December, when I was two-and-a-half, I could recite the entire *The Night Before Christmas*, and would act it out in very animated fashion for the relatives, even explaining words to them that I didn't think they could understand.

While in primary school I dabbled in magic, and every guest in our home was treated to a less-than-skillful display of legerdemain delivered with a nonetheless inspired level of humor and showmanship and stage presence. My parents thought it was cute and funny, and they encouraged me with their laughter and applause. In fact, they would frequently awaken me from a sound sleep and drag me down the hall in semi-consciousness to the living room to watch Johnny Carson's "Mighty Carson Arts Players" skits on *The Tonight Show* on NBC. He got his start in the same way and at the same age, so I guess my parents figured I'd follow in his footsteps.

Puppetry and ventriloquism intrigued me as a child, and I went everywhere with my vent dummy, "Walter Ego," manufactured by the Pelham Puppet company of England. In 1971, at age 9, my father accepted a promotion and transfer to the U.S. Pacific island territory of Guam, and Walter Ego went with me. I began producing puppet shows for the kids in the neighborhood, with Tammy and our neighborhood friends as the puppeteers, while I hosted the show, directed the action, and improvised the script out front as master of ceremonies, host, and narrator.

Christopher with Walter Ego on July 15, 1969,
and hosting the Silly Willy Show on April 22, 1972.

A school play in 1972, called *The Magic Egg*, was staged at Tamuning Elementary on Guam, and during casting it was determined by the teacher in charge that I would be the director.   It would be probably the only stage production in my life in which I was involved but not actually performing. Without previous experience, I seemed to have a knack for blocking and drama coaching, and actually coached my classmates on the delivery of their lines.

My first stand-up comedy routine consisted of ventriloquism using a Charlie McCarthy dummy, and included my buddy, Keith, as comedic partner.   It was a talent show at Tamuning Elementary School on Guam, and my first exposure to a large audience of several hundred of my peers laughing and clapping.

My second act in the same program was a puppet show in which I again enlisted the assistance of my sister, Tammy.   The plywood and cardboard Punch-and-Judy-style stage was of my design, but was constructed by my clever father, and the curtain was sewn and scenery was painted by my artistic mother.

Keith and Christopher on February 23, 1973
at Tamuning Elementary School on Guam.

Eventually my puppetry evolved into marionettes, with a bigger and better stage built in the summer of 1976 that accommodated both hand puppets and marionettes. I designed the stage, my handy and enthusiastically helpful dad served as draftsmen, and we purchased the hardware with money I saved from my allowance and odd jobs. Dad and I constructed the stage together, while Mom sewed new curtains. I created two separate backdrops, a forest and a throne room, and cut up carpet scraps to fit the stage floor. I typed up scripts, and recorded elaborate soundtracks for my shows on tape in my bedroom using character voices, ragtime music, and home-made sound effects. There was a lava lamp sitting outside my bedroom door with a sign that said, "If the light is ON, I am recording…please DO NOT DISTURB!"

Mother Marilyn is a very talented oil painter, and the walls of our home were covered with her paintings of landscapes, nudes, and clowns. One of the clown faces intrigued me (in addition to the nudes, of course), and I asked Mom to paint my face in that clown design, and henceforth my puppet shows were hosted by a clown. Being the only "Chris" in my class at Tamuning Elementary, my Pacific Rim classmates used to call me "Crisco Oil;" so I became "Crisco the Clown."

*Mom Linnell surrounded by her clown paintings, including
the one that inspired the face of Crisco the Clown.*

Enrolling in St. John's Episcopal Preparatory School in September of 1974, I made new friends, and found a new student body which had yet to see me perform. Enlisting the aid of my buddy, Steve Norton (who later became a professional rock musician and is still one of my best friends today), I performed my new clown and marionette show at the school's annual Halloween carnival, and became a professional entertainer at the age of fourteen, performing at private birthday parties, schools, convalescent homes, company parties, shopping centers, and in the Guam Bicentennial Parade.

My first celebrity impressions were also done in elementary school. I impersonated Elvis Presley, Flip Wilson and his character Geraldine Jones, Tom Jones, Laurel & Hardy, James Cagney, and a variety of other celebrities of the period to the delight of my fellow students, and the constant irritation of my teachers through junior high, high school, and into college.

But when I started impersonating my teachers, as well, I seemed to transcend the status of irritant, and eventually, and arguably, became the sweetheart of the faculty and staff. In the sixth grade at Tamuning Elementary I did a killer impression of Mr. Roy D. Hay, and at St. John's I was imitating math teacher Kuriakose Athappilly (who now has three bachelors degrees, two masters, and a doctorate in educational leadership; he still looks as young and handsome as he did in the 1970s, and is, as of this writing, an instructor in Business Information Systems and the MBA Program at Western Michigan University; visit: www.WMich.edu/business/facultystaff/person.php?pid=3)

Christopher in April of 1974 as Groucho Marx, in October of 1974 as Bela Lugosi's Dracula, and in February of 1976 as James Cagney.

In Casa Grande High School I did impressions of history teacher Phil Avila, chemistry teacher Kenneth Zamvil, and Cuban Spanish teacher Hector Borrego. At Sonoma State University my anthropology instructor, Dr. R. Thomas Rosin (www.sonoma.edu/anthropology/emeritus/rosin.html), actually asked me to fill-in for him *as him* once in the early 1980s, in costume, to administer a final exam to the class on the day when the good doctor couldn't make it to school.

Back in 1976, my junior high school, St John's Episcopal Preparatory School in Tumon, Guam, staged a talent show, and I impersonated my favorite celebrities. James Cagney (on the right in the photo above) changed a baby's dirty diaper ("Yooouuu dirty *brat!*"), Edith Bunker got tipsy at a cocktail party, and Elvis started out singing a beautiful version of "Amazing Grace," then halfway through made a transition into a rock-n-roll beat to which he began swinging and gyrating his hips in characteristic style.

Shakey's Pizza Parlor in Tamuning on Guam was my first public venue as a stand-up comic and impersonator. The restaurant featured a live pianist, and banjoist Jim Turner, who coaxed the crowd to sing-a-long Mitch Miller-style with lyrics projected on a large screen (the group forerunner of karaoke, which hadn't made it from Japan to Guam as of yet).

The Linnells, the Nortons, and the Cottings
at the Shakey's Pizza Parlor in Tamuning, Guam.

The crowd was composed mostly of Haoles (the Hawaiian word also used by Guamanians for Anglo "statesiders"), because most of the Guamanians, Filipinos, Japanese, Chinese, Koreans, Vietnamese, and other miscellaneous Asians and Pacific islanders who made up the island's majority were not familiar with ragtime and sing-a-long. The largely Anglo crowd was *loud*, singing, laughing, playing the Kazoo (they were free at Shakey's), and was split between the families of American company employees (such as the Linnells of Bank of

America, the Nortons of TWA, and the Coddings of the U.S. Government), all of whom were drinking root beer and eating lots of pizza, and servicemen on leave from the three Navy bases on the island and Anderson Air Force Base, most of whom drank lots of *regular* beer and some pizza.

The Linnell family made this a regular Saturday night activity, and the two Straw Hat entertainers became intrigued by their most enthusiastic fan. I even bought a used four-string plectrum banjo from Jim Turner, who gave me private lessons in the banjo arts. They invited me onto the stage one night, and were treated to a Cagney/Bunker/Laurel spiel that wowed the audience and invigorated me with enough self-confidence to make me unbearably obnoxious off-stage, and undeniably engaging on-stage for years.

Linnell & Cotting as Laurel & Hardy.

On February 2, 1977, St. John's hosted a variety show, and I performed as W.C. Fields, with my sister, Tammy, playing Mae West; and then I came back as Stan Laurel with my buddy, Bruce Cotting (today a Maryland realtor), impersonating Oliver Hardy. The task for Stan & Ollie: to change a light bulb. As rehearsed, Stanley took a pratfall off an eight-foot ladder right into the midst of the audience. The crowd loved it...Headmaster Rev. Col. John T. Moore did NOT (he missed the rehearsal)! Nonetheless, I did manage, as editor of the school paper, and president of the student council, to graduate four months later...with the honor of receiving the Headmaster's Award.

As the Linnell family prepared to move back stateside in June of 1977, I participated in an island-wide talent competition in the downtown Paseo of capital city Agaña (or Hagåtña, as it is now spelled), taking second place, and earning a job offer from the M.C., Jimmy Dee (the Guamanian "Don Ho"), of Jimmy Dee Enterprises of Guam (www.JimmyDeeMusicWorld.com), who wanted to hire me to be the opening act at his night club. It was an opportunity of which I was regretfully unable to take advantage, as Petaluma, California, became my new home. But even more exciting opportunities awaited there.

The riverfront Victorian dairytown town of Petaluma had a population of thirty-three thousand, one-third the size of Guam's, and smaller ponds are easier to conquer for growing frogs. I took my stand-up impression act to the other side of town for a talent show at Petaluma High School. Fortunately, the two masters of ceremonies were disc jockeys Barry Brown (now the morning man at KWAV in Monterey) and Jeff Angel (now the host of Angel Burlesque in Indianapolis) from the local community radio station, KTOB 1490AM.

I had met them both a few weeks earlier at a charity walk-a-thon. My dad and I decided to jog the event, and, reaching the finish line first, were interviewed by Barry and Jeff on the radio. When they later saw my stand-up act at Petaluma High, they asked me to come in to the station and audition by reading ads and some news, and then offered me a job. By December of 1979, Barry and Jeff had moved on to other stations, and I was asked to serve as M.C. of the show, doing my fully-costumed celebrity impersonations between acts.

In fact, it was at that show that I met the girl who was to become my first wife. On Tuesday, December 17, 1979, I entered the hallway at the rear of

Petaluma High School's auditorium for the rehearsal for the school's annual talent show, a benefit for the drama club. As I entered the door of the drama classroom, I was met by an absolutely adorable brunette with big, brown eyes and a big, bright smile. A shot of adrenaline raced through my body like a lightening bolt. I've never felt anything like it before or since. It was truly love at first sight. I said hi, and she said hi, and it was obvious that the feeling was mutual; we were both thunderstruck.

I explained that I was to be the M.C. of the show, and she explained that she was a member of the drama club and would be helping me during the rehearsal. It was a partnership that would last eleven years. On the night of the show, I introduced each act costumed as a different celebrity: Johnny Carson, James Cagney as George M. Cohan, Jimmy Stewart, Johnny Carson again as Mighty Carson Art Players character "Floyd R. Turbo, American," Bing Crosby, and George Burns. I wore the same white slacks and dress shirt for each celebrity, but changed jackets and ties and used costuming accessories.

Christopher in December of 1979 hosting
Petaluma High School's talent show.

When I started at KTOB I was just a high school sophomore who rode to the station before dawn on weekend mornings on my bicycle, but for a radio station paying minimum wage to part-time weekenders, I was the perfect apprentice. I began in January of 1978 as the host of KTOB's Sunday morning religious programs, and eventually worked a variety of airshifts, including middays and weekday evenings. In addition to work as an on-air personality, and announcing news, I developed writing and production skills that would be put to use for years to come.

After the station changed hands a few times, and I had worked at various Santa Rosa radio and television stations, I was re-hired 11 years later by owners Dave Devoto and Dan Hess and returned to KTOB from 1993-1995, at first doing freelance production and live remote broadcasts, and then serving as the morning-drive announcer until programming was computerized and then sold to out-of-town investors who used the frequency for programming in other languages.

In 1981 I started working at radio station KSRO 1350AM in Santa Rosa, and I worked at both stations for a while until KSRO offered me a full-time job in commercial production and hosting the evening show. I spent five years at KSRO, and at KREO (which our parent company, Finley Broadcasting, acquired in 1986), working as an on-air personality, commercial writer, announcer, and producer, and, eventually, and finally, as an account executive.

I wasn't very successful doing sales, however, and after six months I gave two weeks' notice in April of 1987, although I continued to do freelance production work and remote broadcasts for KSRO. I should have taken a weekend airshift to stay on the payroll, as, unbeknownst to me, the station would soon thereafter switch to a news/talk format which I would have loved, but I was too busy entertaining and doing freelance contract commercial production on all the other Sonoma County radio stations of the day through 1997, including KZST, KPLS, KMGG, KVRE, and KXFX. In 1996 I also worked as an air personality at KMGG, and simultaneously as an air personality, commercial writer & producer, fill-in news anchor, and default public service director for Q105. The last regular radio work I did was serve as co-host of a weekly talk show on KRCB radio from 2002-2003.

In the 1980s and 90s I also worked as freelance talent on cable television for PostNewsweek, Storer, Viacom, & TCI, and on broadcast television for KRCB TV22, and from 1981-1993 as an air personality for television station KFTY TV50, doing numerous live remote broadcasts and commercials. In 1987 I was also a regular cast performer, doing improv and sketch comedy, on TV50's late-night comedy and music showcase program called *On The Air*, which was taped at and simulcast from a radio station / restaurant / nightclub combination in downtown Santa Rosa known as the Studio KAFE. Along the same lines, in the 1990s, my celebrity impersonations had become familiar faces on the San Francisco late-night television music and comedy showcase broadcast on KOFY TV20 entitled *Late Sunday Night with James Gabbert*.

For the most part thereafter, from 1987-2007, I was self-employed full-time as an entertainer for private parties, promotions, and in corporate comedy, and in such performing venues as Microsoft headquarters in Seattle (eight-and-a-half-feet-tall on stilts, impersonating the blue genie Robin Williams voiced in the animated Disney movie *Aladdin*), Franklin D. Roosevelt's presidential yacht, the *USS Potomac* (pictured on the next page), BART (Bay Area Rapid Transit) commuter trains throughout the Bay Area in a BART promotion impersonating Groucho Marx, and San Francisco record stores for Cema Distribution doing singing impersonations of Frank Sinatra to promote the singer's *Duets* and *Duets II* albums.

Through the 1980s and 90s I also worked the fair circuit, entertaining at dozens of fairs throughout California, Nevada, and Oregon, offering my celebrity voices on request. And I performed in colleges, parking lots, grocery stores, and sporting events on the twelve-state, upper-midwest region Fruitopia Fruit Beverage promotional tour sponsored by Coca-Cola / Minute Maid in the summer of 1994.

Christopher as President Franklin D. Roosevelt
aboard the USS Potomac out of the Port of Oakland.

For most of the 1980s and 1990s I split my time between radio, television, college, and entertaining for corporate and private clients. One day I'd be doing Elvis at a private birthday party in Penngrove, and the next I'd be doing corporate comedy, flying to a national sales meeting in Chicago to provide walkaround impersonations, stiltwalking, audio and video presentations, scripting, and consultation.

On August 14, 1986 I did a Ronald Reagan at a private birthday party in Marin County, and the mother of the honoree, Kristi Miller, grabbed my arm at the end of the performance. She was a very nice, bright, attractive lady in her early sixties who went on and on about how funny my Reagan was. She told me her name was Wanda Ramey, and that she had been the first female news anchor at a major market television station in the U.S. (KPIX TV5 in San Francisco). She said that I should be performing down there, and told me she'd put in a good word for me with her agent, Joan Spangler, of LOOK Talent.

So I began working in industrial films and television and radio commercials regionally, nationally, and internationally, and, in 1987, joined the performing union AFTRA (American Federation of Television and Radio Artists), joined SAG (Screen Actors Guild) in 1989, and performed as a principal in national television commercials for MCI, Roy Rogers Family Restaurants, Pontiac, and Aerial cellular phones, and modeled nationally for the U.S. Postal Service, Charles Schwab, Blue Shield, and Macy's, in *Martha Stewart Living*, the *Wall Street Journal*, and *Image Magazine*.

In the fall of 2001 my corporate comedy business was thriving until 9/11. I had booked a lucrative national sales meeting for Morgan Stanley (to encompass some four full days and evenings of performances), and received a call from my client a few days after the tragedy. He told me they were the largest single tenant in the World Trade Center, and that most of the people for whom I was to perform were victims of the infamous terrorist attack. He was calling to cancel.

In the days and weeks that followed, one after another of my corporate clients followed suit. Nobody was doing corporate travel in the short term, and budgets for even local events were cut drastically for the long term. I realized that my entertainment career would never be the same, and that it was time to find another, more steady line of work, or "pretending to make a living" would amount to just that.

On the advice of one of my loyal entertainment agents, Thomas Schoenberger, who had booked my entertainment services at many corporate events over the years at wineries throughout Napa, Sonoma, the Russian River, and Healdsburg's Dry Creek and Alexander Valleys, I had already begun doing wine tours on the side. I later branched out into tours of Yosemite, Muir Woods, and San Francisco, and this is where I really shined. I had studied history in college, and had considered teaching, so doing history tours of my beloved San Francisco was perfect for me.

I was out and about, meeting and entertaining new people every day, and I was driving motorized cable cars and amphibious ducks (the modern, commercial, civilian version of the U.S. military's DUKWs of World War II) through one of the most beautiful and colorful cities in the world. The best part was that I didn't have to wear makeup, wigs, and costumes, and I didn't have to change clothes at night in the rain in parking lots, and worry about when the next entertainment booking would come. I was still entertaining, but with a regular paycheck, just as in radio, and without being stuck all alone in a stuffy studio.

After a couple of years, however, the monstrous city traffic and long commute were beginning to get to me. Driving in commute traffic each day *to* the city, driving a huge tour bus *through* the city all day, and then driving home in commute traffic *from* the city was too much for me. I mitigated the daily commute by living in my van conversion with one of my dogs three nights a week for a year (I was doing tours four consecutive days a week), and then bought an RV, and, with our general manager's approval, parked it at work with the trolleys and ducks, and plugged into the cable car/duck barn for power.

That worked for another two years. The dog and I were home four nights a week, and camping at work the other three. It was comfortable, but those three nights a week I missed my spouse and our house and our other dog and cats… and hot showers! And every time I got my cable car or duck stuck in traffic behind a war protest, or Occupy protest, or Naked Guys traffic snarl, I thought to myself, "I gotta get outa' this traffic and stay home and write a book."

In years past I had started a number of books and a couple of screenplays, but hadn't ever finished a project, being too distracted by "pretending to make a living." One day I was at a discount grocery store, and saw the name of a former client on a book published in 2006. His name is Joe Eszterhas, and he had called me once several years before from Hawaii and hired me to go to his Tiburon home and perform for his beloved but bedridden father, who was all alone on his birthday, except for domestic staff. More on that later.

Now, I knew that Joe was a famous screenwriter (*Basic Instinct, Jagged Edge, Flashdance, Showgirls*, etc.), so I was surprised to see that he'd written a book. It was entitled *The Devil's Guide to Hollywood, the Screenwriter as God!*, and was a how-to (or, perhaps, how-NOT-to) guide to writing a screenplay. It was cheap, and I was intrigued, so I threw it in the cart. Well, it sat on my desk for a year or more, and then I finally grabbed it in August of 2009 when I was packing for my semi-annual vacation at the legendary Burning Man arts festival in Nevada's Black Rock Desert (visit: www.BurningMan.com).

I read the book in the desert, and decided to write a screenplay instead of a book. I didn't know how I'd get a book publisher, and with the advice in the Joe Eszterhas book I figured I had a head start, familiar as I was with screenplays, having worked on several movies before. For my topic I decided to put into writing a story idea about Burning Man I'd had in my previous visits there.

I continued doing tours through the following spring, saving a war chest of tour earnings for living expenses, and then in the summer of 2010 I took a sabbatical, lived off my savings, and finally wrote my screenplay. I began on the morning of July 29, 2010, writing four pages of dialogue and coming up with the title, and by 8 p.m. I had six scenes written. Less than a month later, on August 23, I had completed the first draft. I printed up several copies and loaded them into the car with me as we packed for Burning Man again.

In the desert we were camped next to a pair of middle-aged brothers. One turned out to be the producer of independent films. I induced him to read the screenplay, and he gave me his feedback. Upon my return home I began editing, and by November was convinced it was ready for the screen. I had read that screenwriters often hosted *screenplay reading parties* to get an idea of how the lines sounded coming out of the mouths of real actors.

With an ad on www.CraigsList.org I found a half-dozen local budding actors, cast them into the roles, and hosted a reading party in Petaluma for my original spec screenplay, *Hell in Heaven*. As of this writing, I have yet to sell it to a production company, although, as I mentioned earlier, it is available for purchase in book form at www.*HellinHeavenTheScreenplay*.com.

The genesis of *Pretending to Make a Living* was a similar story. I'd always wanted to write my memoirs, and on-demand self-publishing makes it easy and inexpensive. When my tour season ended in December of 2012, I took another sabbatical, lived off savings, and wrote this book from January 13 to June 13. I'll spend a few weeks promoting it full-time before taking another day job. I'll be doing an on-going public speaking publicity campaign; if you'd like me to speak to your group, or if you'd like to meet me and get your copy signed, check out my speaking schedule: www.*PretendingToMakeALiving*.com

As for my personal life, since 1977 I have lived in the beautiful Victorian riverfront dairy town of Petaluma, California, in the San Francisco Bay Area, just 35 miles north of the Golden Gate Bridge in the heart of Wine Country in Sonoma County. As I've mentioned, I've been married three times. I love being married. The first relationship, with my high school sweetheart, lasted eleven years, the second just four, and I dated a number of women in between marriages, including two long term relationships with women who'd vowed they'd never marry. When my second wife moved out in 1998 I started dating women and men both, and, in 2002, I met Mr. Right, and have been happily married to Juan since 2003. There's a picture of him with me below.

In my free time I enjoy writing, photography, reading history, political debate, old movies on AMC and TCM, old sitcoms in Nick at Nite's TV Land and Comedy Central, plus tennis, golf, hiking, biking, canoeing, swimming, roller skating with the Midnight Rollers in San Francisco's weekly Friday Night Skate, and, most of all, spending sunny afternoons in secluded woods and near picturesque bodies of water, smokin' a stogy, with my husband and dogs, oblivious to the rest of the world.

Juan and Chris, Gorda y Flaco.

2 - Crisco the Clown

My parents say that I have been entertaining since I was two-years-old. My mother gave me her quick, brilliant wit; my father is the affable, engaging, gregarious clown-like buffoon and king of physical comedy. Both of their fathers had those qualities, and they have been combined in me. My grandfathers were also both cigar-chomping, flirtatious, and charming, yet curmudgeonly, and both were blessed with a child-like sense of humor. My paternal grandfather, Papa Harry, was Groucho Marx and Benny Hill combined, a man who couldn't resist a feigned trip into a door jam, and never posed for a picture without a kooky expression. My maternal grandfather, Papa Fred, was John Wayne and W.C. Fields combined, and couldn't resist the old "pull my finger" routine at the Thanksgiving table. Both became Red Foxx's Fred G. Sanford of *Sanford and Son* as they aged, and neither could be bested in fisticuffs until the day he died. This is, no doubt, why I became an outgoing and self-confident entertainer and improv comic.

In my teen years, most of the other kids in the neighborhood were out playing basketball...with my dad. My poor ol' man tried hard for years to get me to play basketball, or baseball, or football, or any other normal pastime for a male teenager. He installed a basketball hoop above the carport, but while *he* was out with my friends playing half-court, I was in my bedroom/recording studio, with the door locked, blankets hanging on the walls to absorb sound, recording onto cassette tapes the soundtracks for my puppet and marionette shows. My dad didn't really understand me, but he always supported me. He was always ready to give me a ride to my show, help me with my equipment, and provide the biggest belly laughs from the back of the audience.

I started with hand puppets, branched out into ventriloquist dummies, and then found marionettes, which were my favorites. My cast of a dozen marionettes was mainly composed of those manufactured, again, by the Pelham Puppet company of England. We lived on Guam from 1971-1977, where no such puppets were available, but we took two *home leaves* in California during that time, and on each visit we made special trips to the historic old Mr. Mopps' toy store in Berkeley and the toy store in the Vintage 1870 shopping arcade in Yountville so that I could use my hard-earned money to increase my marionette cast. Each character had a distinct voice, either an original or a celebrity impression; for instance, The Wizard was vaudeville and old radio star Ed Wynn, the Big Bad Wolf was movie star W.C. Fields, The King and Queen respectively were breakfast cereal cartoon pitchman Captain Crunch and Jean Stapleton's Edith Bunker character from the television series *All in the Family*, and the Wicked Witch was Margaret Hamilton, the actress who played the Wicked Witch in *The Wizard of Oz*.

The marionette scripts were typewritten, then methodically memorized, and, as I didn't have my own orchestra, I synched my script to the background music I used; mostly Scott Joplin rag played on L.P.s. I hated dialogue with no music background, after growing up watching Laurel & Hardy, who always had music in the background in their scenes. I'd play the music over and over and over again, each time reciting my characters' lines until the crescendos in my show matched those in the music.

I'd create my own sound effects using objects found around the house, and became quite a skilled writer, director, producer, and voice and *foley artist* (i.e., sound effects). I only had one record player and one tape recorder, so everything had to be performed *live* and simultaneously on tape, which meant playing the L.P., doing multiple voices, and the foley work over and over and over again until it was perfect. And it was perfect...don't ever let anyone tell you teenagers can't have Obsessive-Compulsive Disorder. Mine was fully-developed, and it meant I would re-record dozens of times until everything synched up perfectly. This would later prove to be a valuable and distinctive trait when I began a twenty-five year career in 1978 writing, voicing, and producing commercials in Sonoma County radio.

Originally my shows were pretty simple affairs, using hand puppets and a sheet of plywood as a stage. But I was assigned a term paper in the sixth grade and chose puppets as my topic, and the books I found in the library were full of elaborate puppet stages, so I began to upgrade. My first really professional stage was about six feet tall and three feet wide, a sheet of plywood with hinged wings in the back to hold the thing up and provide cover for the puppeteers. My clever father built the stage under my direction and with my assistance. The roof was a huge sheet of cardboard, nailed to the top of the front and creased in the back, folded down and resting on the hinged wings in the rear. The roof therefore also served as a backdrop, and I, along with my assistants (comprised of my sister and my friends), knelt underneath with the puppets above our heads. As I became interested in marionettes and began to assemble a cast, my dad cut a square out of the lower front of the stage, hinged it down, built a separate, stand-alone, plywood backdrop with hinged sides, and my hand puppet stage was transformed into a combination marionette stage. With this equipment I performed at schools and convalescent homes.

What I found was that regardless of the audience, some sort of introduction of the show had to take place in order to quiet the group down and focus their attention. My mother was a skilled oil painter, and our walls were covered with her paintings of landscapes, still-life, nudes, and clowns. It was the clowns that intrigued me the most (as far as my mother knew...the nudes certainly had their merits, as well), and one particular face in the crowd of clowns on the wall was my favorite. I had always been a natural physical comic (part of the Linnell Family heritage), and I asked my mom if she couldn't paint that clown on my face. She agreed, and a star was born! A couple of years earlier, in elementary school, I was one of the few *haoles* in my class (this is the Hawaiian word, arguably, for *foreigner* or *newcomer* that Guamanians had adopted for Anglo *statesiders*), and the kids at school teasingly called me "Crisco Oil." I decided that would be the perfect clown moniker.

Crisco the Clown on canvas, and in the flesh in 1975 and 1989.

On November 1, 1975 I was attending St John's Episcopal Preparatory School in Tumon, Guam, and our school hosted its big annual Halloween Carnival. All the students and their siblings attended, and many of the parents were put to work on various projects. My dad was occupied annually as the Bingo chairman. My mother helped my sister and me prepare my puppet show in the Parish Hall. I was in one of the classrooms when the walls and floor and ceiling began to shake and roll.

EARTH-SHAKING PERFORMANCE

It was an earthquake, and, once again, I was at fault. Or should I say, I was standing right *on* the fault! This was no ordinary fault, either. Guam had been formed tens of millions of years before as the Pacific tectonic plate steadily moved into and was forced under the Philippine Sea Plate, forming the Marianas Trench, the world's deepest spot. The ocean floor to the west was shoved up and up and up out of the water, eventually becoming the Marianas Islands. Perched as we were on top of the world's tallest mountain (if measured from the bottom of the trench), Guam has always had more than its fair share of seismic activity.

The earthquake registered a 6.2 magnitude on the Richter Scale, but it seemed a lot bigger than that at the epicenter. Our school was standing right on top of the fault in which the earthquake was erupting, as the Pacific Plate jolted and nudged its way down into the ocean depths and under the ground on which we were standing. The ground undulated as if we were surfing. I scurried out into the parking lot with everyone else that day. And when the quaking was done, I rounded up as many people within earshot as possible, and led them to the Parish Hall to watch my show.

With clown makeup applied, and a matching orange bow-tie and hat my mother had fabricated and decorated for me, eventually festooned with buttons and pins, I turned down the ragtime music and ran out from behind the stage to assault my audience. Over the years I continued to use the puppets and marionettes, but I found that the clown routine was a bigger attraction, and received a far greater reaction from the crowd. I would interact with the kids in front at the beginning of the show, preview what would take place in the marionette show, go back behind the stage and do the show, and then, afterwards, bring individual cast members from the back of the stage out into the crowd to interact with the kids. They loved seeing the Wicked Witch, who had been a star in the show, come out and cackle her way through the crowd, and they were astounded by the (seemingly) miraculous tricks my marionette dog and horse could do right before their eyes.

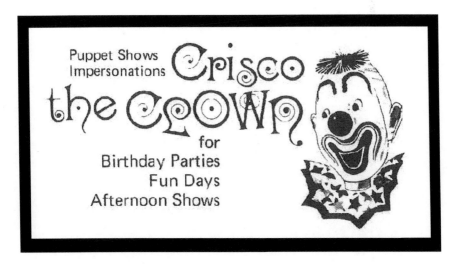

Crisco the Clown's first business card.

This free performance at the school led to my first paid performance at the birthday party for Dana Karasaki, the kid sister of my classmate, Chad Karasaki. I cashed that very first paycheck, and still have the ten dollar bill framed in my office. As more and more jobs followed, I decided that a hat and tie and painted face weren't enough...Crisco the Clown would have to be properly outfitted head-to-toe.

***Crisco the Clown, assisted by Steve Norton, performing
At the Julale Shopping Center in November of 1976.***

My mother sewed up a clown jumpsuit for me, and, armed with a big, loud brass horn fitted with a big, black, rubber bulb, I was ready to round up an audience at any venue. I performed at kids' birthday parties, and was hired by the island's new indoor shopping mall, the Julale Shopping Center, to do weekend clown and puppet shows in their center court in November of 1976. I would come charging down the stairs, and would run the length of the mall, up one side and down the other, running into each store and blasting my horn. The honking and kids' laughter echoed off the concrete floor, walls, and ceiling, and invigorated the entire mall. Like an obnoxious Piped Piper I would be followed by a line of kids who would congregate at center court in front of my marionette stage.

But this was my second generation stage. It was built in the summer of 1976, a very busy summer for me on Guam, to be sure...tragic and exciting.

THE SUMMER OF '76

It started off with Super Typhoon Pamela, generating sustained winds in excess of 115 mph (and gusts up to 150 mph), which lingered over the island at full force for a day and a night, May 21 and 22, dropping almost thirty-four inches of rain on the island (twenty-seven inches in just twenty-four hours). Island residents were first notified about the storm on the sixteenth, and we began to prepare, stocking up on food and filling our bathtubs with drinking water. The day before the Typhoon hit, gale force winds blew as my parents and all the neighbors scurried around securing their homes. Schools were closed, so at this point we kids still thought this was a lot of fun.

Overnight the winds increased to hurricane force, and by morning, the full force of Pamela was bearing down on our neighborhood. Of course, we couldn't see anything but a solid wall of horizontally wind-blown water with huge, mangled objects occasionally flying by. I'll never again watch the tornado scene through the window of Dorothy's bedroom in the *Wizard of Oz* without remembering Pamela…it was exactly what we witnessed.

In the days before the typhoon hit, we had gone to local hardware stores and my dad bought multiple sheets of half-inch plywood, along with washers and bolts. My handy ol' man fabricated wooden shutters for most windows of the house, to protect us from the intrusion of flying debris. He drilled holes directly into the concrete walls and bolted the shutters into place. The one window not shuttered was facing west, in the dining room, which was safely recessed within the carport, and it was through that window that we could see the hell unleashed outside. A wall of horizontal water obliterated the view of anything more than a few feet from the carport, except for occasional objects flying by. While the other windows were all shuttered on the outside, we had to leave them ajar on the inside during the height of the storm to prevent implosion by the monstrous air pressure, and the wind drove water right through the five bedroom house for eighteen hours.

At around noon on the first day, there was a huge crash in the living room, and my courageous dad scrambled into the windy space to find that the huge, heavy living room air conditioner had blown clean out of its housing in the wall and into the room. Furthermore, the sliding glass doors on the east side of the room, covered as they were by plywood shutters, were still under such pressure that the center aluminum frames between the panes was separating a good half-foot! Afraid that the glass would implode everywhere, my dad risked venturing into the carport, into which he'd crammed both our cars, which were rising up and down in the wind, to get from the carport closet a Y-shaped plywood tree prop he'd once constructed of two-by-fours for a papaya tree. He lugged it into the house and propped it against the center of the sliding glass door frame, wedging the frames together against the wind, using the air conditioner and two heavy, decorative, ceramic Asian elephant end tables in the living room on top of the couch to hold it down.

The eye passed over the island in mid-afternoon, and we went out timidly and furtively to take a look up into blue, clear, calm sky directly above, surrounded on all sides by a white curtain of spinning clouds and water and debris. My dad was too busy to admire the view, however, as he methodically checked each of the thick plywood shutters he had securely bolted over the windows and directly into the concrete walls. Pamela had blown a couple off, and loosened a couple of others. My dad re-secured them as best he could, and then forcibly herded us all back into the house before the other wall of the storm approached.

To prevent water damage to the contents of the house, we had stacked in the center of each room a pile of furniture, furnishings, and belongings to keep them away from the windows and air conditioners. Late in the afternoon I took a nap on top of the pile in the middle of my room, which was on the corner of the building and had windows on two sides, facing the east and south, but my parents abruptly awakened me right at dusk because the force of the storm was making four of the bedrooms and the living room, dining room, and kitchen far too dangerous for habitation.

It was a long, scary night as the four of us huddled together in candlelight in the one dry room of the house, a bedroom on the south side of the dining room wall, protected because, like the dining room, it was recessed a few feet from the exterior wall (in an alcove outside in which were housed the washer and dryer below the window). We listened all night, as best we could over the locomotive-like drone of the wind and the crashing of objects flying through the air, to a lone, heroic disc jockey on KUAM radio, stranded alone at the station, and doing his best to process and disseminate official news and information, and keep 100,000 Guam residents company during the storm.

The next morning the sun was out, the skies were clear, and there was no wind. As we cautiously ventured outside we were astounded at the damage. Every square inch of the ground in every direction was littered with torn-up scraps of textiles, vegetation, paper, and mangled objects. The only trees still standing were stripped of their bark and leaning, all at the same angle. All the bushes were stripped bare, and people stumbled about in the mess looking to salvage anything of value. There were huge metal warehouses near our home; some dated back to the early post-World War II era, and others had just recently been completed. The new ones were *gone*, and the old ones, which had been through many typhoons before, stood by in ragged condition, nonetheless seemingly laughing at the ruins of the less sturdily-built newcomers.

Guamanians were used to typhoons; we got two or three small ones each summer, and FEMA would set up shop and thousands in need got money for clothes, furniture, televisions, household effects, and the repair of their damaged houses, or the construction of new ones. Guamanians survived the Spanish, the Japanese, earthquakes, tsunamis, and typhoons…they are a resilient people. All they needed was Spam and San Miguel beer, and they could survive anything. Just as old-time boxing fans compared boxers Jack Dempsey and Joe Louis to Muhammad Ali and Joe Frazier, Guamanians all compared Pamela to the most recent biggie, Super Typhoon Karen in 1962, which was stronger, but passed over the island more quickly.

The damage amounted to $500 million (1976 USD, or well over two billion today). We had no gas for several weeks, and no electricity for six months. Many of my friends didn't even have water. We were fortunate to be living in a concrete house, which was structurally impervious to such winds, and, as such, our damage was confined mainly to carpets and draperies, but over six thousand homes were destroyed or made uninhabitable, and over eighty percent of the island's buildings in general were damaged. The American Red Cross went into debt partly by providing twenty-nine shelters for twenty-six hundred people, and ten million dollars in assistance to some sixteen thousand families; the tab for the U.S. government was $200 million. As a result of Pamela, my dad got me my first summer job, as Supply & Mail Clerk for Bank of America, whose Naval Station branch had lost its roof during the storm, and which needed extra hands to get everything at the branch back in order.

As the island rebuilt after the storm, one morning on the way to work on the navy base, we were stopped at the main gate for an unusual and extensive search of each car by U.S. Marine guards in full battle gear. The date was June 23, and I was shortly to learn that Naval Station Guam was under high security as a result of the disappearance of a base resident: my St. John's classmate and close friend, the darling Susan Sabina Weeks. It wasn't until many years later that her body was found in thick brush on base. She had been kidnapped and murdered. Her father, U.S. Naval Commander George Holland Weeks, was the executive officer of the base at the time, and her mother, Janet Healy Weeks, was a Superior Court judge, yet the criminal mystery, which likely occurred entirely on the fully secured base, was never solved. Susan and her father, who died in 2002, are laid to rest together today at Arlington National Cemetery.

There were also bright spots that summer. July 4, 1976, was America's bicentennial, and, as Guam is situated east of the International Date Line, it was the first American soil to celebrate the happy occasion (Guam's motto is "Where America's day Begins"), and the island pulled out all the stops for the festivities. In fact, Crisco the Clown performed in the Guam Bicentennial Day Parade.

Also, later in the summer, our family took an exciting trip to Japan, visiting Osaka, Kyoto, and Kobe.

Upon our return to Guam, I found more books at the library about puppetry, and in one I found a more elaborate stage that I wanted built. Amateur architect that I was, I drew up a design, submitted it to my draftsman father, and he used his high school woodshop expertise to calculate the exact type, size, and amount of every material we'd need for construction. He was brilliant, and I was convinced that he could build anything. And I was right. With money I saved from performances, my dad took me to local hardware stores and I purchased everything I needed: plywood, 2x4s, bolts, nuts, washers, hinges, hooks, paint, and tools.

My new marionette stage stood six feet tall, six feet wide, six feet deep, and was painted navy blue. It had one opening front and center, two feet tall and four feet wide. The stage floor was painted black; though, when I later realized that the marionettes' feet made too much distracting racket on the plywood floor, I scrounged a piece of green carpeting and trimmed it to fit. Eventually my resourceful dad cut and cleverly rigged a hinged trap door, so that we could use hand puppets on the same stage with the marionettes...a creative and useful innovation.

The 1976 marionette stage in action in the 1980s with Crisco the Clown.

The wooden, free-standing back wall was painted black, as well, and I created two separate removable backdrops of sculpted and painted cardboard: a forest and a castle throne room. Both backdrops had cut-out features, so that they stood out from the black backdrop, the former with trees and the latter with stately columns. I had also accumulated various puppet-sized set pieces to dress the stage: a fallen log and an iron caldron for the forest, and wooden thrones (of my own fabrication) and a miniature grand piano for the throne room. The stage was dressed with a matching blue and white quilted curtain and valence, and a wooden crosspiece was connected the top rear upper corners, and was equipped with a dozen eyehooks that allowed us to hang the marionette cast behind us when they were not performing on the stage.

The finishing touches were a five-foot-wide, heavy-duty, carpeted footstool that allowed the puppeteers to stand up above the backdrop to hold the marionettes out over the stage floor, a cassette and microphone sound system with speakers that sat outside the stage at either corner, and beautifully, colorfully, and creatively printed signs by my mother, the artist, for "Crisco the Clown" and the times and titles of each show I produced. The stage unbolted and broke down into cardboard sheets that just fit my folks' cars, and the entire production could be set up in about thirty minutes.

We would begin setting up the stage a full hour prior to the show, put up the sign, and start the music while I was still in street clothes, and then, as the crowd gathered, I would begin the thirty minute process of applying my clown makeup and then get into my costume behind the stage, so that the first time the kids saw Crisco the Clown was when the show began. My proud dad would drive me all over the island on weekends for my shows, and never complained. I eventually relieved my sister, Tammy, of assistant duties, as she was tiring of being her big brother's hired help, and trained my buddy, Steve Norton, to be my new assistant.

BACK TO CALIFORNIA

In addition to my Julale Shopping Center jobs, I performed at birthday parties, retail promotions, at a company Christmas party for Bank of America (which was also my first performance as Santa Claus), and at a huge outdoor Easter festival at the Guam Hilton Hotel. When my family moved back to California in the summer of 1977 and settled in the Victorian riverfront dairy town of Petaluma, thirty-five miles north of San Francisco's Golden Gate Bridge, I bought my own cars and drove myself to shows, eventually enlisting my long-suffering and ever-helpful first wife as assistant, and we performed all over the Bay Area. I had also started working in radio, so I recorded new show soundtracks, and re-recorded some of the old ones, in the production studios of the stations at which I was working, giving the soundtracks an even more professional sound to them.

Over time, however, despite my love of marionettes, and all the work, money, and resources I'd put into my shows and equipment, I realized that the clown was more of a draw than the puppets. The kids were enthralled by Crisco, but were distracted during the marionette-only portion of the show, and eliminating the stage was a lot less work, so I raised the price of the fully-staged show, and offered the clown and puppets *without* the stage at a reduced rate.

For these performances I originally packed my puppets and marionettes into a foot locker, with the marionettes performing on the top, but this necessitated a lengthy process of unpacking each marionette from its individual box, unwrapping it, unwinding the strings, and then reversing the process, all during the performance in front of the audience, which really slowed up the show. The solution was a piece of equipment of my own original design: a traveling showcase box.

I hired the son of a local cabinet maker to build a four-by-four-foot wooden box that hinged open in the middle and stood flat, and was fitted with a big, sturdy carrying handle on the center of the long end. The "stage" side prominently featured "Crisco the Clown & Friends" professionally hand-painted by a local sign painter, and the backstage side featured individual slots for each marionette with a hook at the top, carpeted on the inside to protect the marionettes in transit. With this box, my marionettes were all hanging, ready to go as soon as I opened the box. At the bottom of the box were separate compartments for my boom box, hand puppets, and assorted props and animal balloons. Though this box weighed about sixty pounds (empty) and was rather large and cumbersome to be carried as a suitcase, I was young and strong, and it was one piece equipment that paid for itself over and over again for years.

Crisco the Clown performing at an elementary school in the 1980s.

In fact, I continued using that traveling showcase box as I solicited, booked, and executed performances at schools. This was the first time in my life that I had done any outside sales. I prepared pictures and printed materials, cold-called school principals right out of the phone book, and then went in coat and tie to meet with the principals prior to the shows. And this was for a bargain basement price of $50, because I figured they were public schools and couldn't afford any more. I also figured that I'd get referral business from the kids' mothers, which did, indeed, pan out. I traveled all around the North Bay for several years doing this, augmenting my private, promotional, and corporate work with school shows.

In order to make this an "educational" show to make it attractive to school principals, I actually started the show in a coat and tie without clown makeup.

I'd introduce myself to the kids as an entertainer, do a little lecture about the international history of puppetry and clowns, and then put on my clown makeup and costume right in front of the kids in the assembly room. I'd then trot out one after another of my puppet characters, and conclude the shows with the kids excited to such a fevered pitch that the teachers couldn't handle them for the rest of the day.

The kids were always receptive, but the faculty was often difficult. School teachers like to maintain control and a sense of quiet decorum in their classrooms. Even more so in school assemblies, at which peer pressure made the teachers corral the kids in an even more disciplinarian fashion, out of fear of appearing to their colleagues to be too lax. This, of course, didn't jibe with *my* standard operating procedure, which was to whip the kids into a state of excited bedlam. I was a CLOWN...hel-LO. I liked the kids laughing and interacting and having fun. A lot of the female school teachers weren't used to that, and couldn't handle it. They'd get very "cross" and try to get their kids under control right when I was trying to make them laugh and have fun! After all, this wasn't a *class*...it was supposed to be entertainment; as far as I was concerned, anyway.

LEARNING SIGN LANGUAGE

The Crisco the Clown in Schools program got off to a rough start, too, at Dunham Elementary in Glen Ellen, in the north end of the beautiful Sonoma Valley. The principal was very nice and enthusiastic when I met him in the initial sales call. I think he was overjoyed that I was willing to come all the way from Petaluma and perform for the school's several hundred kids for a lousy fifty bucks. But the morning of the show I made a dreadful mistake. There are three ways to reach Glen Ellen from Petaluma: 1) around the south of the Sonoma Mountains through Sonoma, 2) around the north of the mountains through Santa Rosa, and 3) directly up, through, and over the mountains via Petaluma Hill, Grange, and Bennett Valley Roads. The latter was always my preferred route, because it was more direct, shorter, had less traffic, was far prettier, and, generally speaking, much faster.

On this day, however, after I had already committed myself to option 3, I turned onto Grange Road, and was confronted with an ominous "BRIDGE OUT AHEAD" sign. I took this road all the time, to and from my Santa Rosa radio jobs, tennis, golf, and skating outings, and to visit my beloved maternal grandmother. I had never seen the sign before, and knew of no recent weather that could possibly have swept away a bridge. So I assumed that the sign was either for an ancillary road, or was simply a mistake, and I foolishly pressed on. I mean, "BRIDGE OUT" sounded like cheap fiction, not a true obstacle. Ten minutes later, after crossing the Bennett range, the road dead-ended at the intersection of Bennett Valley Road...or, rather, *near* the intersection. The bridge, at the end of Grange, literally one hundred feet from the intersection, WAS OUT! OHMYGOD! I got out of the car and desperately searched for a way to drive my vehicle through the damned creek and up the embankment...but it was a lost cause. The bridge was, indeed, out...and I was screwed, as this was a few years before I had my first cell phone.

I flipped a bitch, hurriedly backtracked, and then headed north toward Santa Rosa on Route 2. My heart must've pumped a hundred beats a minute as I watched the digital clock on the dashboard click off minute after valuable minute. When I arrived at the school, thirty or forty-five minutes late, the kids were all in the auditorium, screaming their heads off, bored stiff, as one poor, harried, neglected teacher improvised "story time" with a kiddy picture book. The principal was livid, the teachers were enraged, and all I could do was apologize, press on with all vigor, and try to learn from the experience. Now when a sign says "BRIDGE OUT" I err on the side of caution.

OH, THOSE KIDS

Private birthday parties were Crisco's bread and butter over the decades, and they were the most fun. With a large audience in a huge auditorium, the noise level was high and there was little time to interact with each child. But at private birthday parties there were only usually a dozen kids, more or less, and I could devote individual attention to each child. I remember one performance at Christmas time; I asked the kids, "Does anyone know what holiday Jewish people celebrate in December?" Now, "Hanukkah" is not an easy word for children to pronounce when they've only seen it written, but one of the more enthusiastic boys shouted out his very sincere answer without a moment of thought: "Hanu-KA-KA!" That was when I first thought about writing this book...I remember telling the party mom, "That one's gonna be in my memoirs!"

As for the full marionette stage, we still got plenty of use out of it over the years. Mostly I used the showcase box for private birthday parties and schools, and the full stage for the generally larger audiences at retail promotions, company parties, and street fairs and community festivals. I still to this day have the stage, scenery, props, and puppet cast, all carefully packed and preserved...last did a full marionette show at a company party with my second wife as assistant sometime between 1994-1998.

By the late 1980s my radio work and the celebrity impersonation services I was originally offering on the side began to account for more and more of my income. My weekdays were light, and I did my bookings and marketing in my office during the day, easily accommodating occasional early morning, lunch hour, or evening bookings, usually for company meetings and office parties. My weekends were FULL, though, with no breathing room. Typically I would do one to three adult parties on Friday night, two or three kids' parties or promotions on Saturday afternoon, three or four adult bookings Saturday night, and then two or three more kids' parties on Sundays.

And I did all this while I was frequently juggling weekend airshifts at one or two radio stations, *and* doing freelance production work on-call at several other stations. Also, after 1987 I was driving down to San Francisco two or three weekdays a week for commercial auditions or modeling 'go-see's. It was the clown shows that were really wearing me out, though, requiring so much raw energy and adrenaline just to keep ahead of the rambunctious kids that I'd come home in a sweaty heap, thoroughly exhausted. And *then* I'd have to unload the van, jump in the shower, eat, dress, prep, and then reload the van for my evening performances. I was fed up with the makeup, too, which took a half-hour to apply, was a sloppy mess while it was on and while I was working hard and sweating, and was always an absolute nightmare to remove, especially when I was in a hurry.

I frequently left the clown makeup on after jobs at home and at the radio stations, procrastinating in commencing the torturous process of soap and hot water and scrubbing and rescrubbing until my face was clean...and raw. Numerous pictures in the family albums during that period reveal me in street clothes sitting with friends and family at the table or on the couch or the patio, still wearing my full, runny clown face. I finally began performing the same act *without* the makeup, wearing a straw skimmer hat, plaid coat, and bow tie, but was still worn out at the end of the day, and still needing to wear a cup to defend myself from the kiddies' fists. The necessity of this unique costume accessory was made painfully apparent to me one sunny afternoon.

At a backyard private birthday party, one of the kids, in his fevered enthusiasm, took a full swing at my groin with a closed fist and hit me square on target. I gasped, and the blood rushed from my painted face and down to the insulted area. I dropped to the ground and whimpered in the fetal position on the lawn with tears in my eyes for what seemed like hours. The mother/host jumped up instantaneously, and, after a moment spent staring at me through a pained expression, moved into action. With a forced smile she said in an overly cheerful, Sesame Street voice, "Oh...uh...OK, kids, let's let the clown take a little breather while we open the presents."

The very next day I went to a sporting goods store to buy a cup, and at the next performance I gleefully took one shot after another without so much as a smirk. The damned thing wasn't very comfortable, but I reasoned that wearing it meant I could still have kids of my own some day…if I wanted to. I never did.

THE CLOWN IS HUNG

I also began to note with disdain a new trend in the birthday party clown business. We were now being regarded almost as educators or ministers, and I didn't like it. I always wanted to entertain professionally because I like to make people laugh. But the world was changing…it was filling with new, "yuppie" parents who were constantly vying with their peers to prove that *they* had the most intelligent, advanced, motivated, and ambitious children in the soccer van.

These young mothers would call me on the phone, and, after I described my act and quoted my fee, they'd say, "Well, gee…is that *it*? Puppets and balloons…you just make them laugh? My girlfriend had a clown for HER party and HE taught the kids American Sign Language!" Or Judo, or reading, or Bible stories, or…Jesus Christ. You name it, these moms were trying to cram school and church down their kids' throats…at a birthday party. They wanted to have non-credentialed party clowns *teach* their children something…yikes!

As a result, almost every other clown I knew was incorporating lessons into their routines, and playing up their credentials: clown college, clown ministry, clown MD, clown PhD clown MFCC; whatever! I just wanted to show the kids a good time. I thought, "Can't kids these days even have fun at a birthday party anymore, without having to be force-fed some structure?" Television's Mr. (Fred) Rogers once said, "Play is often talked about as if it were a relief from serious learning. But for children play IS serious learning. Play is really the work of childhood."

Bra-VO, Mister Rogers! Frankly, in childhood I was a fan of Captain Kangaroo, who was my main influence, along with W.C. Fields and Lucille Ball, in my fourteen-year career as a professional clown. As a kid I thought Mister Rogers was for babies, and I didn't watch him. But as an adult I learned to respect the man in the sneakers and sweater. And he was *so* right about this. Too bad more "experts" on child-rearing and education don't understand this simple concept. I was getting tired of swimming upstream, repeatedly telling those young mothers, "SCHOOL is for education, clowns at birthday parties are for having FUN."

So, the decision was made to stop performing as a clown. This was a big shift in my business, and I was taking a big risk eliminating a service for which I was fully prepared, equipped, and experienced, and for which there was still a huge demand. But I really wanted to focus on my other services, and so I figured that if I was going to do this, I should do it BIG TIME, and publicly dump the clown character forever. On October 31, 1989, therefore, on the eve of the fourteenth anniversary of my first performance as Crisco the Clown, at Petaluma's venerable and historic old vaudeville house, the Phoenix Theater, I *killed* the clown in a very public manner. But first, some background.

THE PEOPLEOLOGIST

Our hometown newspaper, the historic *Petaluma Argus-Courier*, with roots dating back to 1855, had a columnist who, over the course of his five decade tenure, had become a local legend. His name was Bill Soberanes, born October 19, 1921, and he was descended from the famed General Mariano Guadalupe Vallejo, founder of the town of Sonoma, and the man who served as commandant of the San Francisco Presidio, military commander of the northern Mexican frontier, and the man who in 1834 secularized the northernmost Spanish mission of the twenty-one mission chain on El Camino Real in what was then referred to as "Alta California."

Soberanes was born and raised in Petaluma, living precisely between what was then east and west Petaluma. In fact, when he married his beautiful wife, Jane, he moved from the house in which he was born and into his uncle's house right next door at 423 East Washington Street. He lived all of his eighty-two years across from the train station, which was in his youth where all the important visitors to Petaluma arrived and departed. Furthermore, just beyond the railroad yard was the Petaluma Turning Basin which was the hub of transportation, commerce, and industry when San Francisco was being developed in the 1800s. The train station and the turning basin had truly been the center of activity in Petaluma for a century. While Bill lived in that spot all his life, he also traveled the globes to spread word about Petaluma, the "Egg Basket of the World."

Bill was my buddy and my hero. A pipe-smoking old-style journalist who'd do anything to get a *scoop*, Bill's claim to fame was that he met and was photographed with more famous and unusual people than anyone else in history. Forty-five thousand, to be inexact. His column appeared in every edition of the *Argus* from June of 1954 to the week after his death in June of 2003, and featured daily stories about, and pictures of him with, the likes of The Beatles, Frank Sinatra, Sammy Davis Jr., Bill Cosby, Jack Dempsey, Billy Graham, Jimmy Hoffa, several US Presidents, including Nixon, Ford, and Reagan, plus Hells Angel biker Sonny Barger, sports figures, gangsters, and boxcar hobos.

Peopleologist Bill Soberanes in the 1960s, 1980s, and 1990s.

Bill attended Petaluma High School with actor Lloyd Bridges and my maternal grandmother and her younger sister, Marie, and their baby brother, shipmaster Barney Lieder, about whom I'll talk more later. Bill worked as a cowboy, served in the Merchant Marine during World War II, toured as a prizefighter, and founded the sport of "wristwrestling." He literally put Petaluma on the map by luring ABC's Wide World of Sports to our town for several consecutive years in the 1970s to cover the competition between wristwrestlers he'd invited from around the globe. He coined the term "peopleologist," and delighted in the stories of anyone having anything to do with Petaluma.

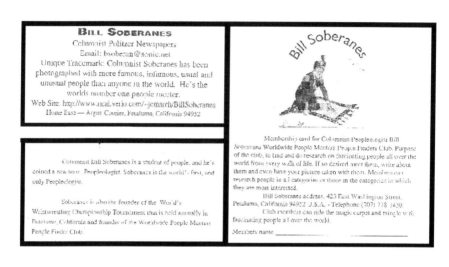

Bill Soberanes' famous fold-over business card.

He was also fascinated with Harry Houdini, and knew practically every professional magician who ever pulled a rabbit out of a hat. To that end, when the American Society of Magicians stopped hosting the annual Halloween séance atop Hollywood's Knickerbocker Hotel, which was begun on the deathbed orders of Houdini by his widow, Soberanes took the reigns and brought the séance to Petaluma, attempting each year to contact the late Houdini in that great theater in the sky. Bill's annual séance, which was the quintessential annual Petaluma Halloween tradition, was held in a variety of locations, including a number of Petaluma mansions alleged by some to be haunted. It brought even more notoriety to our town, and attracted a long list of, as Bill would say, "famous and not-so-famous" attendees, each year netting a fair amount of regional, national, and international media attention to our town.

What is the connection to Crisco the Clown? Hang on. As a teenager I read Soberanes' column, saw him frequently around town, and always wanted to get my name in his column, a real distinction that proved one was a true Petaluman. Bill would scurry into our hometown radio station, KTOB, where I worked, as part of his regular daily rounds, on foot, looking for scoops, puffing on that gnarly pipe, and lugging a heavy man-bag, which generally contained the following: his Kodak Instamatic camera, multiple roles of new and used film, mangled Reporter's Notebooks filled with page after page of scoops scribbled in his indiscernible scrawl, pens and pencils, copies of his column in the *Petaluma Argus-Courier*, a number of copies of his annual World's Wristwrestling Association programs, and several bags of pipe tobacco and books of matches.

Bill Soberanes on his front porch writing his column.

Bill typed his column from his notes on an old manual typewriter perched on the bannister of the high front porch of his raised bungalow house. Bill would be puffing on his pipe and typing as passersby waved and honked and shouted. Bill would wave back, and if it was someone he recognized, that person would find his or her name in the column in the following days. After Bill was finished, his beautiful, doting wife, Jane, would retype his column, cleaning up the spelling, grammar, and punctuation. Eventually she used a computer and sent the column daily via modem to the *Argus-Courier* office.

One sunny November day in 1978 I saw Bill standing at the town's main intersection, on the southwest corner of Washington and Petaluma Boulevard North, one door east of KTOB, across the street from the corner to the north where the first wristwrestling tournament occurred in 1953, across from another building to the east that today bears a beautiful Petaluma Heritage mural, in part depicting his famous progenitor, General Vallejo, and kitty-corner from the spot on the northeast corner on which today there is a statue of wristwrestlers and a brass plague bearing Soberanes' handsome visage and a few words of tribute to him. I saw Bill standing there, puffing his pipe, deep in thought about his next column, and I said to myself, "Chris, this is your chance to get into his column and be famous!"

I stepped up to him and said, "Hello, Mr. Soberanes. I'm a big fan of yours…I read your column every day. I attend Casa Grande High School, I work at KTOB, and I'm a clown…here's my card." I handed him one of my Crisco the Clown business cards, which my mother had printed for me as a gift on my fifteenth birthday. Without looking at it he shoved it into his pocket, handed me one of his cards (pictured a couple of pages earlier), and said, in his rapid-fire Bill Soberanes way, "Yeah, sure…good to meet you. I'll write about you in my column." And he did. Proudest day of my life at that time. That revered first column mention follows.

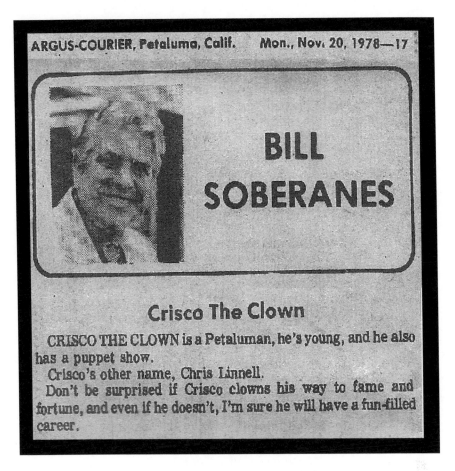

ARGUS-COURIER, Petaluma, Calif.   Mon., Nov. 20, 1978—17

BILL SOBERANES

Crisco The Clown

CRISCO THE CLOWN is a Petaluman, he's young, and he also has a puppet show.

Crisco's other name, Chris Linnell.

Don't be surprised if Crisco clowns his way to fame and fortune, and even if he doesn't, I'm sure he will have a fun-filled career.

Christopher's Holy Grail in 1978.

Some time later I ran into him again in the office of his newspaper. I was at the front counter talking to my friend, Martin Brody, who was the managing editor of the *Argus-Courier*. Martin noted Bill's mention of me, and interviewed me, and wrote two full-page feature articles about my clown services and celebrity impersonations (the first on March 26, 1981 ["'I like to have fun,' says Crisco, the clown, in one of nine voices"], and the second on April 15, 1983, ["Stargram delivers special messages with a flourish"]). I had worked-up a very good impression of Bill's iconic vocal delivery, and was getting giggles from Martin and the office staff when the door opened behind me and Martin suddenly straightened up and whispered, "THERE'S BILL!" I stopped in mid-sentence and turned around as Bill approached. He looked at Martin and then kinda' glared at me in feigned disdain and mumbled, "Whaddareya tryin' to do...put me in your act?"

Christopher and Bill.

What is the connection to the killing of Crisco the Clown? Bear with me. I was horrified and humiliated, scared that I had offended The Great Man, but Bill was a good natured fellow with a great and very dry sense of humor (unrecognized as such by those who didn't know him well), and he appreciated the fact that I apparently thought he was so famous that I should add him to my list of celebrity voices. We became friends over the years, and I assumed the role so many of his other friends had assumed before me: acting as his chauffeur.

Bill never drove...didn't even own a car. Jane did, and she'd drive them to the grocery store and the doctor and to other miscellaneous errands around town. His house was right in the middle of Petaluma, and he walked back and forth across town for five decades. But when he wanted to go out of town for a press conference or big event at which he could obtain new scoops and even more pictures of himself with big celebrities, he would rely on his friends to give him a ride.

On October 8, 1988, at 12:30 p.m., two plaques and a statue were dedicated in his honor downtown, and the evening before at 6:30 p.m. the whole town turned out for a tribute dinner for Bill and Jane at the Veteran's Memorial Auditorium. They both looked fantastic, and I attended, doing my new fully-costumed impersonation of my old hero.

Bill Soberanes meets his twin on October 7, 1988.

Bill loved it, and when the people in our town of thirty-some-thousand learned that there was a Bill Soberanes impersonator for hire, I was deluged with bookings as Bill, including at a party for Congresswoman Lynn Woolsey.

Christopher as Bill Soberanes preparing
Congresswoman Lynn Woolsey for life in Washington D.C.

To acquire the appropriate Soberanes costuming I cruised the thrift shops and bought two matching red, plaid, polyester sport coats (the 1970s style for which Bill was most known), and Bill and I frequently attended local events together. People would always joke that they couldn't tell which one of us was which, so he'd wear a nametag which read, "Christopher Linnell, Celebrity Impersonator," and I'd wear one reading, "Bill Soberanes, Columnist & Peopleologist." I think that Bill and I enjoyed these events even more than our audiences did.

The Name-Tag Tag-Team.

So what's the damned connection to the killing of Crisco the Clown, already? Ok, ok…we're there. On the fourteenth anniversary of my first performance as Crisco the Clown, I had already served on the Board of Directors of the World Wristwrestling Association, served as M.C. of the competition, impersonated Bill at the competition, and I had taken over the production of Bill's annual Halloween Harry Houdini Séance. In fact, I figured the latter would be the perfect event at which to kill Crisco the Clown. I asked Bill if I could incorporate that headline stunt into the evening's festivities, and he was only to happy to approve.

I contrived an elaborate scheme to make this very public shift in my business from clown shows at kids' parties and into celebrity impersonations at adult parties, and I promoted it relentlessly through newspaper ads, publicity, and direct mail. I asked for assistance from two local magician friends Bill and I had in common, Nahmen Nissen and Dick Quierolo. (By the way, this raises an interesting coincidence I just learned while researching this book: unbeknownst to me was the fact that Dick was the step-son of the aforementioned Wanda Ramey, the woman who three years earlier had suggested me to her agent.)

I told Nahmen and Dick that I wanted to kill my clown at the séance, and that I had devised a unique illusion for the task. I needed their assistance. I began promoting the event several weeks prior, in the *Argus-Courier*, and to my client list, and the *Press Democrat* published a feature article about it complete with a picture of Bill and me tied up Houdini-style.

Houdini séance publicity.

On Halloween I welcomed the attendees as they entered the lobby. I was in full makeup and costume, and I led them into the theater. I stepped to the stage, explained the thirteen-minute séance that would commence precisely at midnight, and then announced that I was retiring from the clown business, and that this very show would be Crisco's last appearance. I said, "Tonight, in a few moments, magicians Nahmen Nissen and Dick Quierolo will magically make me disappear right before your eyes!" The crowd laughed incredulously. I then introduced Nahmen and Dick, and left the stage, as they each, in turn, did a few illusions.

When I stepped back onto the stage, still fully-costumed and wearing my Crisco the Clown face, I stepped directly into a metal ring on the floor, attached to which was a six-and-a-half-foot-tall round curtain laying crumpled beneath. I waved goodbye, and Nahmen and Dick each grasped the ring on either side of me, and then raised the curtain above my head. They said the "magic words," and then dropped the curtain, and standing there before the audience was Christopher Linnell, wearing no makeup and a completely different set of clothes!

Magicians Nahmen Nissen and Dick Quierolo
make Crisco the Clown disappear.

As the shocked crowd applauded and cheered I dropped to my hands and knees, feigning some kind of attack, coughing and wheezing. The suddenly silent crowd simultaneously pondered how this illusion had been done and what was happening to me, and at that moment a man's body dropped fifty-feet from the ceiling at the end of a rope with a noose around its neck. A huge thud was heard that made the audience scream and gasp. The body hanging in in that noose was Crisco the Clown!

Christopher gasps, Nahmen assists, Crisco hangs; and the séance.

Costumed just as I was a few seconds before, still wearing full makeup, Crisco dangled there as the audience laughed and cheered and applauded. Nahmen and Dick and I stood there and looked at the body hanging above us, and then looked down onto the stage floor below it. The loud THUD that thunderously echoed throughout the old theater was Crisco's right leg, which had been ripped off the dummy by the force of gravity when the body hit the end of the rope, and had crashed onto the wooden stage floor.

What the audience didn't know is how Crisco got up to the ceiling and into the noose while Christopher was standing right before them behind the round curtain. My father was our secret accomplice up in the attic. He later told me that while he was preparing the body of Crisco for the drop, one of the legs of the dummy I had constructed had become loose, and he wasn't able to fasten it properly before his cue to drop the body. The THUD of the wooden leg on the wooden stage floor was a mishap that actually accentuated the surprise.

The illusion worked perfectly, and what YOU will never know is how we did it. You see, a magician never reveals his secrets.

ARGUS-COURIER, Petaluma, Calif.   Sunday, November 5, 1989—9A

bill soberanes

Columnist-peopleologist

The end of the clown

Although Chris Linnell shelved his Crisco the Clown act some time ago and became Christopher the Impersonator, it wasn't until he took part in the Harry Houdini Seance that Crisco was permanently replaced by Christopher the Impersonator.

The Death of a Clown, as Chris Linnell's pre-Houdini seance act was billed, wrote the final chapter in one phase of Linnell's life and added a new twist to Christopher the Impersonator. Those who witnessed Linnell's dramatic finish of Crisco were taken by his acting ability, which means he could have a third career in the hopper.

They say Lon Chaney was a man of a thousand faces; Chris hopes to surpass him. If Chris is successful in adding faces to his impersonating voices, Petaluma will have a star whose voice and faces could be shown and heard all around the globe.

Nahmen Nissen, standing, looks up at dummy; Crisco the clown is on the floor

Now, I know this is a big order, and I think Chris Linnell is capable of fulfilling it.

Interesting sidelight: Back on Nov. 20, 1978, I had the following article in this column:

Crisco the Clown is a Petaluman, he's young, and he also has a puppet show. Crisco's other name: Chris Linnell.

Don't be surprised if Crisco clowns his way to fame and fortune. But even if he doesn't, I'm sure he will have a fun-filled career.

3 - STARGRAM^{SM} Singing Telegrams

As a teenager in junior high, I listened to popular songs on the radio, and delighted in rewriting the lyrics for humorous effect. I did this with dozens of popular songs, writing about my friends and teachers and current events, and sang the songs to my classmates at recess. I was really good at writing lyrics, but had no way to actually use them in my professional performances...at first.

Singing telegrams were invented by Western Union public relations director George P. Oslin. He asked one of the company's operators, Lucille Lipp, to sing over the phone a birthday telegram from a fan to crooner Rudy Vallee on July 28, 1933. While Western Union ceased the delivery of telegrams sung *a cappella* by their uniformed messengers in 1974, singing telegrams by others were all the rage in the 1980s.

The year was 1982, and I received a call from a Mrs. Karen Brennan who had seen me perform somewhere. Her husband, Jim, was celebrating a birthday, and she wanted something fun. She said that he was a supervisor with Pacific Gas & Electric, and also a musician member of the famed Bohemian Club. He was a tubist who played Dixieland jazz with the Fourth Street Five, Red Garter and Three Easy Pieces Plus Two jazz bands out of San Francisco. The performance would be at a party at 8:30 p.m. on November 27 in their home in the wooded Mark West Springs area northeast of Santa Rosa, California, just twenty miles north of Petaluma.

When she asked what I could do, James Cagney was on my mind. He was one of my heroes, and I had recently read his autobiography, *Cagney by Cagney*, plus I had just watched his biopic about legendary vaudevillian, songwriter, and Broadway producer George M. Cohan, entitled *Yankee Doodle Dandy*. I suggested to Karen that I come fully-costumed as Cagney as Cohan, and sing a song to Jim, with custom lyrics written all about him, and sung to the tune of the title song of the Cagney movie. She said that would be great.

And it was. In fact, it went so well that I decided that singing telegrams would be a great sideline to my Crisco the Clown shows. I had already assembled costuming for thirteen celebrities, and all I needed was a name. They were STARs delivering singing teleGRAMs, so I coined the name STARGRAM^{SM} Singing Telegrams, and a new business venture had commenced! I hand-drew a logo, bearing a caricature of one of my other big heroes, and another celebrity impersonation I intended to offer, vaudeville juggler and movie icon W.C. Fields. I interviewed my clients on the phone, asking them all sorts of questions about their honorees, and then afterwards I read through the information over and over, looking for lyrical phrases. When a song I'd heard seemed to jibe with the lyrical phrases I'd concocted, I'd go to work incorporating into the confines of the music the information I'd obtained.

SINGING TELEGRAMS

I photocopied my STARGRAM^{SM} logo onto reams of canary-yellow sheets of paper, leaving a space for the lyrics, and dressed up the page with a caricature of the celebrity the client and I had chosen for the performance. I then typed the lyrics I'd written onto the sheet, and made two copies: one for my client and one for my files. Originally I performed the songs a cappella, but with the advent of karaoke, I was eventually able to find popular music *without* lyrics, which I'd play from a cassette tape on my Crisco the Clown boom box.

At some point in the early 1980s I found a book which I found extremely useful over the decades: *The Complete Rhyming Dictionary and Poet's Craft Book* edited by Clement Wood (Doubleday and Company, Inc., Garden City, New York, 1936). You look up a word, and listed is every other word with which it rhymes. In fact, the book is rather specific in that it has several sections, depending on which syllable one wants to rhyme. For instance, "cat" rhymes with "hat," but "catapult" rhymes with "difficult," and so and on. I'd choose a couple of tidbits of information (for instance, "she likes to dance to disco," and "she eats crackers in bed"), and then I'd rhyme it and match the syllable count to the line in the song (e.g., "She likes to dance to disco, but her bed's like a box from Nabisco!").

All this seems rather pointless without some kind of central theme. And that's why I eventually developed a "storyline" for my performances, usually falling into three general categories: A) investigating and questioning them about some imaginary crime, B) hiring them for something or asking something of them, or C) selling them or suing them for something. For instance, if I'm told that the honoree is a police officer who likes deer hunting with friends at a hunting lodge at which they love to drink Pabst Blue Ribbon, I would offer my client several storyline ideas and several characters for each storyline:

> A) Lt Columbo, Sgt Joe Friday, or Sheriff Buford T Justice works for the ASPCA and is investigating drunken deer roaming the area near the lodge; OR

> B) Rodney Dangerfield, Pee Wee Herman, or Benny Hill is an independent film producer who wants to make a movie about redneck male bonding; OR

> C) Groucho Marx, Johnny Carson's Art Fern, or Raymond Burr's Perry Mason is an attorney for Pabst Blue Ribbon, and they are prepared to take legal action if the honoree doesn't cease defaming their product.

Over time I found that spending thirty to forty-five minutes or more on the phone soliciting information from my clients about my honorees was a poor use of my time and theirs, so I developed a written questionnaire for the purpose, which I originally mailed, and then, as technology improved, faxed, and then finally just posted on my website and e-mailed to my clients. This generally elicited the bulk of the information I required, and, after I'd worked-up storyline and character suggestions, I'd call or e-mail my clients, explain my ideas, sometimes tweak them a bit, ask any additional questions, and then ask for their choices. In that way I always knew that my clients were on-board and would not be unpleasantly surprised by anything I said.

I've never been very good, generally, at memorization, and, for some reason, I seem to be terrible at delivering my own pre-written jokes. Furthermore, I have always been an absolute wiz at repartee, so I always improvised almost all of every performance I ever did. I would review my performance materials and sing my song lyrics once in the car before going into the venue, and then, once inside, I'd just improvise my way along as I played-out the storyline that I'd created, and, when I felt that I'd milked it for all I could get, I'd cue the music and conclude the performance with the song, leaving both the honoree and the client with their own copies of the lyrics.

One of the keys to the success of my word-of-mouth business over the decades was my custom of putting a half-dozen or more cards and/or brochures into the hand of my client as I took my payment and exited. I would joke, "Thank you very much, and here are some of my cards so you'll know where to send the attorneys." Another essential key were those lyric sheets, with the celebrity caricature and my business and contact info at the bottom. Party guests would say to the honoree and client, "Oh, lemme see that. Wow! I gotta get this guy for MY party next month!" As a result, the bookings snow-balled, and one booking would almost certainly guarantee at least two or three others from party attendees in the coming weeks, months, or years. I frequently had people calling me and saying, "I saw you at a party twenty years ago, and I've had your card on my fridge ever since."

CAN'T BEAT THE RAP

As "rap" music came to the fore, I decided that a great gimmick would be to perform my singing telegrams as raps, and I used the Quincy Jones instrumental, "Midnight Soul Patrol," which was actually an R&B instrumental, but nonetheless had a very catchy rhythm that lent itself just as well to rap-style spoken lyrics as to sung lyrics. It was perfect for my purposes, and I used it for years, not only for many of my STARGRAMs[SM], but for other acts I would devise later (described in the next chapter). The incongruity of Ronald Reagan or Rodney Dangerfield or Groucho Marx performing rap created additional humor for my performances, and my singing telegrams began to eclipse my clown shows in frequency and revenue.

Being an obsessive-compulsive packrat, I dutifully filed and have preserved every single lyric sheet I wrote over the course of three decades, and would love to publish them all someday, but they would be meaningless without the honoree information I'd gleaned from my clients, which has to remain privileged, obviously. The humor of the performances came from my honorees' personal information being sung in verse in front of their friends, relatives, and/or co-workers. Without knowing and understanding the honoree information, most of the humor is lost.

I not only offered STARGRAM[SM] Singing Telegrams in private settings, I also included them in performances I did at office parties, training meetings, national sales meetings, OSHA safety meetings, and fundraisers. Frequently in corporate performances I was asked to honor as many as a couple of dozen individual people in one song. For this I would use such longer songs as the Scarecrow's "If I Only Had A Brain" from *The Wizard of Oz*, which was widely recognized and ideally suited to my purposes. I would take minimal information about each honoree, and then devote two lines to each, usually incorporating a single joke for each person. This was very effective, for instance, for a sales team, or for the staff of a non-profit, or the faculty of a school. Everyone in the room was mentioned in the song, and everyone received a copy of the lyrics, which, as I mentioned above, was a fantastic marketing tool for me.

DR. HACKENBUSH

It was Groucho Marx who performed a song for the aforementioned bedridden father of screenwriter Joe Eszterhas. As I said, Joe had called me from Hawaii and was upset because he could not be with his ailing father in his home in Tiburon on the old guy's birthday. Joe said that his dad was all alone, except for the domestic and medical staff which cared for him 24/7 in Joe's absence, and that he wanted me to go cheer up his old man. With information Joe gave me about his dad, I wrote a song for Groucho, and rang the doorbell.

The home was a monstrous mansion on a picturesque cliff in Tiburon in southern Marin County with a spectacular view overlooking the Golden Gate Bridge, San Francisco and the bay, the Bay Bridge, and Alcatraz, Angel, Yerba Buena, and Treasure Islands. There was a maid and butler and nurse, if I remember correctly, and they very politely giggled and whispered as they led me into the elder Eszterhas' bedroom. He was propped up, awaiting something, apparently, though obviously not exactly what was coming his way: Groucho Marx, as the character Dr. Hugo Z. Hackenbush from the 1937 Marx Brothers movie *A Day At The Races*.

Dr. Hackenbush in the movie was a horse doctor who was just one step ahead of the law as he treated and wooed the wealthy old dowager, Mrs. Upjohn (played by Groucho's frequent film foil, Margaret Dumont). This was one of several Groucho characterizations I offered my clients on a regular basis over the years. Dr. Hackenbush attempted to do a fully nonsensical examination of the elder Eszterhas, eliciting laughter from the honoree as well as from his loving staff of caregivers. As always, the performance was concluded by the STARGRAM^{SM} Singing Telegram.

GOVERNMENT *IN*APPROPRIATION
Or CABINET SNATCH

Several years earlier, I was doing one of my many repeat performances at The Rocks & Shoals Club on the U.S. Coast Guard Training Center base at Two Rock just west of Petaluma, and the head physician instructor on the base (one of "TranCen's" course specialties was medical training) grabbed me by the arm at the end of my Groucho-as-a-doctor performance. In my Dr. Hackenbush performances I was equipped with an old leather doctor's bag I'd found at a thrift shop, filled with all kinds of goofy pseudo-medical equipment, such as a stethoscope and tongue depressor and blood pressure tester, as well as huge horse pills, syringes, condoms, lube, Vaseline, and my grandmother's enema bag. Yeah…for reals.

The Coast Guard doctor said, "C'mere…I've got something for you." He led me to a nearby building and through the labyrinth of classrooms and laboratories to a wall filled floor-to-ceiling with tall, stainless steel cabinets. He opened one of the doors, and pulled out a wide drawer absolutely overflowing with important and expensive-looking stainless steel medical devices and tools. He reached in and grabbed a particularly odd-looking duck's beak device, and handed it to me, saying, "Here…take this, and stick it in your bag, and the next time you do your doctor routine, Groucho, you pull this thing out and I guarantee that you'll get a big laugh." He absolutely refused to tell me what it was, but the next time I did a Dr. Hackenbush, I pulled it out, and sure enough, I got a *huge* laugh that wouldn't subside. Later I was told the device is called a "vaginal speculum." Needless to say, I still have it in my bag to this day.

TIM McGRAW, THE MACHO MAN

It was many years later, early in the morning on May 1, 1998, that I got a call from the staff of legendary country artist Tim McGraw. They told me that he and his new wife, country artist Faith Hill, were at historic and picturesque V. Sattui Winery in St Helena shooting a music video, and that he was trying to ignore his thirty-first birthday…they wanted to surprise him. They already had the storyline worked out for me, too. "We tease Tim a lot that he's a bit of a homophobe, and he's petrified of gaining weight and looking out of shape for his fans. So we thought it would be funny if you came in today as RICHARD SIMMONS!" I told them that I couldn't have constructed a better storyline myself.

Needless to say he was surprised, and I gave him and his wife and their staff and the video crew and the winery staff a performance they will never forget. Faith Hill, five months pregnant, was not wearing any makeup (and, by the way, that sweet lady is absolutely gorgeous without makeup), tending to baby Gracie Katherine (who was herself just four days shy of her first birthday), and laughing her head off as her husband was tortured. Richard Simmons had Tim McGraw prancing around the room with him to the tune of the Village People classic "Macho Man," as Richard poked Tim in the belly, saying, "C'mon, Timmy...I've seen better lumps in oatmeal! Let's start sweatin' to the oldies!"

A couple of months later I received a nice letter from Tim's staff, along with the autographed photo of the two of us, shown below. You'll note that Tim signed on *my* chest, so the next time I run into Richard Simmons, I'll have him sign *his* name on *Tim's* chest.

Tim McGraw with Christopher as Richard Simmons.

PRANKS A LOT

I have a colleague in San Francisco who has made pranks his life's work. His name is Brian Wishnefsky of "Pranks for the Memories" at www.Pranks4U.com, and he is one of the fastest and funniest comedians I've ever met. He is the king of relentless puns, and offers as many characterizations as I offer celebrity impersonations. In other words, I may do an event as John Wayne or Jack Nicholson, but he performs as a nerd or a biker dude. I refer clients to him all the time, but I rarely want to perform at events *with* him, because on the few occasions on which I have, I found that I couldn't get a word in edgewise with him around. And that's saying a lot. But as he doesn't do celebrity impersonations, we are not generally competing with each other directly. In fact, our services complement each other nicely. For instance, whenever someone calls for a prank, or a practical joke, or to ask me to pretend to be someone or do something *real*, I invariably refer them to Brian.

On occasion, though, I have been talked into doing a prank or two by an eager client with a "great idea." And I've hated it and regretted it almost every time. There's something about pretending to be a famous celebrity or character, such as Lt. Columbo or Popeye, that's very easy. The character is well-known, and pretty obvious when you walk into the room. Everybody knows why you're there, and they're ready to laugh. Portraying a real person is different. People react differently when someone they perceive as real begins behaving in an odd fashion. They get nervous. They get upset. They get mad. They start getting defensive. And, after all, I'm there not to make them cry, but to make them laugh.

One time a large and prominent electrical contractor in the town of Novato in affluent Marin County called me up and said, "You've performed for us so many times before, we wanna have you again. But this time we've got a different idea. This gal we're honoring has been having some tax problems lately. We want you to come in as an I.R.S. agent and pretend to do an audit right here in our conference room." I resisted, but they persisted, and seemed very enthusiastic about the idea, so I relented and we made some rather elaborate preparations.

They wanted the performance videotaped, so I had them set up the camera in their conference room at the far end of the conference table in plain view, and I was in a suit and tie, and had piles of official-looking papers in manila envelopes laid out on the table. They brought the honoree/victim into the room and I told her that we had some questions about her returns and informed her that I would be video-taping the proceedings to document her responses. And she started crying. Not the laughing kind of tears, mind you, which I frequently got out of both women *and men* when they were simultaneously laughing hard and embarrassed and surprised, but the anguished kind of tears you see in courtrooms and funeral parlors and hospital E.R.s and actual I.R.S. audits, I would imagine.

Furthermore, contrary to my express instructions, the staff had almost immediately assembled outside in the hallway in plain view through the floor-to-ceiling windows. They stood and laughed while she cried. It was horrible. I ended the thing as quickly as possible, and never heard from that formerly good client again.

On the other hand, I actually did a similar performance that went quite well. In this case the staff had told me their boss was in big trouble with the I.R.S and they wanted me to come in and kick him out of his office. I explained that this scenario wouldn't be too feasible, as an I.R.S. agent would have documentation to prove his identity, and I couldn't prepare something that would be realistic enough to fool a prominent real estate developer into vacating his company's headquarters. I suggested that I say that I'm an I.R.S. contractor who handles I.R.S. collections procedures. I had a private security badge in a basket-weave police wallet, and I created paperwork and an I.D. card that contained the identical name and logo found on the badge. I also put a spare answering machine on the fax line in my office with a message done by a professional-sounding female accomplice identifying my fax number as belonging to my fake private security firm. And it's a good thing I did this, because he did call my office to verify that I was real.

I went into their offices in downtown Sebastopol in western Sonoma County, and asked to speak to the principal of the firm. I explained that due to his existing trouble with the I.R.S., the agency had contracted with my firm to foreclose on his offices. He would have fifteen minutes to vacate himself and his staff and all of their personal effects from the premises, at which point I would chain the doors and affix official seals. He was flustered and perturbed, but fearfully compliant, and I supervised while he informed his staff, who managed to maintain their composure beautifully despite the incredible inconvenience of this elaborate practical joke which they had all planned.

Individual employees asked me questions about what was a personal effect and what was business (e.g., purses and jackets and personal photos could be taken, but potted plants and wall art had to stay, etc), and the entire staff of a dozen people packed up everything in sight and we all went out to the parking lot. I wrapped and locked chains around the doors from the outside, and then pulled my cassette boom box out from behind a nearby bush and hit "PLAY." As the music played, the poor fellow looked at me, totally perplexed, and then I pulled my STARGRAM^{SM} Singing Telegram lyrics out of my jacket pocket and began to sing them to him. I actually got three or four lines into the song before he finally figured out what was going on. The staff laughed as he said, "Oh, NO…you have GOT to be shitting me!"

GRIN AND BEAR IT, COUSIN

Another prank that actually went quite well was for my cousin Susan. She was celebrating a birthday, and was recently divorced. My dad's older brother, Uncle Curtis, and his wife, Aunt Ann, asked me to come and do a STARGRAM^{SM} Singing Telegram for her. I said that I'd have to create a pretty intricate storyline and a very distinct characterization so that she wouldn't recognize me, and asked that they tell me everything she'd been up to lately. They told me at some length about how involved Susan had become in prayer circles and chat rooms online. We devised a very funny storyline that evolved into a rather evil prank.

Her online pseudonym was "Mama Bear," so we decided that I would pose as an online stalker named "Papa Bear" who had been lurking in chat rooms and was becoming infatuated with her. I created a fake profile online, writing that

Papa Bear was a disabled Vietnam vet about a decade older than she was. He was also a recovering substance abuser with a long prison record, anger management issues, and a number of other exceptionally undesirable qualities. A real catch! And then I actually began stalking her online, following her from one chat room to another for a few days, saying hello to her in each one, and professing love and an inextinguishable passion for her. I promised that we would meet. Despite her constant rejections, I persisted.

On the appointed day, she had arrived at her parents' house with her sons for her birthday party, and her parents and siblings and nieces and nephews were telling her about the phone calls they'd been getting all morning from Papa Bear, and they were all asking her if she had a new boyfriend. In fact, Uncle Curtis said that Papa Bear told him he was coming by later to meet Mama Bear, and that's all she needed to hear. She grabbed her boys and headed for the door, just as I rolled up the driveway…in my wheelchair.

The question was whether Susan would recognize her own cousin. She didn't. As Susan scurried out the front door, Papa Bear rolled up the driveway, wearing black leather boots and motorcycle chaps and a vest, and a hooded sweatshirt, and a gray Willie Nelson ponytail wig and a bandana on his head, plus thick glasses and Billy Bob teeth. Oh, and the Santa pillow I was wearing underneath the sweatshirt added about twenty-five pounds to my look. She didn't have a clue. She freaked! In fact, she turned tail and ran toward the door to call the police, but the family stopped her and the kids ooh'd and aah'd and Uncle Curt said, "Don't run off, Mama Bear…Papa Bear wants to get acquainted!" He pulled the blanket off his lap to reveal a boom box, and, as the music played, Papa Bear sang a love song to his dream girl.

I was several lines into the song before she even realized that this was a singing telegram, and I actually finished the song before she realized it was her cousin sitting there before her. Papa Bear said, "Oh, don't get upset, Mama Bear…we're only cousins. I mean, it ain't like I'm your brother!"

4 - Christopher & Co. Celebrity Impersonations

Doing celebrity impressions was fun, but the first time I dressed up in costume to impersonate a celebrity, the response I received was so gratifying that I decided that full costuming was, to paraphrase Jim Backus' koala bear cartoon character in the old Qantas Airlines ads, "the oooonly way to fly!"

CAPTAIN LIEDER

My maternal grandmother's youngest sibling, Barney Lieder, was a ship captain for Pacific Far East Lines. He was himself W.C. Fields, Ernest Hemingway, and Johnny Cash combined, and he was a hard-drinking bar buddy, Merchant Marine colleague, and high school pal of the late, great *Petaluma Argus-Courier* columnist and "peopleologist," Bill Soberanes. While we lived on Guam in the 1970s, Uncle Barney sailed into the island's huge commercial port, Apra Harbor, roughly twice a year en route to "the Orient," and my parents would pick him up at the ship, begrudgingly pour the cocktails he expected, take him to dinner, pour him back into the car, and carry him onto the ship.

One time, after a few cocktails at the house, my folks took Captain Lieder with us kids to M's Steak House, our favorite Saturday night family dinner spot, and the old coot got roundly intoxicated with cocktails before, during, and after dinner, loudly and brashly telling ribald tales and incoherent anecdotes and making characteristically prejudiced remarks loudly enough for all around to hear. My parents were humiliated, but were helpless to stop him, and, as we left the restaurant, they apologized profusely to the manager, who was so familiar to us he was almost like family. He politely brushed off the apologies, saying, "Oh, don't worry...it happens all the time. It's just too bad that pastor and his family were dining at the table next to yours."

Later that evening, upon returning Captain Lieder to the port, we were stopped at the gate by two huge Guamanian security guards. Now, we'd been in and out of that gate numerous times over the years with Uncle Barney, and had come in just hours before that evening to pick him up with no problem whatsoever, but on *this* occasion the guards told my dad that they had to inspect our car to check the dates on our FIRE EXTINGUISHER! My dad said, "Fire extinguisher? I don't have a fire extinguisher. We just came through this gate four hours ago!"

Before my poor dad knew what was happening, Uncle Barney had bounded out of the passenger door, ambled around the front of the car, and was getting into the guards' faces. Or, their *chests*, actually, because Barney was only about five-foot-five, and these two monstrous, professional-wrestler-lookin' island boys were easily six-feet tall. "What the hell's the matter with you, you God-damned jungle bunnies? Don't you recognize ME? I'm Captain Bernard Lieder, master of the *Hawaiian Bear!*" There was a scuffle, and, as my mother squeezed my sister and me in the back seat of the car in terror, my dad somehow managed to wrestle Barney out of a scary situation, back into the car, and then through the gate and into his stateroom on his ship. Don't ever let it be said that my dad can't be charming, diplomatic, *and* forceful when necessary.

I was pretty impressed with my Uncle Barney. He was loud and funny and opinionated and we visited him on his ship once, and all the sailors saluted him and got out of his way and said "Aye, aye, Captain!" He traveled between the lowest and highest points in the contiguous United States, going from Badwater in Death Valley to the peak of Mt. Whitney; he traveled alone through Alaska; yawned at the aurora borealis; sailed the world at the helm of the largest freighters…he saw it all and did it all, and had a brash, outspoken opinion about everything and everyone under the sun. I was an impressionable teenager, and he seemed to me to be truly larger than life.

Christopher with Captain Lieder.

One night he sat on the couch guzzling his gin and ranting on about the how the unions were destroying industry, the Jews were running Hollywood, and how the Modern Woman was emasculating and feminizing men. All the while, in my bedroom, I was hurriedly dressing in my father's old, discarded sport coat and a battered, black, felt hat, and searching for my big rubber cigar. With all costuming and accessories in place, I strutted down the hallway, and, upon entering the living room said "Ahhhh, yes..." in my already perfected W.C. Fields voice, and without batting an eyelid the inebriated old salt shouted "W.C. FIELDS" and literally burst into uproarious laughter.

I was hooked. I mean, if The Great Captain Lieder recognized and applauded my impersonation, I knew I had found my true calling.

THE CLOTHES MAKE THE MAN

Doing impressions of celebrities on stage was easy and fun, but once I'd been fully-costumed as a celebrity and had been fully immersed in that character's personae, I could settle for nothing less. The next best thing to *being* John Wayne is looking like him and sounding like him and acting like him and having people treat you like him. To me it was just a game of pretend, which sounds childish, but my audiences loved it and were entertained by it, so I was yearning to do fully-costumed impersonations of all the stars in my stand-up act.

Living on Guam made a lot of things difficult, particularly finding costuming. Guamanians didn't save clothing...they didn't even *wear* much clothing. Women had a couple of *muumuus,* men had pants and island shirts; but there were few sport coats, ties, tuxes, top hats, or cowboy gun belts to be found on the island. Bottom line: there were no thrift shops. Flip-flops and swimsuits are what everybody wore on a daily basis. How was I gonna be W.C. Fields, Groucho Marx, James Cagney, John Wayne, Johnny Cash or Elvis when I had to do it wearing jeans and boots and a flowery cotton blouse?

When my family moved back to California in 1977, we stayed in San Francisco for a while before making our way north to Petaluma...and I was in heaven. The Haight-Ashbury neighborhood is more than a tourist attraction, more than the center of the universe for hippies, more than just a great place to smoke dope, drink coffee, and get free treatment for STDs. The Haight is THE place for costumes! There are more fantastic vintage shops on Haight Street today than anywhere else I can think of, short of Hollywood Boulevard. If there had been a Haight Street on Guam, my parents may never have gotten me into that plane back to California.

I started with just a few hats and coats and ties, and eventually found myself buying every piece of clothing I found that I thought I could one day use. And I almost never threw any clothes out. Every time a client asked for a celebrity I didn't already offer, I'd check my closets and then head out to enthusiastically hit the thrift shops with checkbook in hand and see if I could put it all together for them. Originally my list of celebrity impersonations numbered just thirteen, but the number grew and grew and grew until thirty years later I have complete costuming for well over one hundred stars. I built four closets in my garage, and only two of them contain costumes I used on a regular basis. The third contains characters I'd only done once or twice, and the fourth contains costume pieces I bought and never used, as well as my old personal clothes that I thought I might one day be able to use.

In addition to STARGRAM^{SM} Singing Telegrams, I also offered a similar performance, including a fully-costumed celebrity impersonation, but without the STARGRAM^{SM} Singing Telegram, and at a reduced rate; I called it a "Celebrity Impersonation." These were for parties or meetings for which the client didn't have the budget for me to write a song. And I offered a program called "Walkaround Impersonations" in which I performed fully-costumed celebrity impersonations on an hourly basis for promotions and large parties with hundreds of attendees, typically for retail promotions, in corporate settings, or at fundraisers.

BARKING AT THE COMPETITION

My first professional Walkaround Impersonation on July 29-31, 1982, was for a small store called EarthMart on Petaluma Boulevard North, right in the heart of the downtown business district. The store across the street, Lombardi's Western Wear, had purchased expensive regional print and broadcast advertising to promote a big sidewalk sale that weekend. EarthMart was a small mom-and-pop, hippy, crystal, batik, and tie-dye store, and proprietor Paul Mailloux figured he could avoid spending tens of thousands of dollars on advertising and still attract shoppers to his own sidewalk sale by simply hiring yours truly to stand on their sidewalk directly across the street and *shout* across the street in character. He was looking for a town barker; I recommended my old hero and comedic role model, W.C. Fields.

This was a summer weekend in July, and temperatures soared into the upper 90s. I was costumed as Fields' Professor Eustace P. McGargle, the carnival barker character from the 1936 movie *Poppy*, dressed in black dress shoes and white spats, black-and-white herringbone polyester slacks, cotton t-shirt, white dress shirt, nineteenth century necktie, long Navy-blue wool overcoat with a fur-lined collar, black felt top hat, and a big rubber nose. And, of course, I wore my tailor-made Santa Claus belly pillow, because I wasn't yet up to full W.C. Fields girth at the time. (I've since grown into the character, of course, and no longer need the pillow to look the part, unfortunately.)

Christopher as W.C. Fields in downtown Petaluma in July of 1982.

I juggled balls, balanced my cane on my toe, juggled my top hat, and used a small P.A. I brought, but it did little good. As crowds across the street perused the tables filled with Wrangler jeans, Western dress shirts, silver belt buckles, and all sorts of cowboy hats, I barked Fields gibberish across the drone of main street traffic...all day Friday, Saturday, and Sunday. Needless to say, my voice, which I have always been told by derisive school teachers "carries," nonetheless was all but *gone* by the end of the first day. Sunday I was screeching, as the sweat rolled down into my collar and soaked every single garment I wore. By sunset Sunday, I was a hoarse, sweaty, stinky mess.

In fact, my voice remained painfully hoarse for *weeks* thereafter, which made it difficult to do my radio airshifts and other performances, and I was truly worried that I had permanently damaged my vocal cords, so I visited a doctor, who referred me to a voice coach. This woman, who taught budding opera stars how to project without straining, scared the living hell out of me by warning me of polyps and throat cancer, and telling me that the only way to regain my voice and manage its use was by paying her an on-going retainer on a permanent basis. I didn't have the funds for this, and thought for sure that I had destroyed what I had always thought would be a lifelong career in the performing arts. Fortunately I resisted her sales pitch, drank the warm honey-and-lemon concoction prescribed by the M.D., and within a few weeks I was back to normal...almost. I still got hoarse on busy weekends, but, three decades later, have yet to develop the life-threatening conditions that voice coach promised. Thank goodness.

PRESIDENTS AND THE SECRET SERVICE

U.S. Presidents are always popular character selections by people planning private and corporate events alike. Ronald Reagan was president when I began offering celebrity impersonations as a regular service, and I did a killer Reagan. I wore a blue pinstriped suit, red silk tie with a full Windsor knot, American flag lapel pin, black wig, and a hint of red rouge on the cheeks to give me that characteristic Reagan blush.

I did Reagan everywhere for everybody...he was one of my top ten busiest characters. My favorite Reagan, though, was an absolute gas! I was hired by Cathy Smith-Markusen, eldest of nine children of the founder of Argonaut Construction, a large general engineering contractor, to help celebrate the firm's upcoming thirtieth anniversary, and was asked to perform on August 23, 1986, at the annual company picnic in the Keiser Grove out in the beautiful Russian River area west of the then-unincorporated hamlet of Windsor in Sonoma County. They had an ample budget, so we went all-out.

I chartered a black stretch Cadillac limousine from Lon Kaufmann, proprietor of "Lon's Limo Scene," and adorned it with a pair of small American flags mounted on the front fenders. In recent years, of course, there have been stretch limousines everywhere in Wine Country. Every wine tour, quinceañera, wedding, graduation, birthday, anniversary, and Red-Solo-Cup party could rent a limo for just a few hundred bucks. (This will probably be changing soon, as the industry had been moving away from stretches and into SUVs and "executive coaches;" coincidentally, two stretch limousines fires occurred here in the Bay Area in early 2013, the first resulting in the deaths of passengers trapped inside. Most people won't touch them with a ten-foot pole anymore.) But this Reagan job was back in the good old days when the only people riding in black stretch limos were either movie stars or the president of the United States; when you saw one, you turned your head and snapped a few pictures.

Christopher as Reagan in August of 1986 with Lon's "Limo Scene."

To complete the illusion, I talked Mrs. Markusen into providing four male staff members, in business suits, to pose as Secret Service agents. I equipped them all with reflectorized sunglasses and old-fashioned white earplugs. Two rode inside the car with me, and two outside jogged alongside the car. I'm tellin' you, we looked good. Of course, today the president is escorted by a phalanx of dozens and dozens of black SUVs, all with machine gun-toting agents peering out of open windows, but in the 1980s it was convincing enough seeing one lone black stretch limousine with fender flags and Secret Service agents jogging alongside outside.

The job itself was fun and fast. Our presidential limo pulled into the grove, escorted on foot by the jogging agents. The car stopped in front of the crowd, and the jogging agents took up positions at the front and rear bumpers, looking vigilantly in all directions, and talking into their cuffs. The agent at the rear cautiously opened the rear door, and the other two agents sprang out, scanning the crowd for unfriendly faces, and then escorted President Reagan as he stepped out of the car to the cheers of the crowd. Reagan shook a few hands as the Secret Service agents suspiciously pushed the people back, and he made his way to the stage where he greeted the crowd on mic, made a short, humorous speech, presented a plaque to Clyde P. Smith (1926-2000), one of the company's founders, and then retraced his steps to the waiting limo.

We finished in such short order, in fact, that we felt kind of let-down. My agents all wanted to do something else, their earlier nervousness all gone as they bathed in the afterglow of their Secret Service illusion glory. We still had plenty of time left on the limo, so I told Lon, "Let's all go downtown and get cool, refreshing beverages."

We returned to "downtown" Windsor, which, prior to incorporation in 1992, was a stereotypical small town, consisting of only a half-dozen buildings, half of which were vacant, bearing old-west facades, huddled around the main street where it crossed the railroad tracks, and including only the old train station, a restaurant, a diner, a Laundromat, the post office, a feed store, the Odd Fellows' Hall, and a tiny, family-owned grocery store called Pohley's Market.

Our presidential limo slid up to the front of Pohley's, and the four agents jumped out of the car. Two stood at either end of the car on the sidewalk, doing sentry duty, while the other two went in to "sweep" the store. I had told them to play this up to the hilt, checking out the whole store for assassins, terrorists, and miscreants of any variety. When they returned to the car, the agents opened my door, and then escorted the president into the store. Inside a clerk was behind the counter, and four customers were in line, including a couple of Latino vineyard workers, and two nice Latina matriarchs, one holding a baby. Our official-looking procession gave them pause in their conversation (in Spanish), and we proceeded, in formation, to the refrigerators in the rear of the store. We each selected a bottle of pop, and then headed to the counter. Reagan stood in line right behind the ladies, with the agents lined up behind.

Christopher's Secret Service detail.

The customers in line in front of Reagan tried to pretend as though they didn't notice, and they didn't say anything directly to our group, but they all meekly smiled and shot indirect glances toward Reagan, the agents, and the flag-adorned limousine out front. One of the ladies was heard to whisper to the other, "¿Por qué esta el presidente en Windsor?"

We all paid for our soda bottles, and headed out the door and into the stretch, which pulled away from Pohley's and into the annals of Windsor lore.

YOURS TRULY AND THE SECRET SERVICE

Speaking of the U.S. Secret Service, I had an indelibly intimate personal experience with them one day in 1988. They arrested me...sort of. And all I was doing was "research." A little background is necessary first.

In an attempt to absorb as much of each of my celebrities' mannerisms and motivations as possible, I would try to improve my knowledge of each person and his or her history. But there was no Internet available to me in those days. Today I can Google somebody, and I get pictures, video, movie scripts, and complete biographies online in an instant. But in the 1970s and early 80s I had to glean what I could from memory, so I relied on newspapers, magazines, library books, and radio and television broadcasts. But, of course, that meant passively waiting for a desired celebrity to show up on television, and then hope that no one else in the family was watching anything else. I didn't own a VCR until 1984, so, before that, when a movie or television show featured a celebrity I wanted to impersonate, I would hold a cassette tape player up to the television speaker to record his or her voice.

I maintained separate files on every celebrity I offered, or would ever consider offering, with clippings from magazines and newspapers. That way, when somebody called and wanted a particular star, I would check my files and assemble costuming and accessories based upon the pictures I had of each star. I also assembled a large library of books, trying to purchase at least a biography, or, when available, a "filmography" of each star. I have filmographies of W.C. Fields, James Cagney, Laurel & Hardy, and the Marx Brothers, to name a few, each containing synopses, photographs, and cast lists for each movie the star made. These were particularly helpful for celebrities of whom I offered multiple characterizations.

For instance, several celebrities are listed below, each followed by their multiple characterizations that I offered:

HUMPHREY BOGART
Sam Spade from *The Maltese Falcon*
Rick Blaine from *Casablanca*
Charlie Allunt from *The African Queen*
Lt. Commander "Captain" Phillip Francis Queeg from *The Caine Mutiny*

W.C. FIELDS
Sheriff Cuthbert J. Twillie from *My Little Chickadee*
Professor Eustace P. McGargle from *Poppy*

GROUCHO MARX
J. Cheever Loophole, Esq of *Animal Crackers*
Professor Quincy Adams Wagstaff from *Horse Feathers*
Captain Geoffrey T. Spaulding from *Animal Crackers*
Dr. Hugo Z. Hackenbush from *A Day at the Races*
As himself in the 50s from the radio and television game show *You Bet Your Life*
And as "Kris Lipschutz", the Jewish santa, aka "Santa Klez" (my own creation)

JACK NICHOLSON
Jack Torrance from *The Shining*
Darryl Van Horne from *The Witches of Eastwick*
Randall Patrick McMurphy from *One Flew Over the Cuckoo's Nest*
Colonel Nathan R. Jessup from *A Few Good Men*
President James Dale of *Mars Attacks!*

JOHN WAYNE
Marshal Rooster J Cogburn of *True Grit* & *Rooster Cogburn*
Captain Wedge Donovan USNR of *The Fighting SeaBees*

Offering multiple characterizations expanded my storyline options exponentially. If a client wanted Jack Nicholson, for instance, I could choose which of my five Nicholson characterizations to use, based upon the storyline I created. Therefore, my files were essential to me in character preparation. Of course, the very best way to impersonate a celebrity is to actually SEE that celebrity in person. And that brings us back to the story I promised about the U.S. Secret Service.

I had to stay on top of pop culture, because people always wanted the latest thing. I had to watch television, go to the movies, listen to the radio, and read the newspaper. And one day in the paper I read that one of the celebrities I wanted to offer would be appearing LIVE and in person just twenty miles from my house! What an opportunity! I had to go. It was research!

In 1988 the Reverend Jesse Jackson was making his second bid to become the first African-American president of the United States. His Rainbow Coalition was popular in liberal Sonoma County, and he decided to make a campaign stop in the county seat of Santa Rosa, just north of my town of Petaluma. I had been doing a Jackson vocal impression for some time, and recognized that if he won the election, offering a Jackson impersonation would be a must. When I heard Jackson would be appearing in Santa Rosa, I planned to go to the outdoor rally at the Sonoma County Fairgrounds. I mentioned it to a buddy of mine, whom I'll call Robert. Which brings me to another sidebar...

I met Robert almost ten years before while working at KTOB. Like me, he had started at the station as a teenager; but, unlike me, Robert had previous disc jockey experience working at Cal Skate in Rohnert Park as a roller-skating disc jockey. I worked Saturday nights at KTOB from 6-10 p.m., and Robert worked 10 p.m. to 2 a.m. Being the same age, having roller skating in common, and working together at the radio station, we became fast friends. Robert and I also had another very important characteristic in common: a quick wit. Robert was a wiz at repartee, loved practical jokes, and had the balls to do any kind of prank suggested. We skated together, worked together, and, when I dated and married my high school sweetheart, we became a threesome, going everywhere together: dinner, skating, skiing at Tahoe, the Russian River.

Furthermore, Robert had just as busy a schedule as I did in those days. We both held several jobs simultaneously, and both of us were self-employed entertainers (Robert ran a successful mobile DJ service). In addition to his roller, radio, and mobile DJ jobs, Robert was a volunteer fireman, and later left disc jockey work completely to become a professional full-time firefighter in Santa Rosa. We also both attended college; I wanted to teach history and political science, Robert wanted to one day become a fire chief. This didn't take all of our time, however...we both loved pulling costumed pranks. I actually hired Robert several times to help me in my performances, once impersonating The Blues Brothers.

Several times I entered my entertainment business in local parades, for such annual local festivals as Petaluma Butter & Egg Day, Sebastopol's Apple Blossom Festival, and the century-old Santa Rosa Rose Parade. I would typically decorate my car as the presidential limo, with fender flags, my dad would drive the car, wearing a Jimmy Carter mask, and my mother and wife would stand up through the sun roof wearing my business suits and ties and rubber Nixon and Reagan masks. Robert and I would be dressed as Secret Service agents and escort the car on roller skates. We wore dark business suits, sunglasses, and earplugs. We always got big laughs, and Robert enjoyed the fun as much as I did.

You can see where this is leading, right? At 2 p.m. on Wednesday, May 11, 1988, the lifestyles editor of the *Petaluma Argus-Courier*, A.L. Landers, arrived in my mobile home office to interview me for a feature story about my entertainment business, when the phone rang. I asked Ms. Landers to pardon me, and answered the call using my desktop speakerphone, "Good afternoon, Christopher & Company."

"Chris...it's Rob. Are we still on for tomorrow?" I answered, "Yeah. Have you got your suit and tie?" Robert responded, "Yeah. Have you got the sunglasses and earplugs?" I said, "You bet. Pick you up tomorrow at 6:30." Robert said, "Cool. See ya," and hung up.

The puzzled reporter queried, "What was THAT all about?" I explained that I was picking up Robert for golf the next morning, followed by lunch, and we'd be formulating our plans for an upcoming Jesse Jackson rally. We were going to go in our Secret Service getups. Ms. Landers said, "What?"

I explained that Robert and I were going to the Jesse Jackson rally that Friday so that I could see and hear Jackson in person for my impersonation of him, and that we were going to go dressed as Secret Service agents as we'd done at events so many times before. I explained that seeing Jackson was important research for me as a celebrity impersonator, but told her, regarding our costumed prank, "Hey, there's no reason not to mix business with pleasure." She was intrigued; she giggled and asked, "Lemme know how it comes out, ok?" I said,

"Will do."

Early the next morning I picked up Robert for golf, and we played at the beautiful Bennett Valley Golf Course in Santa Rosa, and then had lunch at the Annadeli and planned our upcoming Secret Service gig. At 1:00 that afternoon I was in the production studio at KSRO working on an ad for one of my loyal clients, Ted Fullmer's Unocal 76. Ted had been using my production services since I was still on staff at KSRO, and I did dozens of goofy ads for him, using a wide variety of character voices. *Argus-Courier* photographer Scott Manchester met me at the station during the session to take pictures of me in the studio for use in Ms. Lander's article. (By the way, Scott still shoots for the *Argus-Courier*, as well as other papers, and as recently on May 4, 2013, he shot pictures of Christopher & Co., including yours truly along with my partners Karicia Aventura, Mark Bellinger, and Karen Aviles, in a benefit lip-synch show called "The Who's Who Revue.")

On the following day (which was, as a matter of fact, Friday the thirteenth), I picked-up Robert in the afternoon and we headed to the home of my maternal grandmother, who lived a short walk from the fairgrounds, where Jackson would be speaking. Grandma loved having me stop by, in- and out-of-costume, as my grandfather had died a few years before and she loved the companionship. I would come at all hours of the day and night, in all kinds of crazy costumes, and she would laugh and ask me about the job I was doing. Sometimes I'd come when she was hosting her bridge group, and all the elderly ladies would get a kick out of a clown or movie star coming in and interrupting their game. In fact, as I pulled a Saturday night radio shift 'til midnight at KSRO in Santa Rosa, and another one on Sunday morning, she would let me come over and sleep in the extra bedroom so that I didn't have to drive all the way back to Petaluma on my measly six-hour break between airshifts.

We parked at Grandma's house so that we wouldn't get stuck in the crowd of Volkswagen vans and Volvo and Audi station wagons inching their way into the fairgrounds. Our family always parked at Grandma's for events staged at the fairgrounds, including the fair. She laughed at our costumes, and told us how official we looked, and, as we headed down the driveway, she called after us, teasingly saying, "Be careful not to get caught by the G-Men!"

Robert and I arrived sometime after 5 p.m. at the expansive grassy area that hosted the carnival each year at the Sonoma County Fair, and we were surprised by the huge crowd of enthusiastic Jackson supporters awaiting his scheduled 6 p.m. appearance. Estimated by the *Santa Rosa Press Democrat* to be about two thousand strong, the crowd was largely composed of Jackson's targeted demographics, namely: African-Americans, Latinos, Native Americans, hippies, the working poor, LGBT folk, and, in general, hard-core capital "L" Liberals (aka white progressives). I fit into this group on a personal and political level much better than Robert, but both of us stuck out like sore thumbs on this hot, sunny day, wearing suits and wing-tip oxfords in a sea of batik and Birkenstocks. They'd all formed into a monstrous semi-circle around the stage on the lawn. Robert and I moved as one, side by side, never smiling, *surveiling* the crowd through our sunglasses.

We mostly stood at the outside perimeter, trying to look the part. It wasn't just the suits, sunglasses, and earplugs that put us into character, mind you. We both wore American flag lapel pins, as I'd noticed in photographs that Secret Service agents wore some sort of lapel pin, and we both carried "accessories." I always carried a basket-weave police detective's wallet with a badge inside. I used it in performances of many of my cop characters, including Lt Columbo, Inspector Clouseau, Jack Webb's Sgt. Joe Friday of television's *Dragnet,* and Raymond Burr's Chief Ironside. And it was a great gag when I wasn't performing, as well. Additionally, I carried a pocket-sized cassette tape player, and Robert was wearing a telephone. Not a cellular phone, mind you, which few people in our socio-economic level carried at that point, but the green handset of a wall phone, with the cord tucked into his belt. Periodically he'd pull the phone out, ala Maxwell Smart, and make imaginary phone calls to his "colleagues."

The response we got from the people surrounding us was a gas. Most of them "got" the joke, and laughed when they saw us. Some people stared and whispered, and some people came up and actually asked what we were doing there. One middle-aged white guy, in an island shirt, shorts, and Birkenstocks, obviously a life-long "Progressive," seemed rather indignant, and peppered us with questions, which we dispatched with staccato Jack Webb-style non-answers. He apparently either finally figured it out or got tired of the routine, and left us alone. One lady, who seemed to be "in" on the joke, asked me, "What are you listening to on your earphones, fellas?" Without looking at her, I shot back, in my best Sgt. Friday, "Ball game, Ma'am."

We were having a ball, although you couldn't tell from the stoic expressions we tried desperately to maintain, but we were getting too hot and too sweaty and very tired of standing in our suits and oxfords in the hot sun. It was close to 6 p.m., and we were glad to finally see some activity at the front near the stage, as more and more uniformed SRPD officers joined the crowd, and a phalanx of black, secretive-looking, Government-issue cars and SUVs pulled up behind the stage. Suddenly there were men in suits *everywhere*, and that's when Robert and I started to realize that we weren't the only single men standing on the perimeter.

As we looked to the right and left from our position directly in front of the stage but way out at the back edge of the crowd, we both noticed there were single men spaced a few yards apart all the way around the outside of the semi-circle. Mind you, they were dressed like the rest of the people in the crowd, but they were all wearing sunglasses, and we both got the distinct impression that every time we looked over at them their eyes darted *from* us to straight ahead, as if they were looking at us when we weren't looking at them. We didn't notice them taking up those positions…they just seemed to simultaneously and motionlessly *appear*.

Now we were getting nervous, and realized that we had probably milked all the laughs out of our little prank that we could, and that it might be time to consider a strategic retreat back to the milk-and-cookies safety of my Grandma's kitchen. I voiced this thought to Robert, and he heartily agreed, saying, "Hey, man, I know some of these guys from work." He was referring to the uniformed local police officers that received paychecks from the same city coffers that paid him as a fireman. "We gotta get outa' here, right NOW," he said, desperately, and started to turn around.

I grabbed his arm and whispered, "WAIT, Rob...don't move too fast. It might not look too good. If they're actually looking at us, we better just stay right here and not look too suspicious." Robert said, "You stay if you want to...I'm outa' here!" And, with that, Robert made a rapid gait toward the gate a few dozen yards behind us, and was out of sight in seconds. Now I was really nervous.

Just then two uniformed police officers approached. No sunglasses, no earplugs, no attitude. They came up and both stood directly in front of me. They smiled and nodded, and were actually quite polite....even friendly. "Pardon me, sir. We couldn't help but notice you're wearing a suit, sunglasses, and an earplug. What are you doing here?"

Only too glad to explain myself at this point, and in my most personable way, I responded, "Well, see, I'm a professional entertainer. I do celebrity impersonations, and I wanted to come see Jesse Jackson. See, I do clown shows and singing telegrams. I've entertained for your chief, Sal Rosano, and many times for the CHP, and for most of the public safety departments in the county. Here's my card."

I handed him my two business cards. One about Christopher & Co. Celebrity Impersonations, and the other about Crisco the Clown. One officer studied the cards while the other used his hand-held radio to talk to a supervisor. The first officer said, "Listen, we understand, but would you mind coming over to the stage to talk to the Secret Service...they'd like to ask you a few questions." Heart thumping on the inside, cool, calm, charming, and compliant on the outside, I said, "sure thing."

They walked alongside me through the crowd (which now really thought our little prank was funny, no doubt) and over to one side of the stage, where I was approached by half-a-dozen men in their thirties who looked exactly like me…except that *their* earplugs were clear plastic, making my white one look *so* obsolete. ("Note to self: Time to upgrade my equipment.") A handsome, black, 40ish, Secret Service agent stood directly in front of me (as his fellow agents surveiled the surroundings and talked into their sleeves; "Note to self: Dump the pocket phone. They use sleeve mics.") and said, "Mr. Linnell, I am Special Agent Wilson" (flashing a badge that looked just a tad better than mine).

I was about to make Mistake Two. (Mistake One was GETTING UP THIS MORNING.) I said, "Special Agent? HaHa. Really?"

Now, don't be too quick to judge me here. I mean, I always thought that "Special Agent" was what they put on the plastic badges and decoder rings in cereal boxes…I didn't know that was an official Government title. I was trying to be funny to kind of lighten the mood. It didn't work. Special Agent Wilson stared right at me without expression, and then asked, "Where's your partner?"

"Okay," I was thinking, "he knew my name. He knew about Robert. Guess I was right about those guys on the perimeter being *on the job*." I sputtered, "Uh…partner? Robert? You mean Robert, my buddy. Uh, he had to go." Wilson shot back, "Where?" I reluctantly answered, "Uh…my Grandma's house. She lives around the block. That's where we parked. 1063 Stevenson Street."

The radio chatter immediately escalated as these now *dozens* of "Special Agents" surrounding me were *all* talking into their sleeves. Wilson conferred with a couple of them, and then turned to me and asked, "Will you take us there?" I answered, "SURE…no problem." Wilson then said, "Take him," at which point I was grabbed firmly by both arms (I'm thinking, "Who's taking *whom* here?"). Being a peaceable, law-abiding fellow with nothing whatsoever to hide, and not wanting a mouthful of soil, or grass stains on my best suit, I immediately said, loud and clear, "Ok, guys, I'll give you no problem. You tell me what to do and I'll do it!"

They frisked me but good, and started removing everything that wasn't attached, including my sunglasses, earplug, car keys, business cards, and my WALLET AND BADGE. "OOPS," I thought, "that's gonna be hard to explain..." Special Agent Wilson said, "What's this?" I said, "well, you see, I do celebrity impersonations . . . Lt. Columbo, Sgt. Friday, Inspector Clouseau--"

They cuffed me and put me in the back seat of an SRPD patrol car, my first and only time in that situation, fortunately. Once is enough, though. Dozens of Special Agents filed into several cars, and we all sped out of the fairgrounds towards Grandma's house. As we drove away at 6:10 p.m., I looked out the back window and caught a brief glimpse of presidential candidate Rev. Jesse Jackson taking the stage to thunderous applause. So much for watching him speak.

My squad car was in the middle of the procession, and when we turned the corner onto Stevenson Street the first couple of cars were just coming in for a landing in my grandmother's front yard. Literally hordes of Special Agents, like clowns from the tiny VW in the circus, absolutely *spewed* from all four doors of each of the cars. Poor Robert was standing at the foot of the driveway, hands in his pockets, jacket slung over one forearm, trying his best to look sweet and innocent. They apparently didn't think him so, and they didn't give him the gentlemanly treatment I had managed to talk my way into. They pounced on him and threw him onto the ground, groping every fabric and biological orifice, and then cuffed him and tossed him lengthwise into the back seat of one of their *Men In Black* sedans.

My grandma burst from the front door just at that moment, waving her hands above her head, shouting, "Stop it! Robert? He didn't do anything!" Inside the patrol car I shouted against the rolled-up windows, "GRANDMA, I'm HERE, I'm OK!" She couldn't hear me, though. Hell, she was seventy-seven-years-old; she couldn't normally hear me when I was standing right next to her! Grandma blurted out, "Who ARE you men? Where is my grandson?" One of the agents walked up to her, flashed his badge, and said, "We're federal agents, Ma'am. Your grandson is with us."

With that, the entire entourage filed out of Stevenson Street and three blocks away to the Santa Rosa Public Safety Department where we would be interrogated...and where Robert was employed; though for how long was anyone's guess.

They stripped us of our shoes, belts, and neckties, put us in separate holding cells, and then interrogated us individually for *four hours*. I don't remember much of what was said during that four-hour-long blur in my life, but I do remember, "Do you belong to any clubs or organizations?" I answered, "Petaluma Area Chamber of Commerce, Petaluma Valley Rotary Club. Oh, and the Clowns of America."

Finally they reunited me with Robert and sat us down together in an interrogation room. They explained that what to us may have seemed like a harmless prank, was, in actuality, an expensive and time-consuming ordeal in a meticulously planned operation. Special Agent Wilson told us that most of the agents were from other parts of the country and would now miss their plane(s) and would have to be replaced with other agents called in to cover for them. Wilson, himself, in fact, was planning to be home with his wife in Atlanta that night, and would now be delayed because of our little prank.

I apologized profusely, and said that I was sorry for all the trouble we had inadvertently caused them, and that we meant no harm, and I pointed out that we had stayed away from the stage. I said that I was surprised that they had paid us so much attention...that if we had any idea that we would have caused them all this trouble, we certainly wouldn't have done it.

As they led us to the front desk, Wilson queried me about how I knew about the lapel pins (Hey, I'm a professional!), and somewhat sincerely complimented me on the earplugs, though he added, "We use clear ones...you'll really have to upgrade." (That's what I thought!) At the front desk they returned to us our shoes and ties and belts and sunglasses and earplugs and cassette player and telephone (the badge, Wilson told me, had somehow, regretfully, been "lost"), and one of the SRPD officers asked us, "Which one of you is Linnell?" I meekly answered, "That's me." The officer slyly said, "We got a phone call from your grandmother. She said to release you...you're a 'nice boy'."

Outside Robert told me that he'd see me later...much later. He was worried about losing his job. They had given him quite the talking to. As for my grandma, no need to say that she was relieved to see us. As usual, she was right...we should have worried about the "G-Men." Back in my office on Monday morning, I got a call from A.L. Landers from the *Petaluma Argus-Courier*, saying that she was up against deadline and wanted to know how it all came out on Friday. Mistake Three: I told her the whole story. Live and learn. Everything you tell a reporter goes into the story. And this certainly did. In fact, it accounted for about a third of the story. The article was in the "Lifestyles" section, which was Page 12, on Wednesday, June 8, 1988, and was entitled, "Celebrity impersonation man adds zing to life; His experiences could fill a book" (well, she was obviously right about *that*).

It wasn't just in the newspaper...it made radio, too. My own former co-workers at KSRO called me up and interviewed me about the incident for their newscasts. Well, I figured, as urban legend erroneously has P.T. Barnum saying, "any kind of publicity is good publicity." For *me*, of course, it was, but Robert wasn't too happy about it.

In fact, he called me a few days later...for the last time. Thanks to his union he managed to keep his job, but his dream of one day becoming chief would never come to fruition. He blamed me, but I reminded *him* that Special Agent Wilson told us that if we had both stood our ground (i.e., if he hadn't split), they would have questioned us on-site and nothing more would have happened. Robert said it was a learning experience for him, and that his costumed prank days were over. In fact, the word from the police chief and the fire chief and the city manager was that if he wanted to keep his job in the future, he should stay away from his "wacko buddy." Which he did. Never heard from him again. Too bad...he had been the Best Man at my first wedding four years earlier...and I had two more weddings yet to come!

A week or so after the "Secret Service Affair," Special Agent Wilson paid me a visit in my rural mobile-home office (pictures of which follow in a couple of pages), and he was much friendlier and more candid. He told me that this had been Jackson's first public appearance after receiving a death threat from a white supremacist group, and that there we were, two white men, dressed as Secret Service Agents. No wonder they got so upset.

He said that we *could* have been charged with "Impersonating a Federal Officer" (U.S.C. Title 18 > Part I > Chapter 43 > § 912: "Whoever falsely assumes or pretends to be an officer or employee acting under the authority of the United States or any department, agency or officer thereof, *AND* acts as such, or in such pretended character demands or obtains any money, paper, document, or thing of value, shall be fined under this title or imprisoned not more than three years, or both."), which he told me carried a penalty of a one thousand dollar fine and/or one year in a federal prison. Today, however, I understand the penalty is stiffer: three years in prison. Of course, they would have had to prove criminal intent, and there was none.

Wilson also said that as this had occurred on a Friday after 5 p.m., they *could* have held us until Monday to go before a federal judge in San Francisco. Hell, on Saturday, May 14 I had two clown shows during the day (three, actually; one of which I assigned to my wife, Carrie, to perform as Pippa the Clown), plus in the evening I had a singing telegram, *and* I emceed a retirement banquet for six officers of the California Highway Patrol...missing that day of work would have been serious and costly!

Before leaving, Wilson had me sign one form saying that I had been given all my stuff back (which was a lie, as my "lost" wallet badge, of course, was *not* listed on the form), and a form acknowledging that we had NOT been *arrested*, but merely "detained for questioning." If I refused to sign the forms, he reminded me, they could still charge and prosecute us. This one was a no-brainer...I was certainly not looking to file a charge of false arrest.

I was also amused to read in the paper a few months later about Secret

Service agents being disciplined for having their badges and guns and radios and other equipment stolen from a hotel room while they were all partying in the lounge downstairs. I remembered how sternly they told us that our prank was irresponsible, and I thought how ironic it was for such *responsible* men to be so careless with their own gear. Well, I figured, if they lost *their* badges, at least they had *mine* to use.

So, despite our "support," Rev. Jesse Jackson failed to win the Democratic primary, and George H. W. Bush won the general election and followed my beloved Ronald Reagan as POTUS (that's the Secret Service acronym for President of the United States; I said that whole fiasco was a learning experience). I say "beloved" not because I saw Reagan as flawless, nor because I *liked* Supply-Side Economics (or "Voo-Doo Economics," as Bush had referred to them eight years prior), nor because I would have commended him on his choice of staff. (Has anyone ever hired more crooks and scumbags to high-level jobs?)

I loved Reagan because in 1980 he was the first president for whom I voted, and because he was a tough, active, affable, humorous cowboy whom the *Ruskis* and the Chinese and the Iranians respected/feared. I loved him because he took a bullet and joked with the hospital staff while they pulled it out, I loved him because he loved his wife and he loved our country, and I loved him because he stared down the "Evil Empire" and stood in Berlin and said, "Mr. Gorbachev, tear down this wall," and they did. But mainly I loved him because I could impersonate him and he was handsome and funny and iconic and a very popular president with the clients who put bread on my table.

BUSH LEAGUE

As far as learning the vocal impersonations was concerned, some were easier than others. The first time I heard radio commentator Paul Harvey, I could mimic his voice perfectly...and immediately. President Ronald Reagan was another easy one, but when George H. W. Bush became president, I was stumped. I couldn't even get close at first. I recorded his inaugural address on video and audio tape, and took the text of the speech from the newspaper, and then sat down to work on it in my own office recording studio.

Christopher & Co. office at 171 King Road.

This was a fairly professional affair, by the way, which I originally put together using home stereo components, eventually updated with obsolete radio station equipment chucked into the garbage at various radio stations. Its first location at 171 King Rd was in the bedroom of a single-wide mobile home in a rural area several miles west of Petaluma which I rented from my future in-laws beginning in 1983. My executive desk, credenza, and file cabinets were in the living room, theatrical makeup and wigs in the bathroom, and costumes in the closet. The back bedroom was a recording studio for puppet show soundtracks, sample tapes for clients, and freelance radio production work.

When my sister-in-law wanted to use the mobile home as a residence, I moved into a 576 square foot downtown office I rented at 154 Keller Street across from the Phoenix Theater in 1988-89. I used room dividers to create a large space for my desk, credenza, chairs, and file cabinets, and a smaller space for a nap couch, microwave oven, refrigerator, and makeup vanity table and mirror. There was a bathroom, and there were two separate, smaller rooms. The smaller of the two was my costume closet, and the larger one, with windows at the top of the wall, was my recording studio.

Christopher & Co. office at 154 Keller Street.

Back to Bush. I had Bush on the television, Bush in my headphones, and the speech text in front of me, and I read the entire address over and over again with the president into a microphone, recording the results each time, until I'd gotten as close as I could to the Real Bush. And then, after all that work, Dana Carvey did his OWN Bush on *Saturday Night Live*, and I realized that my clients would actually expect *me* to impersonate *his* Bush, rather than my own. So I did. The first Bush I did was for Bank of Marin, complete, again, with faux Secret Service agents.

As the Bush months wore on, I was still not completely comfortable being Bush, especially after eight years of my flawless Reagan. So I simply told clients asking for the president, "You know, it isn't very feasible that the actual president of the United States would come to your event, but it is feasible that a presidential candidate might." I went on to tell them that some of the presidential candidates did keynote speaking engagements worldwide at corporate events for big bucks, and at fundraisers for extraordinarily exorbitant *honoraria*, so telling event invitees that a former presidential candidate was coming would seem like an actual possibility. You see, I did a killer Bob Dole, and I was always a big fan of the senior senator from Kansas, so, when someone wanted a presidential visit, I would talk them into a Senator Bob Dole impersonation, and he became my most popular character right through the

Clinton Administration. I had a "DOLE in 1992" sign made, and I crossed out the year every four years and updated it with each election. More on my use of Bob Dole in Chapter 7, entitled "Corporate Comedy."

TROUBLE WITH ANOTHER WILSON

By the way, I didn't know it at the time, but a few years later I learned that the State of California has its own "secret service" that protects the governor of California. And, yes, I had a run-in with them, too. But this time, I was impersonating a specific cop.

I received a call from the local office of the California Republican Party for a job right in my town of Petaluma. California Governor Pete Wilson would be attending a lavish fundraiser in the rural garden homestead of the rather wealthy Goltermann family (described as: "A 1913 farmhouse, cottages and suites on a six acre country estate with beautiful gardens, lake and forest for weddings, meditation retreats, business meetings and social events;" visit: www.VisitPetaluma.com/Goltermann-Gardens). In addition to the governor, a whole slew of state, county, and local elected officials and bureaucrats would be in attendance, along with several hundred local, wealthy Republicans.

This was gonna be a great job. Especially since they wanted an appearance by my all-time favorite character, Peter Falk's LAPD homicide detective, Lt. Columbo, the cigar-chomping television icon for forty years in the filthy, rumpled trench coat, whose friendly and seemingly sloppy manner instilled in frequently high-profile and celebrity murder suspects a carefree attitude as they misjudged him to be an idiot from whom they had nothing to fear. I always felt that Columbo was the man that the LAPD should have assigned to investigate O.J. Simpson.

Lt. Columbo made his entrance on a warm, sunny, spring Saturday at around noon, and stunk up the entire bucolic garden with his cheap cigars. He made the rounds of the guests, asking inane and sometimes embarrassing questions, picking through the buffet, stumbling over every flower bed, and spilling every unguarded beverage at the party. Despite this, Columbo was well-received, as usual. One of the reasons that I loved doing Columbo so much was the fact that he was so polite and personable and innocuous...everybody loved him. Furthermore, the costume is comfortable (as I never have to worry if my tie is straight or my shirt is tucked-in, because the sloppier you are, the more Columbo you look), and he is one of the easiest voices for me to do. My Columbo is perfect. In fact, in the days before I wore a beard, I looked just like him. He was exceptionally well-received at this particular occasion because I had long been an active and visible member of the Petaluma Area Chamber of Commerce and the Petaluma Valley Rotary Club, and several of the city council members, bureaucrats, and public safety officers on hand were clients and friends of mine.

Christopher as Lt. Columbo.

The highlight of the event, of course, was the arrival of Governor Pete Wilson, and, as the activity level in the parking lot increased, my client hustled me to the center area specifically so Governor Wilson would get to meet Lt. Columbo. And the governor made his entrance, shook a lot of hands, and took one look at me and said, "LT. COLUMBO!" He laughed and bounded toward me and pumped my hand, and Columbo said, "Geez, Governor, it's a great pleasure to meet you, sir! Hey, I love that necktie…is that silk? Can I ask you," leaning in to him to whisper in a nonetheless purposefully audible tone, "how much did that thing cost you, sir?"

At that moment two men in suits, sunglasses, and earplugs (the white kind, like I used, by the way) grabbed the governor and whisked him away, while several others absolutely descended on Columbo and dragged him over to the far side of the garden. The men were members of the Protective Services Division (PSD) of the California Highway Patrol. Radios ablaze, they peppered me with questions about who I was, how I got in there, and what I wanted. They obviously weren't as big fans of the show as was the governor. In fact, Columbo often got that kind of treatment in restaurants and parties. People who weren't paying attention to Columbo's patter, or who were not fans of the show, often threatened to call the police, thinking Columbo to be some sort of nut or homeless transient. In fact, at several events over the decades, the clients and guests were laughing so hard about the error that Columbo was hustled right out the door before finally being rescued by the person in charge, telling the errant staffer, "It's OK… that's Lt. Columbo… we HIRED him to be here!"

This client was a bit quicker on the draw, however, and was able to extricate the good lieutenant from the clutches of disaster, assuring the governor's PSD officers that Columbo was, indeed, an invited guest. The fact that Wilson approached *me*, shouted Columbo's name, and shook *my* hand was lost on these guys, who were just trying to do their job by keeping the governor safe. Among the hundreds of Petalumans in attendance that day were Mayor Patti Hilligoss (1924-2000), City Councilman Brian Sobel (www.SobelCommunications.com and www.*TheFightingPattons*.com), and Petaluma Police Chief Dennis Dewitt (1937-2009), all three of whom were friends and clients and well aware of my much-publicized "Secret Service Affair" of 1988. This gave them new ammunition, and they teased me at the event and for years afterward about "getting hassled by the Secret Service…AGAIN."

As my Columbo story illustrates, of course, the celebrity impersonation business isn't always just about the president. There was quite a diversity of characters on my list. Everybody from Edith & Archie Bunker of *All in the Family* to Ralph Kramden and Ed Norton of *The Honeymooners*, plus Laurel & Hardy, Cheech & Chong, the *Ghostbusters*, Dame Edna, Inspector Clouseau of the *Pink Panther* series, and Jackie Gleason's Sheriff Buford T. Justice of *Smokey & the Bandit* fame.

THE GREAT D-BATE

Frequently local politicians gained enough celebrity to be requested as impersonations. Such was the case when I received an e-mail on January 25, 2002, from prominent San Francisco realtor Ilse Cordoni, who wanted me to impersonate San Francisco Supervisor Tom Ammiano for a political fundraiser on February 8. Ammiano was involved in a campaign, named Measure D, to shift the power of appointing San Francisco planning commissioners from powerful Mayor Willie Brown and to the board of supervisors. Cordoni was a member of the No on Measure D camp, and thought it would be funny to have Ammiano present at the party to defend himself from Mayor Brown and others who would be in attendance at the fundraiser in the beautifully restored Victorian home of Richard Reutlinger.

Now, gay men and lesbians are prevalent in San Francisco politics, and in most cities you'd find them on the same side of the political isle fighting against the "Establishment." But in San Francisco, the LGBTIQ community *is* the Establishment...and the Anti-Establishment, and every other "-ment" there is. San Francisco is such a gay haven that gay men and lesbians can be found all across the political spectrum: liberal and conservative, religious and secular, activist and conformist. Ammiano is gay and Reutlinger is gay, yet they were on opposite sides of the isle, on this issue, at least. Willie Brown was seen by most California conservatives as an activist liberal during his thirty-year tenure in the California State Assembly, reigning as speaker for half that time, ruling the proceedings with an almost Huey Long style. Yet during his first term as San Francisco Mayor from 1995-1999, many viewed Brown as a pro-development conservative and reviled him as a turncoat to their cause. Tom Ammiano was a last-minute write-in candidate against Brown in 1999, but his $300,000 war chest couldn't match the $3.1 million Brown had amassed, and Brown prevailed.

Impersonating Ammiano was rather easy for me, as he is a white man of average height and weight and a full head of gray hair. He typically wears expensive suits and fancy silk ties, so with a wig and a suit and a tie, I looked a little like him. His voice was a cinch, too, because he has a very nasal whine with a bit of a lisp, speaks with a distinct New Jersey accent, and, as a professional stand-up comic and teacher who never misses an opportunity to speak into every mic and mug into every camera, everyone in the Bay Area is very familiar with his personae.

Seven years later Ammiano would become familiar to many people nationally because of the five minutes of fame he earned in October of 2009, heckling Governor Arnold Schwarzenegger at a Democratic party fundraiser at the Fairmont Hotel. Mayor Willie Brown had just introduced the Republican governor, when Ammiano started shouting that Schwarzenegger's appearance was just a "cheap political stunt." The governor attempted to respond, and Ammiano shouted, "You can kiss my gay ass," and stormed out of the room. The sound byte went viral in the media, and was seen all over the country. According to www.Gawker.com, Schwarzenegger took the heckling in stride, and retorted when the laughs died down and Ammiano had left the room, "Compared to the reaction I got in Hyannis Port when I told the Kennedys I was marrying Maria, (that reception) was fantastic."

Back to 2002. My Tom Ammiano arrived at the No on D party and lit into Mayor Brown immediately, whining, "Mayor Brown, you've sold out to the developers! We're gonna stop you in your tracks, though! You wait...you'll see...Measure D will pass and then *I'll* be the one to decide who builds what and where!" Brown went into hysterics, unable to respond. Seeing Willie Brown at a loss for words is a rare thing, too, but the two battled, more for laughs than for points, for some time in front of the large and wealthy crowd of No on D supporters. Mayor Brown, like the real Ammiano, has a fantastic sense of humor, will laugh at almost anything, and is also not afraid of a microphone or a crowd…the two were perfectly matched.

By the way, I ran into Tom Ammiano in an alley once after he was elected to the California State Assembly and handed him my card, telling him that if he ever needed a doppelganger for an event, I was the guy who debated Mayor Brown *as him* at that No on D fundraiser in 2002. He laughed and pocketed the card, but I have yet to hear back from him. I have run into Mayor Willie Brown several times during performances over the decades, and he's always a good sport. Once I was performing my Kermit the Frog in a Tree impersonation (I wear a *Wizard of Oz* / enchanted forest-style tree with a Kermit puppet on my arm/branch…a rather clever and convincing gimmick) at a fundraiser for Marin Day Schools at Fort Mason in San Francisco, and Mayor Brown stopped by to verbally taunt Kermit for a few minutes.

I also saw the mayor in San Francisco one evening standing in front of the (now closed) Chevy's Restaurant on the southeast corner of Van Ness and Golden Gate. It was getting dark and cold and he was all alone and appeared to be awaiting a passing cab, so I pulled up to the curb and said, "Hey, Mayor, do you need a ride?" He said, "Sure," and hopped into my van.

As I pulled away from the curb and headed east on Golden Gate I puffed away on my stogy and asked my distinguished guest where he was heading, telling him that I was on my way to the weekly Friday Night Skate. Brown said "anywhere near Union Square" a few blocks ahead of us would be fine. I handed him my card and reminded him about that No on D party in 2002, and he got hysterical again, saying, "Shit, I thought that *was* Tom Ammiano who walked into the room that night! You had me going, man…I didn't know *what* to say!" I dropped him off at Union Square, and told him to look out, because I was going to work on a Willie Brown impersonation, and he said, "Oh, no you don't. You stick with Ammiano…you're much better suited to the part!"

GETTING BLUE OVER BILL GATES

Getting black would be tough, but I found that getting BLUE was even tougher. Back when Robin Williams provided the voice for the huge blue genie character in the 1992 animated Disney movie *Aladdin,* I got a call from Microsoft headquarters in Seattle. They were hosting an *Aladdin*-themed special event on April 10, 1993, they needed a bigger-than-life-size blue genie, and I was only too happy to comply. I had been offering stiltwalking characters for some time, so I started working on costuming. I already had tailor-made blue pants (with a sixty-seven-inch inseam) for my stiltwalking Uncle Sam, so I had a costumer make me a big red sash. I then bought a mess of blue body paint, which was nasty, and a big brass earring. I was all set.

Microsoft flew me up to Seattle, picked me up at the airport, and set me up with a room in the hotel in which their event was being hosted. I was able to get fully-costumed, stilts and all, inside my room without a hitch, but the makeup was a problem. I got on my stilts and into my pants and put on the sash. I pulled my short, normal, male, hair into a little, tiny middle-aged-bald-guy-trying-to-look-hip-and-artsy ponytail, put on my earring, and then started putting on the blue paint. I'd been using greasepaint for years on my face as a clown, but not on my neck and chest and shoulders and arms…and my…BACK! Yikes! I was alone in the room, half-naked and painted blue, and I had a hairy, UNpainted, Anglo back!

How the hell was I gonna put the makeup on my BACK? I was alone in the room! I looked out the door…no maid. How the hell was I gonna find someone to put blue makeup on my BACK? The clock was running, they'd be expecting me downstairs soon, I just *had* to finish up…and fast! I took the makeup and a few towels and my keys and my phone and I headed for the elevator. The bell rang. The door opened. There was no one in the car…thank goodness. I bent down (because, remember, not only was I half-naked and blue, but I was also friggin' eight-and-a-half-feet-tall), stepped in, pushed the convention center button, and listened to an instrumental Muzak version of Billy Joel's "Don't Go Changin'."

Christopher as Robin Williams' blue genie.

The car stopped. The door opened. A lady stepped in…looked at me…I smiled…she stepped out. The doors closed again and the car continued its descent. The car stopped again. This time it was two women and a businessman. The women giggled, the guy laughed out loud. They all got in, said nothing, turned their backs to me, and the doors shut again. Finally we got to my floor. I said, "Excuse me," as I passed between them, trying to be careful not to get blue paint on anyone's nice business clothes. I ducked through the door and walked through the foyer past innumerable puzzled stares.

I finally reached the meeting room in which I was to perform, and it was abuzz with preparations prior to the arrival of the guests. I went to the stage and asked around for my client. I found him, and he said, "Wow, Christopher, you look great!" I said, "Yeah…except for THIS." And I turned around. With my bare, hairy, tanned, Anglo back staring at him, he said, "What happened?" I said, "I can't reach back there. Can YOU do it?" And I attempted to hand him the makeup. He actually, physically stepped back a foot or two. No, that's not right. He *jumped* back a foot or two. He said, "Oh, no…I've got to…I can't…I'm…this is my good suit!"

After some desperate moments, we finally found an audio technician who said he'd be willing to finish off my back for me. He wasn't happy about it, but he agreed. He was a rather gruff man, in his forties, in jeans and boots and a navy blue sweatshirt. I could tell that he had been working very hard and didn't need this additional task in his already busy day. We found a restroom, and I bent down and put my (blue) palms on the mirror in front of me. The tech got behind me, smeared the blue paint on his hands, and then reached up and started smearing it onto my back. What a "team player" this guy was, eh? So far so good…he was just putting on the finishing touches under my big red sash, when we realized the door had been opened. A man in a suit stood there, looking at us, with the kind of look on his face you'd expect if he'd have caught his grandfather abusing himself in the family bathroom.

The tech stopped smearing. I smiled. The shocked man said, "I'll find another restroom."

Oh, yeah…the performance went great. I was funny, tall, and…blue.

GROUCHO AND THE SECRET WORD

I got a call in the fall of 1991 from a man by the name of Michael Healy. For thirty-two years he was the Media & Public Affairs Director of and spokesman for BART, the Bay Area Rapid Transit system. They were hosting an important promotion in the coming months, opening new BART lines and stations in the East Bay, and they were looking for Groucho Marx for a number of events.

I performed as Groucho at a press conference on October 23 at BART headquarters in Oakland, at which they announced to the media the schedule for the groundbreaking ceremonies for the two new extensions to their system. Two days later BART hosted those ceremonies in Pleasanton and West Pittsburgh simultaneously at 9:30 a.m., after which I performed at a BART VIP luncheon at Pacific Bell's complex in San Ramon. This was actually the first time I met Governor Pete Wilson, who was the guest of honor (no problem with the security guys this time, however). I was again performing as Groucho, and comedian and Bay Area native Ronnie Schell (who played Duke Slater on television's *Gomer Pyle U.S.M.C.*) was serving as master of ceremonies.

From childhood I was always intrigued by BART, as I had watched them building a stretch of the system on a huge concrete elevated railway in the playground of my school in Richmond, Fairmont Elementary. They ran a few test trains by our school, but my family was on Guam when the first passengers rode the system, and the trains had spread all over the Bay Area by the time we returned in 1977. The system in 1991 included 590 vehicles on 71.5 miles of track and 34 stations in 15 communities, and today is still a viable, relatively inexpensive, and environmentally-conscientious means of transportation daily for 375,000 commuters on 104 miles of track in four counties. (I sound a lot like *Dragnet's* Sgt. Joe Friday sometimes, don't I?)

The following May BART hired me as Groucho again, this time on their trains, to boost ridership on their new lines. They would periodically announce a "Secret Word" to the public in advertisements in regional media. As Groucho Marx used to have a Secret Word on his old radio and television game show, *You Bet Your Life*, BART management planned to have Groucho periodically riding their trains. Riders were encouraged to approach Groucho and tell him the secret word. The first seven riders each day to tell Groucho the secret word would receive a year's free pass on BART. I spent five days riding BART cars, May 11-15, 1992, and saw the whole Bay Area from the rails.

Costumed as Groucho on BART trains I wore the trademark glasses, eyebrows, mustache, tail coat, and I carried an unlit cigar, as smoking aboard the trains is not allowed. (Note that while the "secret word" was Groucho's gimmick on *You Bet Your Life*, when he wore plastic lens frames, a gray suit, and a polka-dot bow tie, I knew that fewer people would identify me in that outfit as Groucho Marx, so I wore his more easily identifiable movie outfit.) Some people would ignore me, some people would laugh as they walked by, and kids would peer over their mothers' shoulders at the funny man with the painted-in eyebrows and mustache. And some people would rush over to me and whisper the secret word into my ear. BART employees, incognito, would surround the individuals and make a big fuss, and hand them their passes.

Christopher as Groucho Marx.

On one such trip a familiar face was aboard the train. My cousin, Scott Hodges, a butcher from San Leandro, was riding BART to catch an Amtrak train to see his paternal Grandma Dodo in Mariposa. I asked him if he knew the secret word. He said he'd heard it in the media, but he stressed and strained, and couldn't remember. I told the BART lady accompanying me with the prizes,

"He's my cousin. He said it…didn't you hear it? Say it, Scott, say it!" No luck. No free BART pass. Even for family. Bummer.

BART General Manager Frank Wilson wrote me a flattering letter in October of 1991: "Your performance got rave reviews…the impersonations were terrific, and your enthusiasm infectious. I would give Christopher & Co. my highest recommendation." A very nice thing to say, even if they wouldn't let me sneak a prize to my cousin.

SINGING WITH SINATRA

My phone was always ringing with new jobs that sounded like fun. I got a call one day from a company by the name of Cema Distribution. They asked me if I did Sinatra. Not Nancy, mind you, but Frank. "Sure…I do a killer Sinatra," I said. "Great," they told me, "come on in; we'd like to see it." Turns out Cema was Frank Sinatra's distributor, the company that sold his records. They liked my impersonation, and they told me about an interesting promotion they were planning.

Karaoke was becoming very popular, and Sinatra's songs were among the most popular karaoke songs here in the U.S. and around the world. His new *Duets* album was being released, and they thought it would be a great gimmick to get shoppers to sing duets with Sinatra. They were going to set up a sound system and a microphone in record stores in San Francisco, and they wanted me costumed and singing as Sinatra, using karaoke versions of his songs, and they wanted me to entice shoppers to join me.

It was a kick. *American Idol, America's Got Talent,* and *The Voice* are huge sensations today, but I never would have guessed how many common, ordinary Joes, without any notice or rehearsal, can belt out a ballad in front of strangers in a record store when asked. Dozens and dozens of people came up and sang with me over the weeks of the promotion…some were good, some were bad…some were downright awful, and some were better than I was. And some even sang like Sinatra. Fortunately for me, though, none were as good at impersonating

Sinatra, apparently, because a few years later, when Ol' Blue Eyes released *Duets II*, they hired me to do the same thing again.

I did a lot of Sinatras over the years. I don't look like him (except that I am a white man who had dark, receding hair), my eyes are brown, not blue, and I wouldn't say that my Sinatra sounds exactly like him, either, but I can belt-out a tune just like the Chairman of the Board. One year I was hired to perform as Sinatra, et al., at an elaborate garden party, in a very unusual location, by a very eccentric fellow.

LABOR DAY SOIREE

Bob Pritikin is a unique San Francisco icon. A self-made, incredibly successful advertising executive and author, Bob has become a legend in San Francisco because of the lavish and extravagant soirées he hosted for decades in his two very famous mansions. One, "The Mansion Hotel," a bed-and-breakfast composed of two Victorians connected by a hallway, opened in 1977 in the affluent Pacific Heights neighborhood, and hosted endless wild bashes in the midst of live animals, expensive works of art, and bizarre collectibles, such as Nixon's letter of resignation, Ford's letter of pardon, and Hitler's globe.

The event at which I performed, however, was on September 4, 2000, at his annual Labor Day party at "The Chenery Mansion" (www.PritikinMuseum.org) in the Glen Park neighborhood. The mansion itself is a stately *Beaux Arts* wonder, with Greek columns, monstrous fountains, an indoor swimming pool on the second floor, and a forty-million-dollar collection of fine art. What's most unusual about this house, however, is that it was the largest piece of private property in San Francisco, yet it's not visible from the street, being completely surrounded by residential buildings Bob owned on all sides. Entry is made through a single passageway between the houses, hidden by a huge garage door with apartments on top. Eight hundred guests came every year for decades and were entertained by Bob Pritikin himself, who performs magic tricks and is one of the world's finest classical musical saw players, as well as such diverse entertainment luminaries as Bob Weir, Carol Channing, Mickey Rooney, and Liberace.

Christopher as Frank Sinatra at Bob Pritikin's Labor Day soiree.

I did my "Balladeers" act, which includes songs by my Bing Crosby, Louis Armstrong, Sammy Davis Jr., Jimmy Durante, Tony Bennett, Tom Jones, Nat King Cole, Neil Diamond, Johnny Cash, George Burns, and, of course, Frank Sinatra, in this case backed by the fifteen-piece Rex Allen Big Band (www.AmericaSwingsAgain.com). I was followed on stage that day by none other than 1950s pop icon Eddie Fisher (the real one; not an impersonator), who is a frequent guest at Pritikin's soirées.

Also performing at that event was magician Jay Alexander and Elvis impersonator Dorol Conrad, both of whom I'll mention in just a few pages. Unfortunately I couldn't do the Pritikin party in subsequent years because I was attending the annual Burning Man art festival and encampment in the Nevada desert, along with tens of thousands of others. I went to Burning Man in 2000, too, but I had to race back to the Bay Area early, and perform with a very dry, dusty, sore throat. In subsequent years I resisted the urge to take bookings that conflicted with Burning Man. Even the Pritikin party is not worth missing ten thousand bare-breasted women in body paint.

WALKING AROUND IN PAIRS

Walkaround impersonations were generally much more lucrative than private party gigs, required none of the preparation or research, and were at least as much fun. I did hundreds over the decades. I was hired by I. Magnin in San Francisco's Union Square during the Bill Clinton presidential campaign to impersonate "Bubba" in the foyer of one of their upstairs departments, and bought a $400 saxophone for the part (Clinton played the saxophone on the David Letterman show once during his campaign; and once is all I ever used that stupid sax). I did that job with an Oprah Winfrey look-a-like, and we had a ball.

I should differentiate the term *look-a-like* from *impersonator* here. I was an impersonator; someone who didn't look like any celebrity in particular, but offered one or more fully-costumed impersonations of a celebrity's look *and* sound. Look-a-likes typically, facially, *looked* exactly like one particular celebrity, and dressed as the celebrity, but didn't necessarily *sound* like the star. Some of these look-a-likes are dead-on doubles, and are difficult or impossible to differentiate from the actual celebrity, but they don't always perform in character (I performed at an event one time with Queen Elizabeth and Pope John Paul, and both stood around talking in their own voices about what it's like to be a look-a-like; not the definition of professionalism). The good ones also impersonate their celebrities' voices. They bill themselves as *look- AND sound-a-likes*; they're the best. Corporate clients would often prefer look-a-likes over impersonators because they wanted their guests to pose with the entertainers for pictures, so the sound of the celebrity wouldn't be important. My task, then, was to look so much like each of my celebrities, through costuming and accessories, that I could pass as a look-a-like in pictures.

This is why I spent so much time and money assembling costuming, accessories, hair, and, when necessary, makeup that were as absolutely authentic as possible. The advantage that I had over look-and-sound-a-likes is that they could usually only offer one celebrity, while I literally offered one-hundred celebrities, and could do multiple characterizations over the course of an event. For instance, when I worked with the world's premier Marilyn Monroe look-and-sound-a-like, Diana Dawn, or Greg Williams, a dead-on Clint Eastwood, or Dorol Conrad, the perfect Elvis, Diana, Greg, and Dorol would be stuck doing each of their celebrities for the duration of the event, while I could start off as Groucho Marx, then do Dana Carvey's The Church Lady from *Saturday Night Live*, then Cheech Marin, then Alan Hale Jr.'s Skipper from *Gilligan's Island*, then Peter Seller's Inspector Clouseau of *Pink Panther* fame, and so on and so forth.

In fact, I was able to offer my clients a different celebrity every hour. This was a *huge* bargain for clients who were paying more than $200 per hour for Diana, Greg, and Dorol, netting three walkaround characters, while at just $120 per hour I was offering six different characters at a six-hour event. This was great for me, too, as I never got burned-out doing only one character all day. The downside for me, of course, was that I had to pack costuming and accessories for six characters for each six-hour gig, and return to the van every hour to change clothes. But this was such a huge selling point that I was working a lot more than most of my colleagues, as I've never met anyone in party entertainment who offered as many characters as did I. Rich Little, yes, but he didn't work for $120 an hour, either.

I was frequently hired by clients who wanted Laurel *and* Hardy, Cheech *and* Chong, or Archie *and* Edith Bunker. For these events I would either do one character, such as Jack Benny, asking guests if they'd seen my partner, and then return the next hour as the other character, in this case Eddie Anderson's Rochester, and ask the guests, "Hey, have you seen Mr. Benny?" The guests would laugh in amazement and say, "He went that-a-way!" But if the client wanted the two characters *together*, I would call on a colleague to help me. In the spring of 1995 a department store in the San Francisco Marketplace (a huge, multi-level indoor shopping mall) wanted both Cheech and Chong, simultaneously, so I impersonated Tommy Chong and hired my buddy, actor Joe Peer (aka Joe Voltiera at www.JoeVoltiera.com), to be Cheech Marin.

Joe Peer and Christopher as Cheech & Chong.

I also frequently traded referrals and worked bookings with actor Jeffrey Weissman, who is multi-talented and can impersonate a wide variety of characters. He was also quite successful, working as Stan Laurel and Groucho Marx and Charlie Chaplin at Universal Studios for years. He worked as an actor, too, playing Teddy Conway in Clint Eastwood's 1985 western *Pale Rider,* and he played George McFly, the father of Michael J. Fox's character, in 1989 and 90's *Back to the Future II & III*, and had speaking roles in 1983's *Twilight Zone*, 1979's *The Rose* with Bette Midler, and 1978's *Sgt. Pepper's Lonely Hearts Club Band* and *FM*. Currently Jeffrey lives in Petaluma, works as a writer, director, producer, and actor in independent films, and teaches acting for film, directing, writing, and improv at the San Francisco School of Digital Film Making. His website can be found at www.JeffreyWeissman.com.

THE MILLION DOLLAR WEDDING

One fun job was playing the Desi Arnaz character Ricky Ricardo of television's *I Love Lucy* with impersonator Jean Thomas providing Lucille Ball's Lucy Ricardo. I was booked for a million-dollar Hollywood wedding reception on June 12, 1999, at San Francisco's famed Bimbo's 365 Club. Security was very tight, and I was not told whose wedding it was; but I was told they were using a 1950s theme, and I'd be performing with a full slate of other performers, so I didn't ask too many questions. In addition to being Ricky, they wanted me to serve as M.C. of the stage show, impersonating Ed Sullivan.

After the wedding at Grace Cathedral, the street outside Bimbo's was awash with fans, paparazzi, limos, and searchlights, and my ID was scrutinized in minute detail by very serious and monstrous security guards who looked more like professional wrestlers (mind you, I was not wearing either an earplug or my Columbo garb, so I was relatively safe). I made my way back to the dressing room, and chatted with the other entertainers as we prepped for our performances. I learned that the guests of honor were Courtney Cox and David Arquette of the television sitcom *Friends*. I was at somewhat of a disadvantage, however, as I had never seen the show, and wasn't familiar with those names, but I learned that all of Hollywood was awaiting my Ricky Ricardo and Ed Sullivan behind those doors.

Dressed in my tux and straw hat, with my hair greased back as Desi, Lucy and I entered the huge ballroom, elegantly decorated in 1950s kitsch style, and, as we made the rounds of the room, we were astounded by the number of celebrity entertainers we were entertaining. Lucy was fawning over every celebrity she saw, and Ricky apologetically said, "I'm sorry, but my wife is a screw-ball redhead, and she gets kind of excited around big stars. One time we were at the Brown Derby, and she threw a pie right in the face of Bill Holden!" Lucy would then spy stars at another table and lurch at them, and Ricky would stumble after her, saying, "Luuu-CYYY," and regale each table with her past exploits, including the time she stole John Wayne's footprints from Grauman's Chinese Theater, the time she was caught "snicking" into Richard Widmark's house under a bear-skin rug to get his autograph on a grapefruit, and the time she hid under the breakfast cart in Cornell Wilde's room at the Beverly Palms Hotel.

Over the course of the evening we entertained the likes of *Friends* stars Jennifer Aniston and then-boyfriend/fiancée Brad Pitt, Lisa Kudrow, Matt LeBlanc, David Schwimmer, Matthew Perry, and the groom's siblings, including best man Lewis Arquette, and sisters, Rosanna and Patricia Arquette, as well as the latter's husband, Nicholas Cage (who seemed deadpan until Lucy made a fuss over him, causing him to crack a smile). Also in attendance were *Saturday Night Live* star Jon Lovitz (sitting all by himself at the table and looking kinda' lonely), Richard Benjamin and Paula Prentiss, and Liam Neeson and Natasha Richardson. Also reported by *STAR Magazine* to be in the crowd were stars I don't recall seeing, including Robin and Marsha Williams, director Wes Craven (who directed Cox and Arquette in their 1996 film *Scream*, the project that brought them together), and none other than Paul Reubens, aka Pee Wee Herman (I probably didn't see him because I wasn't performing in the bathroom).

After the cocktail hour walkaround was completed, the other performers took a break as the guests began their steak and lobster dinner, but I was changing into Ed Sullivan, and took the stage to greet the guests en masse and introduce the band. In characteristic style Ed Sullivan introduced the bride and groom to the crowd erroneously, as: "Courtney Love and Wally Cox." The crowd laughed politely and uncomfortably until Sullivan looked at his notes and corrected himself.

Courtney Cox was absolutely regal in her white Valentino silk-crepe gown, with embroidered stripes and a tulle veil attached to a silk-flowered headpiece. The gown was open wide to the sternum, exposing a fair amount of cleavage. Sullivan then rudely asked for someone "to pin up the front of the bride's dress...you can see EVERYthing!" The deadpan, humorless, and painfully conservative Ed Sullivan went over like a lead balloon, and I learned a valuable lesson: famous actors and comedians may tease other celebrities and each other about their apparel, but they don't like being teased themselves by unknown comics...especially on their wedding days.

Sullivan then introduced the band "Pride & Joy", with whom I'd been chatting backstage. I'd introduced them just a month before aboard the *USS Hornet* in the Port of Oakland for the May 7 IPO / sixth anniversary party of Latitude Communications, then a leading provider of integrated voice and data conferencing solutions for geographically dispersed organizations. At that event I was impersonating crooner Bing Crosby, and was backed in song by a full orchestra playing on the *Hornet's* flight deck.

In its four-page, front-cover, full-color article about the Cox-Arquette wedding, *STAR Magazine* detailed the budget at $1,047,850, but overlooked at least $2,500 that was paid to me and my fellow Bay Area entertainers, including unidentified Laurel & Hardy impersonators, Jean Thomas as Lucy Ricardo, and, from Skyana Productions: Groucho Marx, Marilyn Monroe, and Skyana principal Jeanne Lauren as a cigarette girl. I was hired for the event by the Berridge Event Services Team of Jeffrey Best's Best Events of Los Angeles, event producer to the rich and famous.

WHITE ROSES FOR A WHITE RUSSIAN

Back in March of 1994 business was better than ever. I was entertaining, still working occasionally in local radio, and doing union commercial acting and modeling work in San Francisco. My plate was full. So full, in fact, that the

Infernal Revenue Service (yes, I meant to spell it that way) decided to audit my returns. Funny how they ignored me when I scraped-by for years, but when I started actually earning a healthy income, and was paying my fair share to Uncle Sam, they got very suspicious and decided to crawl up my ass with a magnifying glass. Oh, well, that's the price of success. Thank goodness I wasn't that successful for very long.

My first marriage, to my high school sweetheart, had ended in 1991. I was very happy with her, but she became a cop, and after eleven years together I think she figured, as we didn't have any kids, that she didn't need me any more. She was right, apparently, as she's had the same job for more than two decades and owns a home of her own. It was rough for me at first, but I tried to embrace being a bachelor for the first time as an adult, and dated a number of women for a few years, but neither of two "steadies" during that time wanted to get married.

I like being married. Always have. I love entertaining, but it can be lonely to be on stage with all that laughter and applause, and then to have go home to an empty house and have no one to tell about it. Normal people work with other people forty hours a week, but I was self-employed, so I spent my office time alone, and when I was on stage I still wasn't part of the crowd, so to speak. I suppose that's why I have pets, and why I like being married so much. It's nice to come home and have someone there who loves you, not matter what...especially no matter how funny you are.

I went to Santa Rosa's Howarth Park to play tennis on Tuesday, March 1, with my regular tennis pals, and one of them, a Russian realtor and entrepreneur, pulled up in his Mercedes with a gorgeous new seat cover: a tall, thin, beautiful, mysterious-looking Russian woman. I said, "Viktor, who's the babe? You got a new girlfriend?" He said, "No. She is friend of wife of my business partner. She's from Kiev. Talk to her...maybe she'll marry you!" I laughed, but the prospect of a beautiful, single woman sitting right there was too much for me to resist. I sat down on the bench next to her and started to chat. But that's all that happened. After a few paragraphs I suddenly realized that I was the only one talking. She didn't speak English!

This was a challenge, and I love a challenge. I spoke slowly and distinctly using small words and lots of hand gestures and body language. I showed her my business card, and my brochure, and pictures of myself in various guises (I always carried around promotional materials with me in those days; you just never know when you'll meet a prospective client; or a single Russian woman). As I gabbed on and on she smiled disingenuously and nodded and shrugged and mostly ignored me and petted my dog, Cuthbert, the black cocker-fox-terrier who was my constant companion for sixteen years. Ol' Cuthbert never had it so good. She was obviously in LOVE with HIM...and just tolerating ME. I later learned that she hated people but loved animals, and she admitted to me that she married me just for my pets. Anyway, I played my tennis sets (while she sat stroking Cuthbert on her lap), and then bid her and Viktor farewell, and headed for home. See, I loved being married, but I was not about to get too involved with a Russian woman who spoke no English. Especially after Viktor had said, "Maybe she'll marry you." That was a little fast even for ME.

I had a date scheduled the following Monday with a beautiful Latina I had met at a performance. That's how I met most of the women I dated--through my work. Actually, they were usually either clients or audience members. In fact, that's what I thought I was doing wrong.

I met my first wife at a talent show. After that eleven year relationship ended I met an attractive woman at a business party at which I was performing. She had just won a raffle at the party, and said, "I just won a trip to Hawaii for two. Maybe I should take YOU." And she did. A year later I did a performance at an animal shelter, and met a bright, perky, pretty blond. I was very much in love with her. But after we'd been together two years she still wasn't interested in marriage, and I was. In fact, she told me that she'd never get married. So, despite the fact that she was one of the most beautiful, intelligent, and fascinating women I'd ever met, I decided to move on. The Russian gal, however, I met on the tennis courts, not while I was performing. I hoped that difference would make the relationship last.

Sidebar warning: Funny thing happened at a performance at a catholic church school benefit in between wives and girlfriends. I was impersonating Lt. Columbo, doing walkaround, and there was one particularly attractive woman in her thirties who'd caught my eye. Red hair, freckles, blue eyes…tall, pretty, smart, and she seemed very independent-minded…just my type. She seemed to be enjoying my Columbo more than anyone, and also seemed to be following me around. I flirted with her a bit, and she seemed to me to be receptive. After the job the client called to tell me what a great job I'd done, and how well-received I was, and I inquired about the attractive redhead. My client chuckled and said, "Yeah, I wanted to tell you about her, too." Wow, I thought; the feeling was mutual! "She's the principal of the school. She's a nun."

I was lucky I didn't get my knuckles rapped with a ruler! Hey, it wasn't MY fault! How was I supposed to know that nuns could be caught out of the habit? No wonder those in attendance all laughed so hard. Turns out they may have thought I was even funnier than *I* thought I was. It's not good to be the only one in the room who doesn't get the joke…especially when you're the comedian.

Back to the Latina I mentioned above. I had invited her to accompany me to an upcoming performance of the Santa Rosa Symphony. I love classical music, I had season tickets, and each month I would take my girlfriend or lady-du-jour, and if no one was available, I'd take my maternal grandmother (yes, the one who'd warned me about the "G-Men"). Well, that Latina called the morning of the concert and said that she couldn't make it that evening. I was disappointed, and date-less, so I called my grandma. She said, "Oh, Christopher, I'd LOVE to go; you know I always do; but isn't there some nice young lady friend you'd rather invite? How about that nice Russian woman you told me about?"

And then it hit me. This was a Valentine-themed concert featuring romantic music by Russian composers Rachmaninoff, Prokofiev, and Glinka! Russian woman, Russian composers, Valentine's Day theme! Now, I'm not one to believe in the supernatural, but I thought surely this had to be Karma, fate, or destiny. It was too perfect! I thanked Grandma for the great idea, and scrambled through my address book to find the number for Viktor. He gave me the number of the home of his Russian business partner, Spartak, whose wife, Irisha, was the Russian woman's host during her visit. The invitation was made, and the girlfriend, who spoke English with a thick accent, conferred with her BFF off the phone in Russian, and then said, "Hmm, yes, Christopher, I'm think she would like to go to concert with you."

At the appointed hour I arrived in my concert jacket and necktie and with a big smile and a dozen white roses. Irisha greeted me at the door, and giggled when she saw the flowers. We three sat on the couch, and she translated a few sentences back and forth between Svetlana and me, and then said, "You know, in Russia when man bring white roses to woman it's meaning marriage." I gulped, cleared my throat, giggled nervously, and tried to explain that I had no idea about Russian customs...those flowers just looked pretty in the store.

Off we went to dinner. I translated as best I could with a Russian-English dictionary Svetlana brought with her, and we had a nice time. The waitress was amused as I showed my date pictures in the menu, and then scrambled through the tiny Russian-English dictionary and pointed to words during the taking of our orders. Dinner was quiet, but I was surprised at how easily we were able to communicate through looks and nods and pointing at words. After dinner we were off to the concert, which did, indeed, turn out to be quite romantic, with one slight exception. As we entered from the lobby at the back row of the theater, I gestured to our seats up in the balcony to the right of the stage, and we walked down the aisle past partially-filled rows of seats.

When we got to the front row, we turned to the right, toward the stairs to the balcony, and walked right past center stage in plain view of hundreds of people already in their seats, staring at us. I couldn't resist...the Linnell Family Heritage took over, as I feigned a slight trip on the rug, right in front of the entire audience. I acted surprised, garnering a few chuckles out of a few dozen in the audience, but one look at my Russian date revealed that she found no humor in this rank bit of public humiliation. Obviously remembering that I had told her at some length about my years performing as a professional clown for kids, she looked me straight in the eye with that angry Russian stare, and, in exceptionally good English, icily stated, "I - am - not - a - child."

Somehow I must have eventually redeemed myself in her eyes, because, long story short, one month later to the day we were married.

Call me crazy; I dated my first wife four years before we married, and she left me anyway. My parents, cousin, and a good friend all dated four years before marrying, and they were all divorced in the year prior to the date on which my first wife moved out. Furthermore, the other women I met subsequently all thought their careers were more important that I was...how modern of them! *This* one professed to be more old-fashioned. She wanted to be a homemaker. I was sold.

I read the newspaper in English to her every morning, front to back, for three hours each day for six months, explaining the stories as best I could using her Russian-English dictionary, her German (which is closely related to English; she was a German translator and foreign literature teacher by profession), and my superlative and tenacious verbal and physical communication skills. And within six months she was fluent in English. She had a distinct accent, mind you, but for all intents and purposes she was fluent. I learned a little Russian myself, too, but I was not immersed in my foreign language, as was she.

As I said, I married her partially because she said that she wanted to be a homemaker. My first wife became a cop and moved out, and my two recent girlfriends had careers and didn't really need me, so a stay-at-home wife is just what I wanted. "Good Russian woman cooks, cleans, cares for 'dwaggy' and cats...makes 'hwom' nice for husband," she told me, and that's all I wanted to know. This also freed her up to travel with me, as I did a lot of traveling to performances in those days, and I took my new wife on my fun out-of-town jobs with me.

THE FRUITOPIA TOUR

Svetlana and I were married on April 2, 1994, and on consecutive weekends that June I was performing on the beautiful Monterey/Carmel peninsula, home to Clint Eastwood and famous golf tournaments and the 17-Mile Drive and the Lone Cypress. These were lucrative and prestigious corporate jobs, with big paychecks and nice accommodations, and I was doing the walkaround characterizations that I enjoyed doing the most. The job on Friday, June 3, was in Monterey, and the performance on Sunday, June 12, was in Carmel. My wife accompanied me on both trips. She'd only been living with me for ten weeks now, and there had already been numerous trips, including our honeymoon at Lake Tahoe and a business trip for a performance in San Diego. Furthermore, we had moved into a new house in May. She was very anxious to spend time at home to get housekeeping arranged.

However, on Monday, June 13, on the way home from Carmel, I received a call from my agent in San Francisco. I had been offered a contract to perform on a tour of the upper mid-west for Coca-Cola / Minute Maid as part of a thirty-million-dollar promotional campaign for their new Fruitopia Fruit Beverages, designed as head-on competition with Snapple. If I accepted the contract, I would have to fly to Chicago the very next day for a planning meeting, fly back the day after that, and then drive to the start of the tour in Detroit the day after that...on a trip to last the whole summer! We'd only been in our new house a few weeks, had already made four trips out of town, and now we'd have to leave in three days for twelve weeks. It would really have been nice to spend just a few days in our new house.

I had many performances booked that summer, including a county fair in Colusa, California, but this job meant twelve weeks' top pay and great visibility. Best yet, it was my chance to see more of the United States, and my new Russian wife's chance to see her new country for the first time. It was a paid summer vacation, and all I had to do was cancel all my bookings and do three shows a day. Three other entertainers would be traveling with me, in a commuter van, along with a road manager and crew, but they wanted me to leave my new wife at home. That wouldn't work. I negotiated a bit with them, offering to drive rather than fly (at my own expense), as long as I could bring my wife and dog and three cats with me. They agreed.

On Thursday, June 16, 1994, I got home from the Chicago meeting at 2:30 p.m., and at 11:30 the same evening my wife and my pets and I were stopping for the night in Wells, Nevada on our way to Detroit. I was driving in my 1991 Chevy Astro panel van with no air conditioning, loaded with all of our collective gear, plus three cats and a dog, and my new Russian bride, who spoke very little English. This was to be an interesting summer, to say the least.

We stayed in business-class motels, and I was glad that we were driving in my own vehicle, because the van the company provided allowed neither privacy nor personal space for the other entertainers and the road manager and the sound man. We were accompanied on the promotional sampling tour by a psychedelic-colored bus, one of six tripping around the country from Boston to Los Angeles, each with its own troupe of four entertainers. The school bus had been converted for use as a sound and light stage, cargo hauler, and billboard, with hippiesque 1960s-themed artwork depicting the product and fitted inside with huge stainless-steel pig troughs serving as ice chests for thirteen hundred bottles of Fruitopia. An older married couple drove the bus, followed by the company's commuter van, and my Astro van, as we hopped from one town to another. We'd find a parking lot at a college, shopping center, sports arena, street fair, or festival, set up sound and lights and Fruitopia ice buckets on wheels, and local teens would be hired and uniformed to distribute product as we drew a crowd with our music and show.

We were a diverse troupe of performers, to be sure. Pictured in the photo that follows, from left to right, are the Fruitopia entertainers: plunger juggler "Professor" Elliott Cutler, celebrity impersonator Christopher Linnell, master magician Jay Alexander, and African drummer Eli Honsie.

Fruitopians Cutler, Linnell, Alexander, and Honsie.

The show would commence with Eli Honsie, the African drummer, who would draw a crowd by beating his drum and rhythmically shaking his *shekere*, a percussion instrument made of a painted gourd covered with beads. Then magician Jay Alexander (www.JayAlexander.com) would wow the crowd with fiery feats of juggling and legerdemain. He'd be followed by Professor Elliott Cutler, who was costumed as a stereotypical nerd, complete with taped-up broken glasses and a loaded pocket protector. He would do the most amazing juggling and balancing act with a bathroom plunger, all the while narrating his act with rapid-fire physics banter explaining in the most elaborate, scientific, and hilarious terms how the plunger was able to spin and flip and bounce. Then I would bring up the rear, starting off with my characteristic multi-celebrity rap to introduce the idea that I did rapid-fire impressions. I would then hand out copies of my list of 100 celebrity voices and take requests from the crowd. At the end of the show, all four of us would take the stage together and do all our tricks simultaneously to the beat of Eli's drumming.

We drove eighty-five hundred miles round-trip from Petaluma and performed through Michigan, Indiana, Illinois, Iowa, Missouri, Kansas, Nebraska, Wyoming, Colorado, Utah, and Idaho, where the tour abruptly ended in Boise. To save expenses they cut the tour short and gave our remaining dates to another Fruitopia troupe to the east, which was unfortunate, because we were supposed to head back to the east to Wisconsin and Illinois, and at the end of the tour I was planning to drive my little family in the Astro van to the Atlantic coast, down through the old south, and then take old Route 66 back to California. I was disappointed because we didn't get to see as much of the country as I had hoped, and because I had cancelled bookings to take the job, and, while the part of the tour we did was lucrative, I was counting on the balance of the tour to put a lot of extra money in the bank.

The end of the tour came at the right time, however, because we were all chomping at the bit to get home. The summer heat was murder, and my co-workers were getting a little tired of the cramped quarters in that commuter "prison" van. Svetlana was elated because Boise was only one day of driving from Petaluma, where her new home awaited, filled with all those boxes of stuff we had yet to unpack. On the other hand, I was torn.

While the prospect of getting home sounded great, I was disappointed, too, as I had enjoyed the tour, not only because I was well paid to see the country and perform my act, but because it was fun. I had taught Svetlana how to play cribbage, and we sat in our lawn chairs between shows, with a mobile mini-refrigerator between us serving as a card table, plus the dog at our feet and the cats in a huge steel cage, and we played cards and chatted for hours and hours. Best of all, I didn't have to worry about returning phone calls, booking dates, and paying bills. It was virtually my first, brief taste in twenty years of not being self-employed, and I relished the relaxation.

Furthermore, in between shows and on our days off, we visited the Ford Presidential Museum in Lansing, the Indiana Soldiers' and Sailors' Monument, the Indiana War Memorial, the Indy 500 Speedway, the Indianapolis Zoo, the Truman Presidential Library and Museum and Historic Site, the newly completed Independence Temple, the St. Louis Gateway Arch and Soldiers' Memorial, the National Frontier Trails Museum, Kansas City's Pioneer Square, the Eisenhower Presidential Library and Museum, the Colorado State Capitol,

Denver Pioneer Monument, and the Utah State Capitol and spectacular Temple Square in Salt Lake City.

Speaking of the St. Louis Gateway Arch, we were there on July 4, 1994, walking Cuthbert along the riverfront. Since 1981, the arch has been the scene of huge Fourth of July celebrations featuring live music, educational activities, air shows, and spectacular fireworks; truly a demonstration of the slogan, "St. Louis is Where America Comes to Celebrate." We could hear and see that there was a big celebration taking place under the arch, but, being from out of town, we had no idea it included performances by Aretha Franklin, ELO, Foghat, Tammy Wynette, The Beach Boys, and Travis Tritt, among others. Cuthbert was always obedient under voice control, but I had him on a leash that day as we were in unfamiliar surroundings. We sat on a bench at the river's edge, and, while there were hundreds of thousands of people enjoying the festival a few hundred feet away under the arch on the rise behind us, there were very few people nearby on the riverfront sidewalk, so I let Cuthbert off the leash.

Little did I know that directly ahead of us in the river was a barge that was just at that moment about to erupt in a pyrotechnical display of epic proportions. When the first rocket fired, Cuthbert bolted. He tore off away from the sound, past us, directly toward the crowd under the arch. I freaked! My beloved pooch would be gone forever in seconds, and I had to give chase, but my Russian wife had no purse, no wallet, no money, no ID, no cell phone, and little English...just an empty leash. For a split second I weighed my options, and then screamed, "STAY HERE," and charged up the hill after my dog, leaving Svetlana to fend for herself.

When I got up to the top of the rise I could barely see Cuthbert, moving at what must have been almost twenty miles per hour, and I sprinted after him at perhaps half that. As he disappeared into the throngs of celebrants, I thought I'd lose him for sure, so I shouted ahead to the crowd, "WHERE'S THE DOG?" A sea of arms simultaneously and jointly pointed the way as the crowd actually parted for me. Without losing speed I was actually gaining on him, because he was zig-zagging in fear and I was running in a straight line after him. I lost sight of him as he turned corners, but I kept shouting, and the crowd kept parting and the sea of arms kept pointing as I ran.

This memory really does renew my faith in human charity; these people didn't know me or my dog, but with no time to think, their automatic reaction was to help, and in the most basic way: instantaneously and simultaneously moving back and pointing. I wished I could have thanked them all individually. By this time I had been sprinting for what went on to minutes, and I was afraid that I would collapse before I found Cuthbert, but luck was with me, as he'd run into a dead end.

Right behind the stage was a corral of trucks, bounded on the inside by temporary fencing, and measuring, perhaps, forty feet in diameter. There were no people inside, and Cuthbert could not escape, but neither could he hear or obey. The fireworks were still exploding overhead, the music was blasting from the nearby speakers, and hundreds of thousands of people were oohing and awing. Cuthbert was in a complete state of panic, trapped now in this grassy corral, running back and forth and in circles. I couldn't get ahold of him. Svetlana had the leash…even if I did manage to grab him, I wasn't sure that I could hang onto him.

Just then one of the stage technicians ran up and shouted at me, "That dog should be on a leash!" I just looked at him a second, not sure if he was really saying that at this particular moment, and I shouted back, matter-of-factly, "No shit!" Realizing the futility of his remark, he ran to the other side of the corral and we managed to trap Cuthbert between the two of us. The guy whipped off his belt and handed it to me, and I looped the end through the buckle and finally was able to catch Cuthbert and lasso him with the improvised leash. Overjoyed and winded, against the backdrop of the thunder of the fireworks, the drone of the amplified music, and the roar of the crowd, I pumped the guy's hand and shouted profuse thanks. I reached for my wallet, and he threw up his hands to indicate that no reward was required, but I found a ten dollar bill inside and shoved it in his hand and I shouted, "For the belt!" He nodded, and I carried Cuthbert out of the corral as the surrounding crowd cheered.

I didn't realize how far we'd run, as it took several minutes to get back down to the waterfront where, I hoped, Svetlana would be waiting. It actually took more effort holding on to Cuthbert on the way back than it had taken to chase after him at flank speed. While I was a bit more relaxed, he was still in a state of absolute panic, squirming to get out of my grip. I held him against my chest as tightly as I could, praying that I could find Svetlana and get Cuthbert into the van before he got loose. When I got within view of the riverfront bench, I could see that she was indeed still there, sobbing, obviously overcome with relief, anger, and gratitude all at the same time. No words were spoken, but she grabbed Cuthbert out of my hands and squeezed the living hell out of him, and we silently scurried back to our car to get our poor pooch away from the fireworks.

I had to make a split-second decision that day: chase the dog or stay with the wife. Unspoken was the realization to which we both came that day. She had never made any secret of the fact that she married me because she loved my dog. Now we both knew that I cared more for him, too.

5 - The Life of the Party^{SM}

I got a call one day from a female client who'd hired me several times before to perform STARGRAM^{SM} Singing Telegrams, but on this occasion she wanted something different. She said, "We want you to come in as if you're one of the guests, and just *be funny*. You know, kinda' be the life of the party." Wow, I thought, that sounds like a great name for an act! I could do my old stand-up act of impressions at small private parties for the first time. Mind you, I was not too keen on the idea of coming in as just one of the guests and *being funny*, because I'd been doing party entertainment long enough to know that a performance such as that would come off as obnoxious. As I mentioned earlier, I don't like doing pranks, and the few times I've allowed myself to be talked into them by enthusiastic clients, at best they've not gone as well as just doing my regular schtick, and, at worst, they've backfired badly.

But I thought this idea of being the "life of the party" would solve another problem I was having. My STARGRAM^{SM} Singing Telegrams were working beautifully, but I repeatedly had return clients call me and tell me that they wanted *more*. They wanted the performance to last longer. Well, this is another thing that you learn in four decades of entertaining: in comedy, more is not always better. You'll quote a client a price, and they will invariably ask, "How long's that for?" I would say, "fifteen to twenty-five minutes." And they'd say, "Is that all? Can't you stay a little longer? We'll feed you dinner. It's gonna be a great party...and it'll be good exposure!" Ahh, "good exposure." That's what it's always about, isn't it? The owner of every restaurant and nightclub and the planner of every benefit and promotion believes that "good exposure" will be enough of an inducement to do the job for free.

It's always difficult explaining to clients why they should *not* want me to be at the party longer than a few minutes. In almost everything else in life, more is better. If you don't tell them you'll stay longer, they think they're getting ripped-off. But the thing about having a costumed entertainer at your party is that once everybody's seen the character and had a few laughs, it's old. They'll beg you on the phone to stay an extra fifteen minutes or half-hour, but at the performance when the song is done and the gag is played out, it is time to go. Nobody needs Rodney Dangerfield just wandering around being funny all night. Unless, of course, it's for a large crowd. Now, my walkaround program was designed for large affairs at which scores or hundreds of people are in attendance, and I could entertain for hours, changing characterizations repeatedly, without fear of wearing-out my welcome. But at small, private parties with fewer than, say, fifty attendees, once everyone has seen and interacted with the entertainer, his job is done.

Therefore, I was very firm about my time restraints, and I almost never accepted dinner invitations. When they say they will feed you dinner, it doesn't mean you're sitting at the head table with the client and the honoree, it means they have a table out in the kitchen or the garage where the kids and the band are eating. A few table scraps are not worth hanging around another half-hour in costume. Besides, do you eat in-character? I mean, Popeye squeezes spinach out of a can...he doesn't use a knife and fork. Elvis scarfs down peanut butter and banana sandwiches, he doesn't eat salad and salmon. Nobody wants to chat with Inspector Clouseau while eating a gourmet catered dinner...he spills the beverages. And I can't enjoy food when people are expecting me to be funny.

This discussion of my rule against dining at gigs prompts me to include the following admittedly complicated subchapter that pertains to dining, but not to the development of this new act.

THE BIG LITTLE MAN

Back in 1991 I was hired by District 513 of the Rotary Club to perform at a banquet at their annual conference in Sacramento. The evening's theme was the 1942 movie *Casablanca*, a very popular event theme even today, and, as usual, I impersonated Humphrey Bogart's lead character, Rick Blaine. This was one of those occasions on which I could not talk the client out of having me actually eat dinner, as I was, indeed, a Rotarian of that district.

I was seated in a huge banquet room at the head table, which was mounted on risers in front of a crowd of hundreds dressed in black tie and ball gowns. They served us a spinach salad and some kind of fish, neither of which I would have eaten for my mother, grandmother, or wife; but I had to force it down without gagging in front of this crowd of my fellow Rotarians. It was awful...not just the food, but trying to eat with hundreds of people watching me as I tried to remain in character. Fortunately, I was rescued by a munchkin!

Well, actually, it was a wannabe munchkin. Three-foot-nine-inch actor Billy Barty (1924-2000) made a guest appearance at the banquet. He was one of the *Little People* (the term he preferred over "midget" or "dwarf") who appeared in the 1981, Chevy Chase, Carrie Fisher, Eve Arden movie *Under the Rainbow*, a fictionalized story about the 120 little actors who descended upon Hollywood for the shooting of the 1939 movie *The Wizard of Oz* (for which Barty was bypassed as an actor because he was only thirteen-years-old). In fact, Barty had a lead role in *Under the Rainbow*, playing diminutive secret agent Otto Kriegling. Among his many movie credits, in a career spanning an incredible eight decades, was bible salesman J. J. MacKuen in another Chevy Chase picture, 1978's *Foul Play*, one sequence of which I saw shot in San Francisco (that story in a later chapter). Barty also wrote the foreword to the Stephen Cox book *The Munchkins of Oz.*

As the celebrity host of the banquet, my Rick Blaine-Bogart was called upon to welcome Mr. Barty, and it was one of the few times in four decades of entertaining in which I actually stepped out of character, to recite as W.C. Fields a few lines of dialogue with Barty which he had with co-star Rod Steiger in the 1976 movie *W.C. Fields and Me*, in which Steiger played Fields, and Barty played his German sidekick, Ludwig. Screenwriter, songwriter, and Broadway composer Bob Merrill took a lot of flack for the inaccuracies in his screen adaptation of the already notoriously inaccurate and self-serving memoir of Carlotta Monti, Fields' second and final paramour.

This Ludwig character, specifically, was notoriously fictional, but I believe it may have actually been loosely based upon several of Fields' real-life buddies, namely actors Tammany Young, Bud Ross, William "Shorty" Blanche, producer Paul Meredith Jones, and Fields' big, blond girlfriend, Bessie Poole. She was the actual traveling companion, depicted by Barty's Ludwig character in the movie, with whom Fields drove to California in June of 1927 in his Lincoln touring car. Poole was an established Ziegfeld Follies performer when Fields met her backstage in New York, and she bore him a son named William Rexford Fields Morris on August 15, 1917. Poole was killed in a bar fight sometime thereafter.

The scene in *W.C. Fields and Me* involved Fields (Steiger) leaving his buddy Ludwig (Barty) at their jointly-owned wax museum on the Santa Monica boardwalk when Fields went off to become a big star in Hollywood. They are shown playing in the water together, and upon Fields' departure for Tinsel Town, he picks Ludwig up and tearfully admonishes him to be careful in the water, saying, "A gall-darn raindrop would drown ya'."

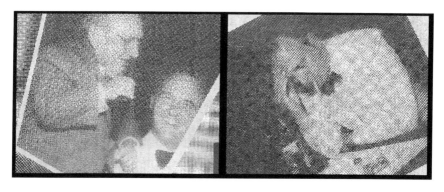

Billy Barty and Christopher as Bogart's Rick Blaine.

After re-enacting the scene with Barty, I returned to my place at the table, and found that my plate had been cleared by the busboy...and with it the remaining spinach and fish. Thanks, Ludwig!

TAKING REQUESTS

Back to the idea for my new act, which I called the "Life of the Party^{SM}." I felt it was going to solve the problem of clients wanting something more or longer than a singing telegram, and also give me a new act to sell to repeat clients. I realized that it also provided me with the opportunity to use all the celebrity voices I didn't get to do when I was fully-costumed as just one character. Clients would hire me to be Pee Wee Herman, for instance, and then say, "You can do your other impressions, too, right?" No...Pee Wee doesn't DO impressions. He goes "AAAAARRRRR" and hangs out in adult theaters. How do you do an impression of Bill Clinton or Edith Bunker when you're dressed as Groucho Marx and have a mustache and eyebrows greasepainted onto your face?

The solution was to start with a fully-costumed impersonation that could be easily removed. It had to be someone widely known (not William F. Buckley), someone polite (not Andrew Dice Clay), and someone who was distinctly costumed but whose costuming could be instantly removed when it was time to do celebrity voices (not Elvis). And then it hit me: Lt. Columbo! He was well-known in the 1970s and 80s, polite, easy to work into a storyline (a policeman can find a reason to investigate anyone), and his costuming was at once distinct and easy to remove: a wig, a cigar, and a trench coat. I could wear a sport coat or suit and tie, and simply put on the trench coat and wig, and I was Columbo. And when it was time to do celebrity voices, I just took them off and I was Christopher Linnell again. Perfect.

So I asked the client to complete my Questionnaire, giving me information about the honoree, same as for the STARGRAM^{SM} Singing Telegram. I would start off as Lt. Columbo, playing out a storyline that involved investigating the honoree for whatever malfeasance I could extrapolate from the information I was given. When I had completed my investigation, I would start music on my boom box, and do an opening song or rap, introducing my audience to the idea that I do rapid-fire impressions. In the first couple of lines of the song, I would remove the Columbo wig and trench coat, and then do a slew of celebrity voices, after which I would distribute my list of one hundred celebrity voices to the audience and take requests. Initially I used Quincy Jones' instrumental R&B tune "Midnight Soul Patrol" and would do the song as a rap. That worked well for years, but eventually I wanted to incorporate more celebrities into the song, so I started looking around for a longer song with a similarly catchy rhythm and an easy cadence for rhyming.

Problem is that most recorded songs have singing in them. I once saw an advertisement for a device called a Thompson Vocal Eliminator™, which was invented in 1976 and promised to remove the words being sung from a recorded song and leave the music intact. But it was expensive, and in my research about the device, I learned that the way this was achieved was by singling out individual tracks of the song and electronically removing the vocal tracks. But most recorded music had the singing still bleeding into the background range of the microphones used for the instruments, so I figured there would still be some residual words. This was fine for someone singing the original lyrics, but wouldn't work for me...I was writing NEW lyrics...the original lyrics in the background would be quite a distraction.

That's when I first heard about "karaoke." It started in Japan in the early 1970s, and by the 1980s had spread throughout Southeast Asia. It was the perfect solution to my problem. I bought karaoke albums for every character I offered. Some celebrities, such as Bing Crosby, Frank Sinatra, Sammy Davis Jr., Tom Jones, Englebert Humperdinck, Nat King Cole, Neil Diamond, and even Johnny Cash and Willie Nelson performed a multitude of songs that were ideal for singing telegrams, and I bought several karaoke albums of each of their repertoires. One of the karaoke albums I found was from *The Wizard of Oz*, and "If I Only Had a Brain" was very long, and had a cadence that was ideally suited to my purposes. Here are the lyrics I wrote for that song (with the celebrity voices underlined or designated in parentheses where not sung):

> (<u>Myself</u>) I could wile away the hours
> Conferring with the flowers

And T.V. shows aren't bad.
I could be tough like <u>James Cagney</u>,
While <u>Eddie G. (Robinson)</u> shot bullets, seeeee?
(<u>James Stewart</u>) You see, Hollywood isn't just a fad.

<u>Long John Silver</u> looks for treasure,
(<u>John Wayne</u>) The Duke's a man against whom to measure
The kind of man you are.
<u>Kate Hepburn</u> rode with him as Rooster,
And rode with Bogie (<u>Humphrey Bogart</u>) as a sister
On the Queen in Africa.

Now, (<u>Sydney) Greenstreet</u> looked for the bird,
And (<u>Peter) Lorre</u> followed behind.
And <u>Boris Karloff</u> was The Grinch,
And do you remember Frankenstein?

And there was more than just one <u>Wolfman (Jack)</u>!
And if <u>Paul Harvey</u> was your newsman,
You knew "The Rest of the Story."
But Uncle <u>Walter (Cronkite)</u> put you in it,
<u>Harry Reasoner</u> took *Sixty Minutes*,
And <u>Robin Leach</u> told rich stories!

Everybody watched <u>Johnny Carson</u>,
A professional humor marksman,
The opposite of <u>Raymond Burr</u>.
(<u>Edith Bunker</u>) But for laughs you turned to The Bunkers,
(<u>Archie Bunker</u>) Less alike than Madison and Unger,
(<u>Edith</u>) Men liked him… (<u>Archie</u>) and women liked her!

<u>Thurston Howell (III</u>) was a tropical isler,
And <u>Fred Sanford</u> the first recycler.
Ooooo, <u>Frank Nelson</u> was glad to help!
But <u>Jack Benny</u> never liked him…
Why didn't <u>Rochester (Eddie Anderson</u>) ever strike him?
Meanwhile <u>George Burns</u> was sucking smoke.

<u>Ed Wynn</u>, the fire chief, you know,
Was the king of silly lines.
<u>Buddy Hackett</u>, a short, fat Jew,
Tells lots of jokes that're kind of blue!

And speaking of Jewish jokers,
<u>Joan Rivers</u> loves to choke us

With gossip laced with laughs.
(Goofy) The only guy she never picks on
Is Disney's pooch with a mental defection
His name is Goofy…ain't that a gas?

Well, my name is (Elmer) Fudd, remember?
I'm an N.R.A. Life Member.
So Snaggle Puss says, "Exit, stage left."
And, of course, you remember Sylvester (the Putty Tat)?
I'm the number one bird molester!
And how 'bout the *Rock & Bullwinkle Show*?

Popeye pleased the kiddies,
And Kermit pleased Miss Piggy,
But Dr. Ruth (Westheimer) just pleasures herself…hehehe!
F.D.R. we've learned had a mistress,
Harry Truman's sex life was listless.
But J.F.K. did Marilyn herself!

While (Henry) Kissinger made peace
'Tween the Arabs and the Jews,
Trickie Dickie (Richard Nixon) stayed at home,
But nevertheless, I made the news!

In the 80s Ronald Reagan
Increased the salaries we were makin',
But George (H.W. Bush) made the increase disappear!
(Bill Clinton) And in the races that followed,
(Bob Dole) Clinton aced that Kansas fellow,
(H. Ross Perot) And the munchkin with the big ears!

This song worked for years, until George W. Bush became president, and the lyrics were, therefore, a bit dated. But that was in 2001, and I was doing tours and not really entertaining as much. I tried rewriting the lyrics with celebrities who were a bit more contemporary, but I didn't like the results as much, and I eventually just dumped the opening song. The pacing of the song meant that I was whizzing through the voices too fast for most people to recognize or understand them, anyway. But the song certainly did generally introduce the crowd to the idea that I did rapid-fire impressions.

When I handed-out copies of my list of celebrity voices to the audience, they would start shouting out names, and I would improvise patter for the characters they requested, using the honoree of the party as the foil or the butt of the jokes, based upon the information given me by the client on my Questionnaire. When I felt that I had milked most of the laughs out of the group that I thought were possible, I would start looking for a finish. And that was important. George Burns often said, "In show business you need two things: a great opening, and a great finish. Then nobody cares about all the boring stuff in between." My opening was Columbo and the song. When I felt it was time to close, if the crowd didn't shout out a funny character, I'd suggest one myself, such as Joan Rivers or Rodney Dangerfield, or the "Copper Clapper" routine Johnny Carson did with Jack Webb as Sgt. Joe Friday of *Dragnet* on a famous 1968 episode of *The Tonight Show*, which I memorized and can still today do rapid-fire:

> JACK WEBB: It was 10:15 am. It was warm in Los Angeles. I was working the daywatch out of Burglary. We got a call from the Acme School Bell company. There'd been a robbery.
> JOHNNY CARSON: There's been a robbery.
> JACK: I see, sir. What was stolen?
> JOHN: Our clappers.
> JACK: Your clappers?
> JOHN: Yeah, that's right. You know, the thing inside a bell that makes it clang?
> JACK: The clangers?
> JOHN: Yeah. That's right. We call 'em "clappers" in the business.
> JACK: A clapper caper.
> JOHN: What was that?
> JACK: Nevermind. Lemme get the facts. Where were these clappers kept?
> JOHN: In the closet.
> JACK: I see. And can you describe them?
> JOHN: Well, they were made of copper. And they were clean.
> JACK: Clean copper clappers.
> JOHN: That's right.
> JACK: Who first discovered your clean copper clappers had been copped?
> JOHN: Well, that would be our cleaning woman.
> JACK: And what's her name?
> JOHN: Clara Clifford.
> JACK: Uh, huh. Tell me, sir, do you have any idea who might have

copped your clean copper clappers kept in the closet?

JOHN: Well, just one. We fired a man. He swore he'd get even.

JACK: And what was his name?

JOHN: Claude Cooper.

JACK: And where is Mr. Cooper now, sir?

JOHN: In Cleveland.

JACK: That figures. Sir, do you have any idea why Cleveland's Claude Cooper would cop your clean copper clappers kept in the closet?

JOHN: Only one reason.

JACK: What's that?

JOHN: He's a kleptomaniac.

JACK: I see. Well, sir, lemme see if I've got this straight: cleaning woman Clara Clifford discovered your clean copper clappers, kept in the closet, were copped by Claude Cooper, the kleptomaniac from Cleveland. Now, does that about cover it?

JOHN: Just one more thing.

JACK: What's that, sir?

JOHN: If I ever catch kleptomaniac Claude Cooper from Cleveland who copped my clean copper clappers kept in the closet...

JACK: Yessir?

JOHN: I'll clobber him.

That was what George Burns would have called, "a good finish." At the conclusion of the Life of the Party^{SM} routine, I would perform a STARGRAM^{SM} Singing Telegram written all about the honoree. The entire performance would last from forty-five to ninety minutes, and was priced significantly higher than just the STARGRAM^{SM}, but it was very popular with my repeat clients, and it allowed me to diversify my services, so that I didn't get burned-out doing the same routine over and over again. Of course, the fact that I was doing improv comedy helped to keep my work fresh for me, as I love a challenge.

The request segment was far from the "boring stuff in the middle" about which George Burns spoke. It was arguably the best single thing I was doing. It was stand-up, impressions, repartee, improv, and audience interaction all in one package. It was fast, fluid, and funny, and it was centered around the honoree and included the audience. Of course, the paper lists of celebrity voices were also a fantastic marketing tool. They were 8.5" x 5.5" (a regular sheet of paper cut in half), and on the back side was my advertising. I printed them on my own office copier, so the cost was negligible. And talk about great exposure! Each attendee at each party was watching me perform for an hour, and each had my list of 100 celebrity voices and a handbill containing my promotional information. This was an incredible marketing tool that reaped a geometric progression of new jobs from each job I did.

The problem I had with stand-up is that I am an improv comic. Not a fake improv comic who performs a pre-written and memorized stand-up act at an "improv club," but a comedian who actually improvises his routine on-site. On the rare occasions on which I've actually written lines and jokes to be recited, the performance has not gone nearly as well as when I just got up and winged it. So, while other comedians fit into the stand-up framework, each writing and memorizing "sets" of stories and jokes, and could easily perform in a nightclub setting, my act was almost entirely improvised, and necessitated close contact with the audience. I found doing club dates extremely difficult. The comedians are on a stage performing for a crowd in the dark. I worked best when the lights were up, and I was performing right in the middle of the audience.

Doing celebrity voices on request worked so well in my Life of the Party[SM] program that I used the same format to perform at county fairs and festivals, as well. And I later created a number of game show programs utilizing celebrity voices on request, which were not only perfect for fairs and festivals, but worked well at parties, in nightclubs, at company parties, and in OSHA safety meetings. But those will be described in Chapter 6 - Game Shows.

I found that while some people did want something more than a STARGRAM[SM] Singing Telegram, they couldn't afford the price of the Life of the Party[SM], so I decided to slice the STARGRAM[SM] out of the Life of the Party[SM], and created an act I called "Christopher & Co. LIVE." I'd start off as Lt. Columbo, then do the opening song, followed by the request segment, and, when I felt the time had come to finish, I'd just wait for a big laugh and say, Thank you, and exit. The LIVE act was perfect for events at which there was no honoree, such as sales meetings, fairs, festivals, and nightclubs.

The request segment usually elicited the majority of the most popular celebrities from my list, but I was always surprised by people who'd shout out names I rarely heard. Frequently people would shout out names they didn't know, just to find out who the person was, such as Frank Nelson (the "Ooooo, Yeeeees" guy with the pencil mustache from *The Jack Benny Show*, *I Love Lucy*, and *Sanford & Son*), Thurl Ravenscroft (Tony the Tiger, and The Grinch's narrator), and Mason Adams (the voice of Excedrin, Smucker's, and the managing editor on *The Lou Grant Show*). One of the great things about my voice acts was that I could involve everyone in the room in the fun. If Grandpa wasn't participating, I could go involve him; if two or three people were participating but everyone else was quiet, I could interact more with the quiet ones to get them involved; and kids were a kick. Kids loved seeing the adults laugh, even if they didn't get the jokes. I performed as a clown and puppeteer for fourteen years, so I made a point of including the kids. I'd hand them copies of the list, too, and it made them feel as though they were a part of the fun.

The kids are always the funniest, too. Teenagers, on the other hand, are the worst age group for which to perform. They are more worried about what their peers will think of them than they are about anything else. They don't laugh unless everyone else is laughing. Adults are like that, too, but most adults are a bit more self-confident than most teens, so they are more willing to let it all hang out and laugh at whatever they think is funny. But kids are the best. They laugh even when nothing is funny. They laugh because somebody else is laughing…or because nobody is laughing. And with my lists in their hands, they are part of the action. I ask them repeatedly whom they want to hear. They're always more willing to respond than adults; and, after all, I don't care if they actually know the names…I just want more requests and to make everyone laugh.

Kids were always making the funniest requests, too. They frequently would shout out names even without pretending to know who they were. Some kids would just stand in front of me and shout out one name after another, which was fine with me. It was easier to just do a couple of lines each of multiple names fired at me one at a time than to try to improvise a storyline for each of fewer voices requested. And the kids would slaughter the pronunciation of the names without any shame whatsoever.

On April 6, 2013, literally just the Saturday night before I wrote this, I performed at the Moose Lodge in Clearlake Oaks at the fortieth birthday party of Clear Lake Police Lieutenant Tim Celli. Nice people, responsive crowd, cute kids. My client, Amanda, Tim's wife, was sitting near the front with several kids surrounding her. She had two daughters, Kristen and Jacey, and a son named Nick, but he was in his dad's lap, and it was some other little boy who made a request. He stood right in front of me with my list looking very large in his very small hands.

I gestured directly to him and asked, "Who would *you* like to hear, sir?" Amanda whispered something in his ear, and then he looked at me and blurted out: "Molester The Stone."

We all laughed, and I asked, "WHAAAAT?" Amanda grabbed him, and whispered in his ear again, and he corrected himself: "Sylvester Stallone!"

6 - Game Shows

The first game show I offered was created to give me something to offer clients who'd already hired my other programs, including my two request acts. I needed a request act with a stricter format. The LIVE act was free-flowing, fast, and fun, but I thought it would be a nice change to offer something a bit more structured. I decided to look for a game show format, and my three favorite television game shows were *You Bet Your Life* with Groucho Marx and George Fenneman, *Match Game* with Gene Rayburn, and *Hollywood Squares* with Peter Marshall.

You Bet Your Life was priceless, of course, but it was only a game show in the mildest sense. They should have just called it, "Groucho Cuts Up on Odd Members of the Public." It was really just a format for Groucho's brilliant and lightening-fast repartee. But I wanted a program that showcased my many celebrity voices, and Groucho was the only star on *You Bet Your Life*.

The show that did the most to form my comedy was *Match Game* with Gene Rayburn. I didn't realize this at the time, watching *Match Game* when I came home from junior high school on Guam in the 1970s, but watching the re-runs today I recognize what an effect the show's star and guests had on my sense of comedy. Gene Rayburn has got to be the most under-rated talent ever on television. I was too young to have seen him when he was Steve Allen's announcer on *The Tonight Show* (Steve Allen, by the way, is my choice as the most brilliant talent ever on television).

I was a teenager when I first saw Gene on *Match Game*, and at the time I thought he was kind of corny, and he certainly did revel in what my grandmother would have termed "base humor." But I now recognize, based upon a broad sampling of his comments on the show, that he was also an intelligent, erudite, extremely well-read man who had a lightening-fast wit, a wealth of characterizations and accents and impressions, impeccable timing, and, most importantly, a child-like sense of humor. Everything was funny to Gene. He loved everybody, and could find the good in anyone.

"DIRTY" JOKES

The risqué humor on *Match Game* is also the root cause of most of the complaints I've gotten over the years from clients and mothers and teachers and employers. I learned what was appropriate from Gene and the *Match Game* panelists. It was a shining example of the use of the naughty *double entendre*. It set the standard for what was appropriate for a family audience on daytime television in the 1970s. I just saw an episode the other day from 1975 in which Gene was standing at center stage with a beautiful and well-endowed young lady who was trying to make the big match with Richard Dawson for $5,000, but, when asked for an answer, she was completely stumped. She said to Gene, "I've got nothing." Gene looked directly down at her blouse and said, "I wouldn't say that." The crowd went nuts.

As with everything in life, the face of comedy changes in waves as the pendulum swings bad and forth. But entertainers have been accused of being too dirty and have been chastised for being inappropriate probably since the days of the court jesters. Examples of naughty double-entendres can be found in classic literature in the works of Homer, Chaucer, Shakespeare, and Dickens, who chose to refer repeatedly in *Oliver Twist* to Charley Bates as *Master Bates*. Vaudeville comics got into movies and radio, and brought their raunchy burlesque humor with them. W.C. Fields was particularly fond of Dickens, as a matter of fact, and reveled in funny-sounding, raunchy names.

In the 1940 movie *The Bank Dick*, Fields was the star and the screenwriter (under the name "Mahatma Kane Jeeves," itself a purposeful misspelling of the line from old stage plays, "My hat, my cane, Jeeves"), and several scenes in his original screenplay took place in a tavern known as the Black Pussy Café.

The censors balked, and Fields was forced to change the name painted on the windows to the Black Pussy *Cat* Café, but director Eddie Cline told Fields to *say* whatever he wanted, that the "front office" wouldn't notice the difference. Fields' character, Egbert Sousè (another double entendre, for "drunk"), repeatedly referred to the café simply as the Black Pussy, and, as Cline said, the front office ignored it. Of course, the movie's title, *Bank Dick*, also certainly at least sounds as if it was another double entendre. "Dick" was a slang expression for "detective" in those days. Now, he could have just called the movie, "The Bank Detective," but he probably figured "Dick" sounded funnier. And it does.

The movie censors fought against writers and actors and attempted to sanitize their jokes. But when Lenny Bruce, Richard Pryor, and George Carlin hit the stage, Fields' vaudeville generation claimed that the new blue humor was beneath them; they claimed that the only good comic is a clean comic. This argument is nothing new. It's nothing more than bullshit hypocrisy, in fact.

I have seen interviews in which Groucho Marx, George Burns, and Bob Hope have all three clearly stated that only "cheap" comics "stoop" to such humor, and each claimed to have always taken the high road. The fact is, however, that they all three have been guilty of this. Groucho Marx in the 1930 movie *Animal Crackers* said, "We took some pictures of the native girls, but they weren't developed." I have a recording of George Burns at the Shubert Theatre in 1974 saying, "I'm at the age now where just putting my cigar in its holder is a thrill." But Bob Hope was the king of pretending to be clean while going for a dirty laugh. He beat the censors at their own game. He spent years battling the censors over his repeated ad-libbed sexual double entendres on stage, in radio, in movies, and on television, yet I saw him in his nineties in an interview stating categorically that dirty comics are at the lowest rank in the industry.

In some respects our society has become more and more politically correct, and less tolerant of toilet humor, sex puns, and racy punchlines. But, on the other hand, comedians have gotten raunchier and raunchier. Big celebrities on national television in primetime can get away with murder, but party entertainers and corporate comedians are held to a higher standard. I've been fired for making jokes that would have been considered mild out of the mouths of Johnny Carson, David Letterman, or Bill Maher.

In fact, I have been fired for making jokes that could be found on afternoon television thirty years earlier on *Hollywood Squares*. This show featured at least nine celebrities on each episode, and they came up with some brilliant ad-libs. Or at least they seemed like ad-libs. There has been some discussion about whether or not the celebrities were tipped to the questions beforehand so they'd have ample time to be assured of coming up with brilliant "ad-libs." According to several sources, including the Internet Movie Database at www.IMDb.com, the stars were not given specific questions or answers, but they were briefed about subject matter prior to each show to allow them to come up with humorous responses and bluffs.

Regardless of that issue, as on *Match Game*, the questions on *Hollywood Squares* were obviously phrased by the producers specifically to elicit illicit answers from the stars. For instance, Paul Lynde was asked what Secretary of State Henry Kissinger was doing in a geisha house during a recent visit to Japan, and Lynde answered, "Negotiating for *piece*." Rose Marie was asked what etiquette expert Amy Vanderbilt says is the maximum length of time fiancés should be engaged, and Rose Marie answered, "Engaged in what?"

Burt Reynolds was asked if his sheep's temperature of 102 degrees was normal, and Burt answered, "People think *I'm* not normal because I keep taking her temperature." Peter Marshall asked Joan Rivers, "Your baby has a certain object which he loves to cling to. Should you try to break him of his habit?" Joan answered, "Yes. It's daddy's turn." And Charley Weaver was asked how many balls are on a pool table, and Charlie answered, "How many men are on the table?"

I was raised in the 1960s and 70s, when television was filled with W.C. Fields, Groucho Marx, Laurel & Hardy, *I Love Lucy*, Johnny Carson, *Hollywood Squares*, *Captain Kangaroo*, Red Foxx on *Sanford & Son*, and Dean Martin's celebrity roasts. While not all were risqué, those shows are how I learned what was funny. In fact, I now realize that *Match Game* and Gene Rayburn were my comedic role models. In the 1980s and 90s people felt that a party and corporate entertainer shouldn't be allowed to get away with the same stuff that was considered appropriate for daytime television just a decade earlier, or for contemporary nationally-known comics on network television.

Today's comedians, such as Bill Maher, Patton Oswalt, and Larry the Cable Guy, were influenced by the legacies of Lenny Bruce, Richard Prior, Eddie Murphy, *Saturday Night Live*, Rodney Dangerfield, and Robin Williams, who were influenced by the previous generation, namely Johnny Carson, Don Rickles, Mort Sahl, Bob Newhart, and Jonathon Winters, who were in turn influenced by Marx, Burns, Hope and their vaudeville brethren Milton Berle, Henny Youngman, and Jack Benny.

Dean Martin's celebrity roasts were the cleaned-up television version of the raunchy off-broadcast Friar's Club roasts. Today *Comedy Central*'s roasts have transcended naughty double entendres and dug deep into truly filthy toilet humor and blatantly politically-incorrect comedy about race, sex, and the raunchiest of topics, performed by the likes of such female comics as Lisa Lampanelli, Sarah Silverman, and even aged veterans such as Betty White, Bea Arthur, and Joan Rivers. How many times have we heard on Comedy Central roasts, "Her vagina is so old/big/dirty, that _____"?

MY GAME SHOW

Back now to my search for a game show format for my celebrity impersonations. The television game show that seemed perfect for my purposes was *Hollywood Squares*. There were nine separate squares, and the humor was derived from improvising jokes about trivia questions, which are much easier to come by than the skillfully-written "So he (blanked) me" questions on *Match Game*. With the help, once again, of my trusty old dad, I built a wooden DJ stand during my radio days, which served a duel purpose as my game board for the game show I created: "Celebrity Squares[SM]."

Just as in *Hollywood Squares*, my game board was filled with celebrities from my list. I would obtain from the audience two contestants (or two teams of contestants), and then ask a trivia question. My contestants would then choose a celebrity square, and that celebrity (or those celebrities, as I would often put multiple stars in each box) would answer the question, either correctly, or with bluff answers. As on television, my contestants would then agree or disagree with the answers given them by the celebrities I impersonated, and they would earn an X or an O for a correct guess, and then play Tic-Tac-Toe until the round was won. The contestants winning two out of three rounds would win the game.

Celebrity Squares[SM] was ideal for fairs and festivals, company parties, and private party clients who'd already availed themselves of my other programs. I even attempted to launch my own local television version of Celebrity Squares[SM], by shooting a pilot in a local nightclub. Many of my local television commercials at Santa Rosa's KFTY TV50 in the 1980s were written, produced, and directed by a lovely lady by the name of Theresa Champagne. I asked her to produce the pilot for me, and asked my friends, the Montero Family, to host the taping in the lounge of their Petaluma restaurant, Sonoma Joe's.

I issued press releases to the local media, inviting the public to the free show, and we shot several games, using contestants from the audience. My dad was in charge of the applause sign. I took the completed and edited video to KFTY and they said that they'd be happy to air the game show on a weekly basis...but I'd have to produce the thing myself, selling advertising to pay for the airtime. I already knew how tough that was, after my experience selling time at KSRO Radio, so I decided to try to hire a professional. I spoke to several, and began working with one, but never found anyone willing to stick with the project, and the television show idea died on the vine. The publicity was great for business, though, and I used Celebrity Squares[SM] for years thereafter all over the state of California.

I also diversified, once again, by creating even more game show programs. I did my own *You Bet Your Life* with Groucho Marx, and, while I still sound just like him, back when I was thinner and had an almost full head of hair, I looked exactly like the 1950s Groucho that the public saw on television.

Christopher as "You Bet Your Life" host Groucho Marx.

Every new act I created meant one or two more times each repeat client would hire me, and the largest crowds for which I performed *You Bet Your Life* were composed of the staff of Pacific Gas & Electric, northern California's utility provider. I performed at PG&E headquarters in San Francisco, in their huge, professional auditorium at 77 Beale Street that seated hundreds. I did two days of shows for their entire roster of field employees who were brought in for training. Members of upper-level management were in attendance, including the company's C.E.O., and I was given rave reviews.

I had also been performing my game shows at OSHA safety meetings (required by the federal and state Occupational Safety Hazard Administrations) for several years at PG&E power plants all over the state. OSHA requires that employees receive safety training, but, as with the D.M.V. and traffic safety school, safety information laced with humor was more effective than just safety information alone. I would be given safety information in the form of questions and answers, and would mix them in with general trivia questions. The employees got their training, and they stayed awake better because they were laughing so hard.

As the years passed, I created "Celebrity Clue[SM]" (which was a game of hangman including celebrity voices), offered *Ben Stein's Money* with my Ben Stein impersonation, and *Do You Want to be a Millionaire?* with my Regis Philbin. I also began offering "Christopher's Murder Mystery," utilizing multiple fully-costumed impersonations, and a program I called the "One Man Pro-Am[SM]," in which I would host and/or play in golf and tennis tournaments utilizing my celebrity voices.

7 - Corporate Comedy

I was notorious at Casa Grande High School. I was the kid from Guam who hadn't grown up with everyone else. I was a clown, and I was on the radio. I impersonated all the teachers, and I did the morning announcements over the school P.A. And, although I knew nothing about football, I was the announcer for the football games, because none of my schoolmates who *did* know about football had the balls to announce the games. They gave me a *spotter*, who told me what was happening and what to say, but I frequently misunderstood or misspoke or repeated speculation that the spotter had not intended for the mic, and the Booster Club parents who sat right in front of the press box would turn around and shout at me and say, "That was a THIRD down, not a second down," and "That was a FIELD GOAL, not a kick-off," and "Are you watching the same game WE are?"

Based upon this notoriety and my brash enthusiasm to make a complete fool out of myself just for fun, I was talked into running for class president in the fall of 1978. As I was a die-hard tennis player and a member of the team, I wore tennis shorts and shoes to school almost every day, and actually won a Legs Contest, beating out several jocks and faculty members, and thereafter campaigned for the presidency as "Legs Linnell." Each year Casa hosted an electoral convention designed to mimic the democratic and republican national conventions. Held in the gym, it featured a lot of festivity and costumes and decorations and cheering.

Each candidate was allowed to produce a demonstration prior to his or her speech, and, clad in my trademarked shorts and a brass belt buckle shaped like a peanut with the name "Carter" upon it, I wore a full-head Jimmy Carter mask and rode into the gym on the shoulders of my supporters, throwing peanuts to the crowd. During my speech I spoke about my plans for the school year, but in a much more humorous fashion than my competitor, athlete and model 4.0 student Steve Cleveland. When Steve got up to make his speech, he wasn't as funny, but he used a much more powerful closing line: "Ask yourselves, do you want to vote for a mature, responsible, capable candidate…or the class clown?" Politics is not for the faint-hearted. Steve won with his *smear campaign*, and politics in America has never been the same since.

Costumed shenanigans at Casa Grande High School from 1977-1980.

I was named Rally Commissioner…better job for me, anyway. We had some pretty creative rallies. Once I enlisted my buddy, John Mangiafridda (who is now a trial technology consultant), and we posed as evangelists and sauntered into the gym during the rally wearing choir robes and jaunty hats and delivered stirring sermons, as pictured on the right above. Also pictured is the 1978 convention and yours, truly, performing at a school promotion as The Unknown Comic.

This was the age of Cheech & Chong, Steve Martin, *Caddyshack*, *Animal House*, and *The Blues Brothers,* so we naturally utilized those themes for rallies, as well. One of my rally conspirators was schoolmate Leonard Luna, who was a magician in high school…and I'm not just talking about pulling a rabbit out of a hat. He was quite the ladies' man. After high school Leonard obtained an electronic engineering degree and got himself into the motion control industry, working for Parker-Hannafin in their Compumotor Division. And that's where my corporate comedy really got started.

I differentiate corporate comedy from entertainment I've provided to corporations for their parties and promotions because it's a completely different kind of service. Entertainment for parties and promotions may simply involve improvising jokes in a walkaround format, or making presentations at meetings, banquets, and luncheons, but as a corporate comedian I am learning about the company's products and/or services to the extent that I could almost sell them myself, and the entertainment is built around the delivery of the corporate message, rather than the other way around.

Leonard first called me from Compumotor and said that he was working in marketing communications and had a training video to produce and wanted a few characterizations to sprinkle throughout. After I had worked in several of his video productions and entertained at a number of the company's parties and promotions, I was called upon to provide a more substantial part of the corporate message. I entertained at Compumotor's national sales meetings, at which factory representatives and independent distributors from around the globe were invited to come together to receive training in new products and applications. At the meetings I wrote, directed, and performed in the opening and closing sessions, did walkaround impersonations during workshop breaks in the foyer, and entertained at company dinners, mixers, and events at local restaurants and attractions.

As Compumotor executives whom I'd entertained moved on to other companies, they called upon me again and I began working for their new employers. Technically OSHA Safety Meetings fall under the corporate comedy category, as well, and, as such, I had already been providing corporate comedy services to Sola Optical, Pacific Gas & Electric, Fireman's Fund, Fujitsu Microelectronics, Genentech, Hewlett Packard, Jandy Industries, OCLI-Optical Coating Lab Inc, Pacific Bell, and Phonic Ear, for instance. But the corporate comedy I did for Leonard at Parker Compumotor, and later at IDC-Industrial Devices Corporation and Cisco Systems, led to work for Danfoss Drives, Graham Drives, and STI-Scientific Technology Inc, and, thanks to the brilliance of fibre optics innovator Don Green, my town of Petaluma became known as Telecom Valley (up until the high-tech and dot-com bust of 2000), conveniently putting me within easy reach not only of Cisco Systems, but of the likes of Diamond Lane Communications, Optilink, DSC Communications, Advanced Fibre Communications, Alcatel, and Next Level Communications, all of whom hired me for their meetings and events.

To give you an idea of what doing corporate comedy at a national sales meeting is all about, let's go back to June of 1998: "Thanks so much for your excellent performance. The entire meeting got excellent reviews from the sales representatives who attended. We're even getting thank you notes from them, which is great. Again, Chris, thanks so much for your time and effort!" That was from Stacey Leggett in marketing communications for Graham Drives (www.GrahamDrives.com).

This was more than just a single meeting…it was a national sales meeting and product kick-off for some three hundred independent sales reps and distributors and their spouses at the MGM Grand Hotel in Las Vegas, at which I performed twenty separate fully-costumed characterizations over the course of three days and evenings of workshops, meetings, dinners, and parties, and for which I provided consultation, scripting, staging, and presentation of the opening and closing sessions, as well as two songs, a PowerPoint Presentation, and a game show. In order to provide these services, I spent five months learning about Graham, and its staff, products, market, and factory reps and distributors.

Graham learned about my services because a year earlier I had done a similar sales meeting for Graham's sister division, Danfoss Drives, at the Downtown Chicago Marriott Hotel on April 16-18, 1997. The parent company, Danfoss of Denmark, was so pleased with my work, it facilitated the referral, and I was hired by event planner Steve Longren of Longren & Parks (www.LongrenParks.com), another former Compumotor employee, who also hired me for similar services for STI-Scientific Technology Inc.

The 1997 Danfoss meeting included an opening session starring my Elwood

Blues impersonation. Events in other venues included my Senator Bob Dole singin' the blues on stage with The Blues Brothers band at the House of Blues restaurant, and my eight-and-a-half-foot-tall stiltwalking basketball player at Niketown, among many other characterizations. I also produced a video presentation that included several celebrity impersonations, including Dr. Ruth Westheimer, *Married with Children* shoe salesman Al Bundy, *Star Trek's* Captain James T. Kirk, George C. Scott's Gen. Patton, Lt. Columbo, of course, and Jack Nicholson.

Here's an amusing side-note about that stiltwalking basketball player character, "Wilt Whitehead," for which I wore a huge, black, kinky, Afro wig and bounced a rubber basketball that was three feet in diameter: the staff of Niketown tried to throw me out! Worried, I suppose, about their liability in having an eight-and-a-half-foot-tall guy walking throughout their store, up their stairs, and in their elevators, a manager came over and started to get butch with me. I looked down at him and said, "Hey, pal, I don't work for you...I work for HIM." And I pointed to my client, who proceeded to chew the manager out.

Apparently the event was booked just before Niketown had made a corporate decision to stop hosting such events in their stores. The Danfoss people told me that after paying a huge fee to use the store for the night, Niketown had been mysteriously less-than-accommodating throughout the planning of the event, so when this further provocation reared its ugly head, Danfoss told the store manager, "If HE goes, we ALL go, and you're not getting the balance of what's owed for the event." Well, the event continued, and Danfoss likely never held an event there again.

Along with writing the opening and closing sessions and songs for these national sales meetings, I also did all the research, writing, and photography for a lengthy and humorous "History of Danfoss Drives" slide presentation for the opening, complete with narration done as a Paul Harvey radio program, which included spoofs of Paul Harvey's characteristically staccato live commercials. Featured were multiple on-location pictures of me as Laurel & Hardy advertising

True Value Hardware stores, and as Crocodile Dundee in a Paul Harvey ad for for Nutragena Hand Cream.

Paul Harvey slide show featuring Crocodile Dundee and Laurel & Hardy.

BOB DOLE DOES VEGAS

Back to the meeting for Graham Drives. The opening session, on May 13th in 1998 at 8 a.m., featured a mystery keynote speaker whom Graham staff had built-up to their reps and distributors as a very exciting celebrity. With the lights dimmed, and the Graham logo on the screen, an off-stage announcer dramatically introduced him thusly:

> "Our special guest was a star high school athlete from Russell, Kansas, who went on to play basketball, track, and football for Kansas University, and was named as Kappa Sigma fraternity's "Man of the Year." He interrupted his medical studies to serve with distinction as a second lieutenant in our nation's military during World War II, earning a Bronze Star and two Purple Hearts for severe injuries as a member of the Tenth Mountain Division in Italy. After the war, he attended the University of Arizona on the G.I. Bill from 1948 to 1951, and earned both his Bachelor of Laws and Bachelor of Arts

degrees from Washburn University in 1952, worked as County Attorney from 1950 to 1958, and was initiated as a Freemason of Russell Lodge No. 177 in 1955. As a public servant he represented the State of Kansas in the House of Representatives from 1960 to 1969, and in the United States Senate from 1969 to 1996. During that time he served as chairman of the Republican National Committee from 1971 until 1973, was the ranking Republican on the Agriculture Committee from 1975 to 1978, the ranking Republican on the Finance Committee from 1979 to 1980, and chairman of the Finance Committee from 1981 to 1985. He was also Senate Majority Leader from 1985 until 1987 and from 1995 to 1996, as well as Senate Minority Leader from 1987 to 1995. He was the Republican party nominee for vice president and President Gerald Ford's running mate in 1976, and the Republican nominee for president against incumbent Bill Clinton in 1996. Ladies and gentlemen, Senator Bob Dole."

I stepped onto the stage, hair greased back, dark eyebrows penciled in, wearing in a blue pinstriped suit, red silk tie, and, of course, carrying a pen in my right hand. According to a number of the reps and distributors, those in the audience believed for the first few seconds that it was, indeed, Senator Bob Dole taking the podium. While a digital slide show flashed on the screen behind his head, he sternly talked about what a bum Bill Clinton was, and about the "Dole in 2000" campaign...

Bob Dole PowerPoint presentation.

...and then, eventually, he did get around to introducing Graham's exciting new product, the VLT6000. He finally interrupted his own speech, though, by saying that this was no way to introduce a product in Las Vegas, Nevada. "You gotta do this Vegas-style!"

He abruptly left the stage, and the thumping intro to Elvis Presley's "Viva Las Vegas" fired up. Two beautiful showgirls, scantily clad in feathers and sarongs, escorted the senator back onto the stage, but he was now wearing a huge silver belt buckle and a sequined, polyester cape, and he started singing the lyrics below to the tune of "Viva Las Vegas."

Bright city lights gonna set your soul,
Gonna set your soul on fire.
A nice Kansas boy sees them desert lights,
knows he's gonna find some buyers!

There's a thousand pretty drivers a waitin' out there,
But they're sloppy and erratic and you need a spare
But startin' today just don't give that a care,
Cuz Bob Dole does Vegas, Bob Dole does Vegas!

Now, the desert sun is mighty hot,
And so's the MGM Grand.
You're all here to find a better A.F.D. (adjustable frequency drive),
And you're sure to find that with Graham.

Oh, there's Graham's newest product,
It's a big A.F.D.
And, brother, it's made for H.V.A.C. (heating, vacuuming, air conditioning)!
It's called the Six Thousand…it's a VLT…VLT 6000, VLT 6000!

If your application is an H.V.A.C.,
The "Real Drive" is the VLT!
Talk about precision control!
VLT 6000 is the "Real Drive,"
It give the other guys the hives!
The only candidate, just like good old Bob Dole!

You're doin' H.V.A.C., ya' need the new VLT,

You want something' good in the housing,
There's only one drive, from Graham, the "Real Drive,"
It's the VLT 6000!

So, it's Bob Dole standin' here telling' you,
If you want a happy client,
Don't play the fool, sell 'em the "Real Drive,
Watch the competition drool!

Bob Dole does Vegas!
Graham does Vegas!
Bob Dole does Vegas!
Graham and Bob Dole do Vegas!

The audience ate it up, and the rest of the ninety-minute opening session was punctuated by other appearances by Senator Bob Dole, as well as four of my other characters during the "Evolution of the Drives" address detailing the history of Graham, delivered by Graham Marketing Director Roger Maves. At 9:30 a.m. the distributors and reps walked off to their scheduled workshops and they chatted-on about how uniquely memorable and entertaining Graham had made its new product introduction.

But, of course, the fun was not over. During workshop breaks, parties, and banquets over the course of the three-day meeting, I provided walkaround impersonations of such celebrities as Richard Simmons, Lt. Columbo, Kermit the Frog, Sheriff Buford T. Justice, Jack Nicholson, Floyd the Barber of *The Andy Griffith Show*, Forrest Gump, and a memorable eight-and-a-half-foot-tall, gun-toting, stiltwalking western bad-guy named Black Bart III.

The closing session was similarly entertaining, with Senator Dole closing things out with a STARGRAM[SM] Singing Telegram that announced and feted Graham's Top 20 reps and distributors (the Top 10 based upon market share followed by the Top 10 based upon shipments) who attended the meeting, all to the tune of the song "If I Only Had A Brain" from the movie *The Wizard of Oz*.

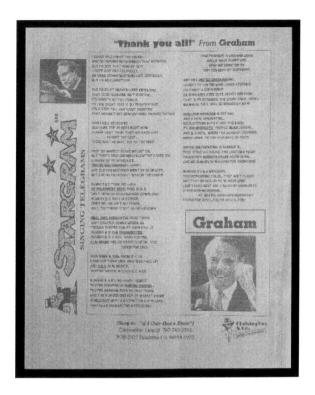

I provided similar services for the national and international sales meetings of these other fine firms: IDC-Industrial Devices Corporation, of Novato, California; Danfoss Drives, of Rockford, Illinois; STI-Scientific Technologies Incorporated, of Fremont, California; Parker/Hannifin-Compumotor Division, of Rohnert Park, California; and SOLA Optical USA, of Petaluma, California. I also provided simple corporate meeting, trade show, and party entertainment and walkaround characterization services to the many other corporations, public agencies, media corporations, and fairs and festivals listed on the Clients and Venues page of my website at www.HireAStar.net.

8 - The Fair Circuit

Through the 1980s and 90s I also worked the fair circuit, entertaining at dozens of fairs throughout California, Nevada, and Oregon, offering my celebrity voices on request. The fairs were quite lucrative, and an entertainer working the circuit could easily book him or herself solid six months of the year and then take the cold weather months off. They were fun, because I got to travel around the western states, and meet all kinds of nice people, and I had an excuse to skip the office work that awaited me at home. On the other hand, the traveling was kind of a drag. I had pets and a spouse and I love where I live. Spending the entire summer working in the heat of the day in small Central Valley farming towns, and living in a trailer or a motel room was fun once in awhile, but I didn't want to make a career out of it.

Weekend fairs within a three-hour drive of home were fun, because I could take my wife with me. But week-long fairs, or those requiring a full day of driving, necessitated leaving my first wife at home, because she had her own career. I did, however, take her with me to one of the first out-of-town fairs I booked in 1988, the Colusa County Fair in the tiny town of Colusa, north of Sacramento. The fair manager, Roger Gibbs, was a tall, handsome, soft-spoken man in a Stetson, and a true country gentleman who tipped his hat and said, "Ma'am" when he met my young wife. I had never seen that kind of behavior before, and was very impressed.

Unfortunately his fair in 1994 was one of the many bookings that I had to cancel to accept the Fruitopia Fruit Beverage tour I mentioned earlier. I felt badly about that, as I knew that old country gentleman figured that your word was your bond. I never did that again, in fact...to my detriment. Sometimes it's just plain stupid to put someone else's needs before your own; namely in business. But I must confess that I still wish that I had not cancelled that fair.

CUTHBERT THE CRITIC

I missed my wife and my pets and my home when I was traveling, but the money was good and steady in the summers. One way I managed to deal with the loneliness of being on the road was by taking my dog with me, as I mentioned earlier. My constant canine companion in those days was Cuthbert, the cocker-fox-terrier, and he loved a road trip. He was a beautiful dog, who looked like a cocker-spaniel but with longer legs, shorter ears, and a long, uncut tail. He was about twenty-five pounds, which was big enough to rough-house with but small enough to carry, and he was the only one in the litter who was jet black...although he did develop a very distinguished white goatee in his later years. He was highly intelligent, understood hundreds of words in English, Russian, and Spanish, and could be walked off-leash without incident until he eventually became blind and deaf, at which point I pushed him around in a stroller.

Cuthbert loved chasing a ball, would swim with me for miles in the Russian River, or ride with me on an air mattress like a sailor, and spent hours in the shallow shore waters chasing guppies. He hiked with me through the mountains, watched patiently by the net as I played tennis, and loved riding the train in Berkeley's Tilden Park. He even accompanied me one year to the Burning Man art festival and encampment in the Nevada desert before they created a rule against that (at which point I boycotted Burning Man until my canine companion passed on).

Cuthbert had his own space in each of my four vans, equipped with food and water and bedding and a clear view out the window, and he traveled with me throughout thirteen states to most of my performances during his entire life, including throughout almost every California county, and repeatedly into Nevada, Oregon, Washington, Utah, and Colorado. He lived with me through three marriages and accompanied me on hundreds of dates. He swam in the Russian River and the Missouri River and every body of water in between. He climbed mountains, played at the beach, explored the desert, and accompanied me to tennis courts and golf courses and chased me as I roller-skated. Cuthbert went with me almost everywhere for almost seventeen years. I miss him dearly.

Christopher and his constant canine companion, Cuthbert the Cocker.

I remember a woman at a fair asking me about Cuthbert once. She said, "What kind of dog is that?" I said, "He's a cocker-fox-terrier." But I must've said it too fast, because the poor gal looked puzzled, and a little put-off. She said, "I'm sorry...what did you say?" "I said, he's a cocker-fox-terrier." And the lady shot back, "What has THAT got to do with it?" After a few puzzled moments I realized that I wasn't enunciating clearly enough, so I said, "He's a COCKER SPANIEL / FOX-TERRIER." She said, "OH...." I guess I never realized how bad that sounded when I said it too fast.

At one fair I had brought a large, steel, collapsing dog cage with me. Summertime in California's Central Valley is far too hot to leave a dog in the car, so I would tie Cuthbert under the tent near the stage while I was performing. He was well-behaved off-leash and wouldn't have strayed, but these were agricultural fairs; I didn't want a cow or a goat or a sheep prancing by and luring him away from my watchful eye while I was performing. Problem was that the kids loved him so much, they would pester him with kindness while I was on stage. I put the cage under the tent near the first row of seats, and he was safe from the kids while I performed.

Cuthbert was a good audience member, too. He would bark when the people were laughing or applauding, and remain quiet when I was talking. I think people liked him better than they did me. I did run into a slight problem one day, however. During my request segment, someone in the crowd shouted out "Edith & Archie Bunker!" I began singing the theme song from *All in the Family*. Cuthbert didn't mind Archie's parts, but when Edith hit her high note in the line, "And you knew who you WOIRE THEN," I must've hit a doggie note, because Cuthbert started to sing with me! The howling stopped when Archie sang, "Goils were goils and men were men, mister we could use a man like Herbert Hoover again. Didn't need no Welfare State," then Edith sang, "everybody pulled his weight," then Archie sang, "Gee, our old LaSalle ran great," then Edith screeched her big finish, "Those woire tha DAAAAAAAAAYS!"

Cuthbert went absolutely berserk, howling away as though he had a speaking part in the show. I was annoyed and embarrassed, but the crowd loved it! So I did it again in the next show, and Cuthbert obliged me with his part, and so on and so on. In fact, after years of fair shows, Cuthbert actually wrangled himself a regular speaking part in the show. Whenever I wanted an extra laugh, I would say, "Hey, CUTHBERT…" and ask him a question, and he'd answer me every time. I should have retired the impressions and just done a dog act.

GRANDMA'S BIG ADVENTURE

One time I took my Grandma Elsa with me to one of the fairs. She was very excited about the offer. My Papa Fred had been gone only a few years, and it was the first time Grandma had gotten out of town on an "adventure" since he died in June of 1981. She packed her bags, and the two of us, with Cuthbert, headed off to the fair in my 1971 Volkswagen van. Although we weren't actually exactly alone.

You see, I had my advertising painted on the side of my panel van, but the back window was a problem. I wanted to fill it, but with something useful and humorous. So I built a small wooden platform to sit above the engine in the back window. Screwed into a sheet of plywood were wooden dowels with crossbars, and on the tops of the dowels I impaled Styrofoam wig heads. I then dressed the crosspieces in black suits and ties, and put rubber Laurel & Hardy masks on the heads.

This was a fantastic marketing tool. As we drove down the rode, and from quite a distance, it appeared as though Laurel & Hardy were sitting and smiling out the back window. In two subsequent panel vans I did the same thing. The third was my 1991 Chevy Astro van, in which there was no room for dummies (except behind the wheel, of course), so I used life-sized, full-color, blown-up photographs of myself as Laurel & Hardy in the back window, and they also looked very realistic from a distance. My previous van was a 1980 Dodge Tradesman with double rear doors, so I cut the plywood platform in half and screwed each to the back doors below the windows. I sometimes swapped other celebrities for Laurel & Hardy, including Popeye & Olive Oyl. And there were two windows on the right side, so I built a Ronald Reagan dummy that was actually waving at passing cars. This caused varying reactions.

Christopher's Volkswagen van with Crisco hanging on, and the Dodge van with Laurel & Hardy, Ronald Reagan, and Popeye and Olive Oyl inside.

One morning upon crossing the Golden Gate Bridge (when there were still human toll-takers), the lady in the booth, who'd obviously seen me pass many times before, said, "Ok...let's see. There's you, and the dog, and Ronald Reagan, and Laurel & Hardy in the back. That's a carpool. No toll!" Another day a police car began to pass me on the freeway in the right hand lane, and then slowed abruptly and let me pass, and then hung back at right my side for a few seconds. He finally got behind me and turned on his red light to pull me over. He came up on the passenger side and cautiously inspected Reagan, and then came over to my window and said, "I'm sorry, I just wanted to see if the president was wearing his seatbelt."

Ok...now back to Grandma. I was doing my Christopher & Co. LIVE act of celebrity voices on request at that fair, and I would start off as Lt. Columbo. Now, my grandmother didn't like the fact that I was smoking a cigar. My grandfather smoked them, but he did a lot of things she didn't want me doing. I didn't smoke or drink in high school...I was a good kid, and I thought doing those things was bad for you. But when I started doing celebrity impersonations, I offered a number of characters who smoked cigars, pipes, and cigarettes. Originally I just carried them around, not actually smoking, but my clients and audiences chided me, saying, "Groucho actually SMOKED those things, you know," as if I was less of an impersonator if I didn't smoke. So to appease the nitpickers and complete the illusion, I would light up just before I went on. Eventually, of course, I got to enjoy the cigars more than the impersonations.

On this particular occasion I was waiting off-stage for my cue, and my grandmother just took it upon herself to do a tough-love intervention, I s'pose, and reached up and grabbed the cigar out of my mouth and stomped it out on the ground. I was furious. Without thinking I barked, "What are you doing? I needed that. My cue will come any second. You go sit in the car." And she did!

Generally, though, we got along fantastically at that fair. Although she was a little worried when we arrived at the motel to check-in on the first night. She was always worried about what other people thought, a product of her German

Lutheran upbringing, I suppose; and this was the main difference between us. Anyway, the clerk asked me, "One room?" Before I had the chance to open my mouth, Grandma chimed in, "Yes, but TWO BEDS!" The clerk and I both laughed, and when we got back outside Grandma said to me, "Well, we don't want to give anyone the wrong idea!" Good notion, Grandma.

The best moment at that fair, though, was one afternoon when we had several hours between shows. It was as hot as sin that day, and I told Grandma that we should go for a ride to a nearby river and see if there was a place we could find a beach. Now, Grandma couldn't swim, but she was always game for an adventure, and Cuthbert was ready, I was sure. We found a parking spot in a promising location, and I spied a secluded path through the bushes. We headed toward the water's edge.

It was a gravelly beach, but the water was fresh and cool and looked refreshing, and Cuthbert dove right in. I snapped a couple of pictures, and then looked behind me. Grandma looked worried. She'd never been a dog lover, and her house was as neat as a pin, so pets were not an option for her, but she did love my cats, and treated Cuthbert almost as if he was another grandson. She was afraid to see him splashing around in the water. As I said, Grandma didn't know how to swim, and her husband and brother-in-law had just a few years before drowned in a fishing boat accident off Point Reyes National Seashore, so she didn't like the fact that I loved to swim, and that Cuthbert was out plying the rushing waters on his own. She stood up on the embankment a few dozen yards away with her arms crossed and a worried look on her face.

I took a couple of pictures of her with my telephoto lens, but she refused to smile. She just stood there, worried that Cuthbert would sink beneath the surface and I would run in after him and drown as well. I said, "Grandma...don't just stand there. DO something!" She shrugged, threw out her arms with her palms facing the sky, and I snapped the picture.

Grandmother Nature

MESSRS. CLEAN

I was always meeting famous people at county fairs. The Orange County Fair in the summer of 1992 was a ton of fun. Beautiful, prestigious, surrounded by other fun stuff to do, and the best part was that they booked me to do one to three shows a night...meaning I had all my days free! I was booked for nineteen days at $350 per day, so I rented a fifth wheel and took my cats and dog with me, and they stayed in the trailer while I was working. Every day was a new adventure. Cuthbert and I would travel all over Orange County during the day, going to beaches and parks. I also went to Knott's Berry Farm on my birthday, and Disneyland, too, while I was "working" that fair.

The best part was my stage, though. I was on the Heritage Stage, a beautiful gazebo right through the main gate, so the majority of the attendees walked right by our stage, and when *I* wasn't performing there were other great acts to draw their attention, including The Goils, a modern version of the Andrews Sisters featuring three pretty girls backed by a guy on keyboard and a guy on bass. (Visit: www.DianeMichelle.com/Goils).

The Goils spoiling Christopher on his thirty-first birthday, July 15, 1992.

By the way, did you notice the caricature of me on the title page of this book? It was drawn at that fair after my 9 p.m. show on Monday, July 20, by artist Jac Rene.

The big draw on the Heritage Stage was the internationally-famous, one-hundred-member All American Boys Choir (www.TAABC.org), which traveled all over the world and performed with John Williams, Bob Hope, Steve Allen, and Victor Borge. At the Orange County Fair in 1992 they were led by their founder, a rather infamous priest by the name of Father Richard T. Coughlin. I didn't care for him personally, because he was crusty and pushy and abrupt and caustic in his manner, but professionally it was plain to see that he was passionate about his show and his boys.

Sadly, Father Coughlin was removed the following January as director of the chorus (which he founded in 1970) over sexual abuse allegations that were made by five men who were in the choir many years earlier. In fact, he had moved to Orange County from the notorious Boston archdiocese in 1965, and twenty years later abuse allegations surfaced from his activities there, as well.

Back to the subject of this subchapter. One night at that fair I was doing my Christopher & Co. LIVE act of celebrity voices on request, and I saw a handsome bald man standing way back in the audience. Now, shaved heads were still unusual in 1992, and so I referred to him repeatedly during my performance as Mr. Clean. Well, at the end of my show as I got off the stage, there he was, waiting for me. I thought, "Oh, great; an over-sensitive twit who wants to get butch with the comedian." I was wrong.

He said, "It's funny that you called me Mr. Clean. See, I *am* Mr. Clean. Really. My name is House Peters, Jr., and I was the original Mr. Clean."

The original Mr. Clean with the future Mr. Clean.

GRATUITOUS BEAVER SHOT

Here's another brief story about meeting a celebrity, and the only reason it's in here is so that I could use that subchapter title for the picture which follows. Mind you, I've performed for many celebrities before; people who are not otherwise listed in this book, including U.S. Senator Richard Gebhardt, U.S. Representative Don Clausen, FBI Director Louis Freh, comedian Tommy Smothers (twice), rock drummer Steve Smith and members of the band Journey, and actors Terry McGovern and Danny Glover; but I don't have particularly funny stories about meeting them. This story is short and maybe not particularly funny, but the title above just had to be in the book.

I was hired by the Greater Chico Chamber of Commerce to provide several impersonations for the Chico Expo on the Silver Dollar Fairgrounds north of Sacramento on October 2, 3, and 4, 1992, and I was told that the special guest on Saturday was going to be none other than Jerry Mathers, the star of television's classic coming-of-age sitcom, *Leave it to Beaver*. I searched all over the fairgrounds for him, and finally found a small group of people huddled around some folding tables at the side of an exhibit building. They were watching him sign autographs. He was exactly as I expected him to be: pudgy, pasty-white, and as Anglo as a guy can get, wearing sneakers, tan slacks, a plaid shirt, his Mayfield High School letterman sweater, and a baseball cap. And he looked exactly like Beaver Cleaver, except that he was forty-four years old.

I was determined to get a picture with The Beav, and when the opportunity arose, I handed him my gun, as I always do for such pictures (when I'm wearing one), and, as I raised my hands over my head as if I was being robbed, I told him, "Ok, now point it at me and look mean!" The Beav looked up at me with the same milquetoast expression I've seen in the eyes of every female authority figure in my life. "Oh, no," he pontificated, "we never point a gun at anything we don't intend to shoot."

Once The Beav, always The Beav, I s'pose.

The infamous "Gratuitous Beaver Shot."

AND THE WINNER IS...

The El Dorado County Fair in Placerville is one of the prettiest fairgrounds in the western states, nestled in the Sierra Nevada foothills in Gold Country and encompassing grassy meadows surrounded by beautiful trees; thus the fair's nickname is "Trees R Us."

Entertainment director Greg Hegwer hired me to perform my Christopher & Co. LIVE act of celebrity voices on request on Thursday, August 4, 1988, at 7:30 p.m. on the main stage between two teen beauty pageants, one at 6:30 p.m. and the other at 8:30 p.m., and to be available to also do two separate fifteen-minute performances during the second pageant as the girls changed clothes. Greg had included in my contract a clause allowing for an extra fifty percent payment if I were asked to also serve as master of ceremonies for the pageants. Just a few days before the event Greg called with just that request, and I was only too happy to comply.

He knew that I had an earlier performance scheduled in Petaluma that day as Crisco the Clown for the annual picnic of the U.S. Coast Guard Training Center-Two Rock in McNear Park in Petaluma, which was to conclude at 2:30 p.m. It's a two-and-a-half-hour drive from Petaluma to Placerville, so, after returning home to shower and change, I hit the road at 3:30 p.m., and should have arrived at 6 p.m. But just east of Sacramento on Highway 80, about thirty miles from the fairgrounds, traffic came to a complete stop. There was a big-rig overturned ahead of me just west of Placerville, and I didn't get my first cell phone until 1992, so there was no way to let Greg know that I was stuck in traffic, without wasting valuable time getting off the freeway and looking for a phone (and then hoping that I could actually get Greg on the phone). I decided to stay where I was and hope for the best. Cuthbert and I were sitting in my Volkswagen van in the sweltering heat behind thousands of vehicles, and the click was ticking.

I arrived at the fairgrounds just a few minutes before the Junior Miss El Dorado pageant was to begin, and Greg was livid. I told him that there was a huge traffic snarl on 80, but it was obvious that he didn't believe me, apparently chalking it up as just the flimsy excuse of another flaky entertainer. He handed me the contestant information and angrily said, "Just get up on that stage!" I complied, but was frustrated that he didn't realize what I'd just been through.

The first contest went well. The girls were cute and the crowd was monstrous. It appeared as though everyone in the county was there. After the first pageant finished, I did my act of celebrity voices, which was enthusiastically received, but I was disappointed because the stage was huge and was raised above the crowd, and didn't allow me the physical interaction I prefer with my audience. As I stepped off the stage to get my contestant materials for the next pageant, Greg approached me and I was cringing, assuming that he was still mad about how late I'd arrived. I was relieved to learn, however, that several acquaintances of his were stuck behind me in the traffic jam, so he now knew that my story was true, and he was very, very nice thereafter.

Christopher at the far right before learning another important lesson.

As I waited for the contestants for the second pageant, I was approached by a middle-aged man who called me by name. "Hey, Chris! I'm Ed Wilson. You know, Rhonda's father?" My mind was in a whirl; I was thinking about the traffic, the pageants, the stage, the crowd; I had no idea who Ed Wilson was, much less Rhonda. I said, "Ed Wilson?" He said, "You know, I lived across the street from you on Columbia Avenue in Richmond when you were a kid. Rhonda was your babysitter."

What a small world! He took me over to his wife, June, who was sitting in the middle of the audience. I had sent a press release and photograph to the fair, and they'd been published in the local newspaper, and Ed and June lived in the nearby hamlet of Pollock Pines and recognized my name and came to the fair that night to see me perform. What a nice surprise! When my sister, Tammy, and I were kids Rhonda had made beautiful Christmas stockings for us, onto which she'd stitched our names; my stocking still hangs by the fireplace at Christmas to this day. We traded pleasantries for a few minutes, and then it was back to work, as pageant time had arrived.

These girls were high-school-aged, and they were gorgeous in their ball gowns. Over the course of the show, one after another, they introduced themselves, answered the standard pageant questions (e.g., "What do you most want?" Answer: "World peace."), made several costuming changes (during which I did my celebrity voices for the crowd), and performed their various talents, and the contest was going wonderfully. I was pleased to be a part of such a professional show and had no idea of the horrible error I would soon be making. One more lesson to be learned as I pretended to make a living.

As the finalists stood on the stage, with all the thousands of loved-ones sitting under the stars waiting for the judges' decision, there was magic in the air. As the crowd held its collective breath, I announced the third runner-up, and the second, and then I announced the name of the first runner-up, and as I began to say, "If for any reason Miss El Dorado County is not able to fulfill the duties of her office--" But no one was paying any attention to me.

The crowd was cheering and applauding, and the girls were screaming and crying and hugging each other, and I couldn't figure out why in Sam Hill everyone seemed to already know who was the winner when I hadn't even opened the envelope and seen the name myself...and then it hit me. I had just announced all the runners-up and was so busy concentrating on what I was doing that I failed to realize that there was only one girl left on the stage: THE WINNER! Hel-LO! Earth to Chris! There were maybe two or three thousand people within earshot of my microphone, and I was the only one who didn't realize that I had already let the cat out of the bag.

As the crowd and the girls and the backstage crew and the fair staff all looked at me in disbelief, I intrepidly continued, "Miss El Dorado County of 1988 is ___," but nobody could hear me because at that moment I was getting my biggest laugh of the night. The lesson learned? At a beauty pageant, always say the name of the winner *immediately* after announcing the first runner-up, without even taking a breath. Where was Bert Parks when I needed him?

Despite this spectacle of stellar stupidity, I received a very nice letter from Greg on August 30:

"Thank you for your help in making the 1988 'Trees R Us' El Dorado County Fair such a great success. Many people commented how much they enjoyed the various performances, and how good the entertainment was this year. You certainly added to their enjoyment. A special thank-you, Chris, for the last-minute help with the M.C. job for the Miss El Dorado County Pageant. You were a life saver. Next year maybe we'll try to put your show closer to the audience. Again, my thanks for a great job!"

Sure, I thought, a more intimate stage...on the other side of the fairgrounds, as far from the pageants as possible. "You certainly added to the enjoyment..." Yeah, I got the biggest laugh of the night.

TALL TEX AND SHORT MEX

I mentioned that business expo in Chico with The Beav, but I should have said that I booked that job because I had performed in previous years at the annual summertime Silver Dollar Fair in Chico. In between my acts I liked to walk around the fairs and watch the other shows, out of professional curiosity and to see if I could get any new ideas about acts I could offer. Part of my success in the fair circuit was due to the fact that, unlike other entertainers who just offered one act or one character, I was able to offer more than just one act, and I offered a multitude of characterizations. In addition to Christopher & Co. LIVE, I offered fair managers and agents Celebrity Squares[SM], and my walkaround celebrities. Sometimes I would do three shows in the afternoon, and then serve as master of ceremonies at a talent show or beauty pageant in the evening. Weekends I would do walkaround as Popeye or John Wayne or some other familiar character.

The Silver Dollar Fair advertised a stiltwalking character by the name of Tall Tex. I had never seen stiltwalking up close, and I made a point of coming to the grand concourse to see the show. He was fantastic! Eight-and-a-half-feet-tall, he wore a big ten-gallon Stetson, a vest, gloves, and monstrous chaps and boots that covered his stilt feet. He was a big, handsome dude with a Texas drawl, silver hair, and bright, blue eyes. He had an extremely engaging personality, and was shaking hands with the men, flirtin' with the women, and liftin' the kids and swinging them back and forth between his legs as they squeeled in delight. He was also armed with a long, shiny, silver, old-western revolver, and fired black powder blanks that exploded with smoke and flames a foot or more out of the end of the barrel and made a deafening roar that echoed against the buildings all over the fairgrounds.

When I started my next act, there he was, sans stilts, sitting in the front row at my stage. During my act he laughed as loud as his pistol, and I tailored my act around the big celebrity in my audience. After the show I came down to meet him, and we chatted for a long spell about performing at the fairs, and about his stilts, and about his gun. His name was Don Cassady, and he said that he was a tradesman who decided to give his drywall stilts a second life and started working the fair circuit.

Don said that he hand-packed his own .45 caliber black-powder blanks, and fired the gun off at all the fairs he visited. In fact, while they were blanks, the flames and percussion that came out of the barrel were substantial enough to do damage at close range, and he said that he did target practice *with the kids*. He'd shoot their balloons, or ask them to throw objects, such as paper plates, into the air, and he'd shoot at them and turn them to cinders. (This was long ago, before the schoolyard and workplace shootings, fanned by fanatical media coverage, that have marred the perception of safety we have in our contemporary society.) I was intrigued. Don's job looked like more fun than mine! He said that he had to get going, because he was doing another set, and he encouraged me to come by and watch again.

Well, I had big plans for his next set, but I didn't tell Don. You see, one of the extra costumes I had packed in my van at that fair was a cowboy outfit, including a recently purchased .22 caliber old-western revolver and holster and belt. I had also purchased starting blanks, which were designed for starting footraces in small starting pistols, but they worked fine in my Western six-shooter, too. I figured I'd go meet Tall Tex in the midway, and test his mettle.

I hurriedly dressed, loaded my gun, and headed off in search of Tall Tex. I found the big cowboy in the center of the concourse, again, chatting up the passersby and amazing the kiddies with his grand scale. I stood at the back of the crowd and shouted, "Hey, cowboy! Yeah, YOU! Boy, you been messin' with my girl, and I'm here for satisfaction!"

The crowd ooo'ed and awe'd, and backed away just as the extras in western movies would back away when two cowboys were about to duel. Tall Tex reared back a bit and said, "What was that, son? It sounded like you were callin' me out!"

"I sure was, Tex, and you're gonna face me right now unless you can get them huge boots turned around and runnin' the other way before I draw my six-shooter!"

Tex said, "I'm from Texas...I never run."

After a few more exchanges the moment of truth was upon us. I drew my pistol and took a few shots at him. He just stood there. "Is that all you got, son?" I retorted, "That's all I NEED, Tex!" He said, "No...you gotta be able to actually HIT me."

I emptied my cylinders in response to this challenge, and when the gun was empty the crowd laughed as Tex just stood there grinning at me.

"Well, I guess THAT's all you've got, boy. So, here's what I'VE got." And with that, he whipped out his Ruger Blackhawk, and the sunlight reflected from the seven-and-a-half-inch barrel as he pointed it toward me and fanned out a couple of shots with the heel of his left hand. Smoke and flames sprung forth and spewed in my direction, and the roar almost knocked me off of my feet. I threw myself back on the pavement and lay motionless with my arms and legs spread wide and my tongue hanging out. The crowd cheered and Tex chuckled. After a few moments I raised my head and then slowly and flagrantly checked myself for holes in cartoonish fashion. Tex bellowed, "Next time you ain't gonna be so lucky!"

Back at my stage I was changed and ready to begin my next show when Don sauntered over, sans stilts again, and had a seat. I came over and said, "I hope you didn't mind. I thought it would be fun to improvise a shoot out." Don laughed and shook my hand and said, "No problem, son. In fact, it was funny as hell. I think you should do that during every set!" I said, "Yeah, sure..." At that moment Don leaned into me and drawled, "One thing, though, son. You better get yourself a bigger gun."

Which is exactly what I did. In fact, I bought several more guns. One was a Ruger Blackhawk .45 like his, and I found a really cool and rare .45 caliber derringer. That's the little pocket pistol that I loved when I was a kid watching Robert Conrad and Ross Martin as James West and Artemus Gordon in the 1960s television series *The Wild Wild West*. James West wore a black hat, bolero-style suit, black leather chaps, and a black gun belt carrying a silver .45 revolver. And up his sleeve he had a .45 Remington derringer on a slide mount. When I was a kid I wanted to be James West. As an adult I finally was able to put the whole outfit together. I later bought stilts, too...the whole get-up, including the stilts, cost me $800. When I bought the derringer, I neglected to tell Don...saving it as a surprise for our next encounter.

We worked several fairs together, and I bought a pair of stilts, which I used at fairs, but I didn't advertise stiltwalking or use the stilts at fairs at which Don was working. I didn't want to detract from his character, and I didn't want fair managers to think that if they hired me I would throw in stiltwalking and they wouldn't need to hire him. Besides, when we did our shoot-outs, if we had both been on stilts, who would take the fall? I decided to play a more cartoonish character, so Tal Tex would have his shoot-out with "Short Mex." I wore a huge sombrero and serape, and put on an extra pair of red polka-dot boxer shorts under my jeans but over my briefs.

The next time we met, Short Mex fired his .22 at Tall Tex, as he did the first time, but when Tall Tex responded with his .45, Mex would draw out his own .45 long barrel from his back belt. Tex would get the drop on Mex each time, though, and would instruct his little amigo to "Drop your drawers so I can see if you're packing any OTHER concealed weapons." I would play this up big time, and the kids would howl with delight when Mex reluctantly dropped his trousers, revealing his colorful undershorts, with both hands clasped at his crotch in shame.

Short Mex got the last laugh, however, because Tex would say, "Take your hands from them pretty polka-dot britches, Amigo, or are you hiding another little gun there?" With this as his cue, Mex would demonstrate that he was, indeed, holding another gun, as he raised his .45 caliber derringer and took two more shots at the cowboy. The startled crowd was thrilled by this surprise, but the act would always end with Tex firing his last couple shots at Mex, knocking him onto his backside. Though the only damage was actually to his pride.

Don was performing at the Grand National Rodeo at the Cow Palace in San Francisco each year. We decided that it might be fun to do the act there, too, even though I wasn't booked. I loved the rodeo, and joined him there, and we did our act numerous times in the center of the big ring. Between shows we'd wander around and chat and look at the cows and the bulls and the horses and the cowgirls.

In fact, we met a couple of pretty cowgirls at the rodeo, and had a grand time wandering around the grounds chatting and flirting. The girls were perfect for us; Tammy was a barrel racer about my age from Oklahoma, Judy was closer to Don's age and from Texas, and both were single. I showed them all three around San Francisco, and then they all came up to my house in Petaluma, where we dined and chatted and flirted some more. By the time the rodeo left town, we had made further plans. I visited my cowgirl at her ranch in Olathe, Colorado, and Don married his cowgirl and they bought an island in Canada and they tour the fair circuit each year to this day.

Romance...western style.

Don Cassady and Christopher as Tall Tex and Short Mex.

BOO!

9 - Radio, Television, Modeling, and Movies

I've already described how I got into radio at the age of sixteen. But this is the chapter in which I'll go into it in a bit more detail. My career in this field spanned twenty-eight years, from my first radio job in 1978 to my most recent modeling job in 2006, so there is a lot to cover.

My family moved from Guam right at the time that I thought I might be getting somewhere in my career. I had been performing all over the island as Crisco the Clown, I won second place in the island-wide talent show, and Guamanian nightclub and recording star Jimmy Dees had offered me a job as his opening act. And then we moved, and my career temporarily came to a halt.

We packed up everything we had into shipping crates. Well, almost everything. I had to leave some cherished friends behind. Namely, Claire Rambeau and Pompeo Posar. Claire was a Playboy Playmate featured in a book of the work of Playboy photographer Pompeo Posar. That book was a part of my "collection"...the most important part. The picture of Claire in that rose garden was all I thought about for most of my teenage years. But one of my idiot classmates told me that the U.S. Customs officials would be searching all of our belongings to be shipped back to California, and if they found any pornography, I would be in terrible trouble, and it would go on my "permanent record." I was petrified.

So I went to school one day with a bag filled with pictures of naked women, and, while keeping a watchful eye for Vice Principal Mrs. Imelda Santos (who, as of this writing, just recently retired after decades of meting out discipline at St. John's Episcopal Preparatory School on Guam), I handed those beloved skin magazines out to all of my buddies. Of course, by the time my family had moved to Petaluma, I realized that the scare story about a customs search was all bullshit, and I was furious, but there was nothing left to do but reassemble my collection.

SAN FRANCISCO'S PACIFIC HEIGHTS

In June of 1977 we island-hopped back to California via Hawaii on the "Island Hopper" milk run of tiny Pacific islands on Continental Air Micronesia, aka "Air Mike," which stopped in (or, more accurately, *on*) the majority of the following islands: Yap, Palau, Chuuk (then called Truk), Pohnpei, Kwajalein, Majuro, Johnson Atoll, and Midway. The islands were so tiny that the landing strips were sometimes the largest features, such as on Majuro.

I believe it was Chuuk where as soon as the wheels touched the tarmac the pilot threw the engines in reverse and slammed on the brakes and we came to a screeching halt. When we pulled our heads out of the seatbacks in front of us, we looked out the window, and as the plane pivoted, the waves were crashing against the rocks...underneath the wing! (There is an excellent illustrated account of a recent version of this trip with stops in reverse order on a site about Air Mike at: www.Airliners.net/aviation-forums/trip_reports/read.main/197642.)

We then spent a night in Honolulu again as we did on the way to Guam in 1971, and finally took a 747 flight back to San Francisco, arriving in fantastic weather right at sunset, on a Japan Air Lines 747 with a nose window...or, at least, so I thought. I distinctly recall during the flight that I made a trip up to the front of the plane to briefly peek through the nose window, which allowed a fascinating and unobstructed view of the Pacific ahead of us, but my fairly extensive Internet research yielded no evidence that such nose windows ever existed on any 747 (or any other passenger airliner, for that matter). So much for the human memory.

We touched down at SFO and disembarked, and I recall the airport and people and their clothing looking exactly as was shown in the climatic sequence of the 1968 movie *Bullitt*, in which Steve McQueen's character gunned down mob informant Johnny Ross in the doors at the baggage claim area at SFO.

My dad's employer was Bank of America, and we were picked up at the airport by a bank executive named Cy, who seemed to me to be rather obnoxious for no other reason than that he was pudgy and smoked the butt of a cigar in the

Chevy Suburban in which he picked up my family from the airport. Little did I know that one day I would be that pudgy stogy chomper. He drove us to the luxurious high-rise Pacific Heights Tower condominium at 2200 Sacramento Street at Laguna Street in San Francisco. On the east side of an upper floor of that building BofA had a two bedroom condominium that was used for traveling bank executives and guests. We stayed there in June and July while my dad prepared to assume a new work territory, and we had a ball.

Our building was one of the tallest in the neighborhood, and our apartment overlooked beautiful Lafayette Park, which was across Laguna Street to the east, and was always full of interesting people and beautiful girls. The building itself was busy with movie shoots, too. The 1973 *Dirty Harry* sequel *Magnum Force* had a lengthy and bloody sequence shot in and outside our building, including five murders by a motorcycle cop, who killed two other cops and three naked people: a fat, old drug kingpin named Lou Guzman, and the young, attractive male and female prostitute with whom he was having sex. But I didn't realize that was our building in the movie until after I had watched it several times on television in the years that followed.

Pacific Heights Tower in San Francisco.

While we were staying at the Pacific Heights Tower, the speeding limousine sequence of 1978's *Foul Play* was shot right below our window. Starring Goldie Hawn, Chevy Chase, Burgess Meredith, Dudley Moore, Brian Dennehy, and Billy Barty, the movie features Chase and Hawn as a cop and a librarian, respectively, rushing through crowded city streets in a black stretch limousine they commandeered/carjacked, bearing two frightened Japanese tourists in the back seat who were petrified until they saw Chase's badge, and then pulled out American flags and enthusiastically said, "Kojak! Bang bang!" The cop and the librarian were headed for the San Francisco Opera to prevent the assassination of the pope, and they jumped their limousine off a mound of dirt the crew carefully constructed on southbound Laguna at Sacramento. My sister, Tammy, and I watched with relish from above as the movie crew smashed up one after another black stretch limousine throughout the afternoon.

THE EL RANCHO TROPICANA

By August we knew that my dad's work territory for the bank would be Marin County, so we moved to accommodations in Santa Rosa to the north to start looking for housing. We had relatives living in both Santa Rosa and the quaint little town of Petaluma, which was south of Santa Rosa and just north of Marin, so my parents were hoping to find a house there. We spent several weeks in a classic old Santa Rosa landmark, the El Rancho Tropicana Hotel (so large, in fact, I called it "ERTH"). This was originally two-to-four separate motels combined into one sprawling hostelry on a ten-acre lot beneath Taylor Mountain (my maternal family's ancestral home) on the east side of Santa Rosa Avenue, which was the Redwood Highway from San Francisco to Oregon, State Route 101, before the freeway was put through in the 1950s.

The ERTH was state-of-the-art for motels in the 1940s, 50s, and 60s, with 180 rooms stretched throughout four separate quadrangle building complexes on ten acres, featuring three separate pools, one in each two-story quadrangle's courtyard, and a large, sixty-room, one-story quadrangle featured a palm-tree decked lawn and children's playground. In the main building was the lobby, a restaurant, and the swinging Bamboo Room lounge, which featured live music most nights. In the courtyard was a pool and a hot tub and guest locker rooms.

The El Rancho Tropicana Hotel...aka ERTH.

The ERTH also boasted a monstrous convention center that hosted conventions, trade shows, huge meetings, and shows by such big name stars as Johnny and June Carter Cash, whose show I attended there, and local theater group the Santa Rosa Players. Another claim to fame of the ERTH was their excellent sports complex, with team locker rooms, training facilities, and two full-sized football fields used for spring training by U.C. Berkeley's Cal Bears, and by the notoriously rowdy Oakland Raiders from 1963-84.

Since moving to Guam in 1971, our family had stayed in motels and hotels in Honolulu, Guam, Taipei, Hong Kong, Manila, Osaka, and Anaheim, so we were pretty much "over" the excitement of hotel living. But I must say, the ERTH was different. All of the hotel's rooms were booked solid most weekends, and the entire complex was absolutely jam-packed with party hounds from dusk to dawn. Classic car and motorcycle clubs, lady bowlers, business conventions, and big-name entertainment brought hundreds every weekend, and Tammy and I were right in the middle of all this activity all summer long.

Beginning Friday afternoon the parking lots and rooms would rapidly fill, and then on Friday and Saturday evenings there was music and booze and laughing and the stench of ganja permeating it all. Saturday and Sunday mornings were quiet, as the partiers slept off their hangovers, but weekend afternoons were an absolute mob scene at the pools and in the playground, with hundreds of kids and dads and bikini-clad girls and women glistening with sunblock and running around on the lawns with bountifully bouncing boobies. As a boy who'd just celebrated his sixteenth birthday, I was in heaven.

Monday morning the huge housekeeping staff would begin the daunting task of cleaning up the debris in the 180 rooms, and the pools, and the lawns, and the playground. Monday through Thursday nights were absolutely dead as the moon and stars sparkled overhead and crickets chirped all around, but weekday afternoons were the best. My dad was working every day, so my mom and my sister and I would each pick our own pool and spend the afternoon lounging about...all alone. After spending the summer in close proximity together with no privacy, the spacious and empty weekday grounds of the ERTH were a welcome sight for all three of us, each craving downtime away from one another.

MEETING MY FIRST BIG STAR

One day I was wandering about on my endless quest for fun, when I saw a familiar face in front of the lobby. A married couple was checking in, and I caught a glimpse of the man's face. He was a distinctive British man in an MGB convertible two-seat sport roadster, wearing a tweed driving cap over curly blond/gray hair. But it was his face that caught my eye...his eye, to be precise. He had protruded and misaligned eyes due to Graves' disease. I had recently seen two Mel Brooks movies, *Young Frankenstein* in 1974 and *Silent Movie* in 1976, and I recognized that face. It was "EYE-gor, " Marty Feldman! He and his wife, Lauretta Sullivan, were checking into my hotel!

I was so excited that I couldn't contain myself. I was a budding young professional comedian myself, and Marty Feldman was about the funniest actor I'd seen of late. He was a big star to me, and the first star I'd ever seen up close.

I lingered at the front of the lobby, and when he came out with his room key, I marched right up to him and said, "Excuse me. Has anyone ever told you that you look like Marty Feldman?" He stared at me, with at least one eye, and quipped, "Yes...my mother." He climbed into the car with his wife and I watched dumb-founded as he drove into the complex toward their room.

I scurried back through ERTH's now familiar pathways until I found their car parked, all alone, beside one of the buildings. It was a weekday afternoon, and there was nobody on the property except the staff, my mother and sister, and the Feldmans. I dawdled nearby while Marty and Lauretta struggled to free the luggage from their bungee-cord-laced trunk rack, and as Mrs. Feldman took the first bag into the room, the suggestion was made that I lend a hand. I don't recall if it was his idea or mine, but I was astounded that I was actually carrying the luggage of Marty Feldman, the greatest comedian, to my mind, since Stan Laurel.

When all the bags were in the room he and his wife thanked me, and as he shook my hand, I said something really stupid and insulting. "Wow...you know Johnny Carson!" Stupefied by this decidedly unflattering remark which clearly subjugated his British movie celebrity to that of another (and an American television celebrity at that), *Eyegore* ushered me to the door without a word, and I reluctantly stepped through and he closed it behind me. I loitered about for some time thereafter, trying to burn the situation into my mind, and as I walked by the sliding glass door of each room facing the interior of the courtyard, I saw Marty Feldman one more time, sitting at the table in his room, gazing out into the courtyard, and staring back at me...with one eye.

Five years later I was saddened to learn that the first movie star I met died at the young age of forty-eight years. If I had only not made that dopey remark about Johnny Carson...

KTOB AT THE "TOP OF THE BAY"

In late August of 1977 my parents bought the house at 1524 East Madison Street in Petaluma, around the corner from where brand new twenty-acre Lucchesi Park was being developed, complete with a community center, senior center, two separate playgrounds, four tennis courts, four handball courts, and a four-acre lake. Throughout my high school years I jogged there every morning, and played tennis there every afternoon, and even went skinny-dipping on foggy mornings in the new lake.

Petaluma is where my mother was born, and where lived the mother of my maternal grandmother, my Great Grandma Lieder, and her son, Barney the shipmaster, at 1009 G Street. Up the street at the northeast corner of Sunnyslope Avenue was Barney's sister, Marie, and her husband, Bob (who, with his father, built the houses from 1009 G to the corner; that's how he met Marie). Marie's daughter, Shirley, and her family, the Oertels, all lived in Petaluma, too. We had stayed in the home of Great Grandma and Uncle Barney during a home leave in 1973. We loved the town, and were very excited to be settled once again.

Well, I don't know if "excited" is how *I* felt. I had been uprooted from one of the most beautiful places on the face of the globe, and brought to a dairy town with thick, cold fog most every morning in the spring, summer, and fall. I was enrolled at Casa Grande High School, which was a brand new school southeast of town in the middle of dry cow pastures, and my first class each morning was gym. I stood out there, freezing to death in the fifty-five-degree fog in my shorts, dreaming with sadness about the sunny eighty-five-degree mornings on Guam. It was truly a tropical paradise with constant views of the Pacific Ocean and the Philippine Sea, a place where I fell in love, not once, but twice, and became a notable local entertainer.

Guam was any kid's dream come true, and now I was back to living in the real world of boring old California. The toughest part was having to start all over again at a new school, with new friends, and with no loyal client base for my entertainment career. I would have to start from scratch again in my career, too, but was determined to make Crisco the Clown as much of a celebrity in Petaluma as he was on Guam.

In October of 1977 my dad and I participated in a walkathon, and finished in first place…because it wasn't a race, and because everyone else was walking, and we were running. Oh, and it didn't matter who came in first. But it did to me. My dad had been running marathons for several years, and he had put me in training with him for several weeks prior to this twenty-one-mile walkathon. I was pretty proud when we staggered up to Petaluma's McDowell Park, gasping for breath. That's where we met two disc jockeys awaiting the walkers at the finish line, Barry Brown and Jeff Angel of Petaluma's KTOB 1490AM.

They congratulated us and interviewed us on the radio. I had been on television once on Guam during the local cutaway from the Jerry Lewis Telethon, but I'd never been on radio before. It was the highlight of my day…even better than finishing that walkathon. My dad and I were drained, and we headed across town to the Swensen's Ice Cream Parlor for a dish called "The Earthquake," which was eight scoops of ice cream, each individually layered with different toppings. I finished that Earthquake, likely wiping out any benefit of all those weeks of training for that walkathon.

A few weeks later, in December, I read in the *Petaluma Argus-Courier* that the drama club at Petaluma High School, across town, was hosting a city-wide talent show. Having had the whole summer "off" from performing, I was starved for a chance to get back on stage. My last performance was at the talent show on Guam in June of 1977 just before we moved away. It had been six months, and I was chomping at the bit to get the momentum on my career rolling again. The best part of doing this talent show was that the two masters-of-ceremony for the show were the two KTOB disc jockeys who'd interviewed me at the end of the walkathon. I hoped they'd remember me, and they did.

In fact, they liked my act so much that they asked me to come back to the radio station with them and read a few ads and a few news stories. The ability to read well was important in radio, and once they learned that this was part of my skill set, they offered me a job. It was the training position at KTOB at the time: Sunday mornings, 7-10 a.m. Weekends were always the training ground in radio, but KTOB had religious programming running on Sunday mornings, with fewer listeners and less actual airtime for the announcer than any other position.

The religious programming on KTOB in the 1970s was pre-recorded, so much of the disc jockey's time was spent just running tapes. Although it was a bit more complicated than it may sound...especially for a 16-year-old boy. Monday through Friday KTOB went on the air at 5 a.m., at which time many people were preparing for work. Petaluma was a dairy town, and dairy ranchers got up a lot earlier than that to milk and feed their cows. Our weekday morning man was Ron Walters, who was exceptionally popular with the dairy demographic. Saturdays we started at 6 a.m. because management figured a lot fewer people were up and around before that, and Sundays started an hour later than that.

I had to arrive at the station at 6:30 a.m., however, because our old one-thousand-watt transmitter needed a half-hour warm-up prior to carrying any sound. In those days the Federal Communications Commission allowed a commercial radiotelephone transmitter to be operated by someone with little skill. No exam was required for a provisional license, which is what I was given on March 24, 1978. It was simply a mail-in deal; the FCC trusted that radio management would vouch for the actions of trainees. In the weeks prior to that, I was monitored by a licensed staffer. I began studying for the exam that was required to obtain a Third-Class FCC Radiotelephone Operator's License, which I obtained on December 28.

The transmitter was located south of town at 2 Rovina Lane near the Veteran's Memorial Auditorium and the bowling alley. It's still there today, in fact, in a little red house with a tall antennae standing in the back yard. I visited one night with engineer Steve Pinch. He needed help in cleaning the thing, but, in the words of Elmer Fudd, "we had to be vewy, vewy quiet" because owner Dave Devoto rented the building as a residence to a Latino family...the transmitter was actually in their kitchen next to the stove! We worked all night, ate Dorritos, cleaned the transmitter, and removed dead rats from the housing. That was KTOB's original studio location, which was featured in the classic 1973 George Lucas movie, *American Graffiti*, in the scene in which Richard Dreyfuss' character comes by XERB to ask Wolfman Jack to do a song dedication for him, although the interior of the studio in which he actually met Wolfman Jack was at KRE in Berkeley. KTOB originated in 1950 as KAFP, which stood for "Krowing Always For Petaluma," and on January 10, 1961 became KTOB for the "Top of the Bay."

KAFP becomes KTOB on January 10, 1961.

Here's a brief side note about the 1973 movie *American Graffiti*. We Petalumans are proud of our movie history, as so many have had scenes shot in our town, including: *Basic Instinct, Peggy Sue Got Married, Heroes, Howard the Duck, Explorers, Shadow of a Doubt, Farmer's Daughter, Bitter Harvest,* and *Mr. Billion,* in addition to many television commercials. In fact, for a week every year in May Petaluma steps back in history as the cars and stars of American Graffiti come back to town for "Petaluma's Salute to *American Graffiti*" (www.AmericanGraffiti.net), featuring classic car shows, and day and evening cruises which close down all of downtown and feature live music, food and beverages, merchandise, and appearances by members of the original cast, signing autographs, including: Paul Le Mat, Cindy Williams, Candy Clark, Bo Hopkins, and Manuel Padilla, Jr.

And I was hired on a couple of occasions to portray Wolfman Jack.

Christopher as Wolfman Jack with the Furrer twins.

Back to KTOB. In December of 1977, when I first visited the station with Barry Brown and Jeff Angel, the studios and offices were located at 21 Washington Street on American Alley (a couple of years later we moved to 58 East Washington Street in the Golden Eagle Shopping Center, and our control room had a window that looked out onto the historic old Farrell House across the Petaluma turning Basin; later KTOB moved yet again to an even smaller space in the center at 21 East Washington), and the transmitter was operated remotely from the studio with a funky-looking device bearing a rotary telephone dialer.

You'd flip a power switch, and then toggle another switch up, and then dial 1-9 to read the various power levels, recording each on a log sheet. The meanings of these readings were vaguely explained to me, but all that was necessary was to monitor the readings every three hours, and trim the power occasionally within stated guidelines to keep our power output and frequency regulated properly. While the transmitter warmed up, I would prep my music. This brings to mind a story about a terrible morning at KTOB.

DONUT DAD

While I generally rode my bike to the station before buying my first car, occasionally my parents would let me take their Volkswagen Squareback station wagon. On one particular morning I was afraid to awaken my family or the neighbors at 6:00 a.m. on a Sunday, so I figured I'd just roll the car down the driveway and start the engine in the street. Well, for whatever reason (teenagers don't need reasons for stupidity), I stood outside the car with my foot on the brake pedal and my hand on the steering wheel, but the car rolled too fast and I lost my footing and had to jump in. But before I could hit the brakes again the hedge forced the open door back against the fender, crunching the door, the fender, and the hedge.

I was panicked! Not only was I going to be in huge trouble, this was going to cost a fortune, and I would be late for work, to boot! I rushed into my parents' bedroom and shook my dad awake. "Dad," I whispered desperately, "Wake up! I really fucked up!" He threw on his pants and followed me outside to see the terrible catastrophe I had caused. He looked at the car and the hedge, both badly bruised after their forced encounter. I was stressed and shaking and sputtering and I probably cringed, expecting my dad to scream obscenities and maybe even belt me, but his reaction completely shocked me: he hugged me and said, "Ok, calm down. We'll deal with this later. Let's get you to work." And with that he put me into the other car and drove me down to the station.

As if the morning had not already had enough drama, we arrived at KTOB to find that somebody had moved all the religious music out of the control room...I had no music! Of all the mornings for that to happen! Murphy's Law prevails! We searched the whole bloody station and finally found the albums buried in one of the production studios, so my dad helped me lug them all back up to the control room. He waited while I prepared my news, cued up my records, and signed on the air. By the time I had finished the news and gotten into my first song I realized that my dad had disappeared, but in a few minutes he was back...with donuts and hot chocolate. I smashed up his car, and he brought me donuts!

Sure, I had to pay for the insurance deductible on the car repairs, which probably ate up my wages for the first six months (I was getting minimum wage, which was $2.65/hour), but my dad demonstrated in the face of my little crisis a level of maturity and sensitivity that astounds me to this day. One of the best father-son bonding sessions we ever had was over that box of donuts at KTOB on a Sunday morning in the spring of 1978...with gospel music playing in the background. I still tear up thinking about it. Dave Linnell was and is just about the greatest dad ever on the face of the Earth.

RIP 'N READ 'N HOLY ROLLERS

So, back to the regular Sunday morning routine. I'd cue up my first two gospel songs on the two turntables, and then clear the old United Press International teletype paper that littered the lobby overnight, pulling together my first newscast. This was the truly exciting part of the job for me. See, television news at that time was delivered only on weekday mornings by San Francisco television stations, and by the networks in the evenings, and Sunday newspapers' deadlines were hours earlier, so on weekend mornings the only truly fresh, breaking news was available in our small town from KTOB's UPI teletype. This meant that I was truly the gatekeeper for regional, state, national, and international news in Petaluma on my workdays.

This was a responsibility I took quite seriously, and it wasn't an easy one, because the UPI teletype news roundups were frequently misspelled and electronically garbled. Furthermore, UPI was competing with other providers and was forced to weigh perspective and veracity against cost and expedience, often sending out arguably less-than-accurate or poorly considered information just to be first. This may have not presented a problem to a veteran journalist, but for a 16-year-old high school student, this could be a major adversary to accuracy and clarity. And as no one had checked the teletype since Saturday afternoon, sometimes the paper or ink had run out overnight and I would come in early in the morning to find I *had* no news.

Finally, reading the news was also challenging for me because international stories usually included the names of people and places that were unfamiliar and extremely difficult to pronounce...particularly when I'd never heard of them before. The station had a dictionary, but no encyclopedia, so there was no way to look up names and places in the days before Google. Prior to airtime I'd try to read through the newscast I composed from the teletype sheets, but sometimes that wasn't feasible. It was definitely exciting to be the first bearer of news in our town of thirty-five thousand people, especially during such major news events as: major earthquakes in Greece and Iran, the Jim Jones "Peoples' Temple" mass suicides in Guyana, the death of Pope Paul VI, the installation and death of Pope John Paul I, and the installation of Pope Jon Paul II, a plane crash in the Canary Islands, and the Iranian Hostage Crisis in 1979.

In addition to "rip and read" news and sports, our top-of-the-hour five-minute newscasts would be concluded by a weather forecast, which came from the National Weather Service in Washington D.C., and would frequently have to be fine-tuned a bit using our station thermometer and barometer. We'd sign on at 7 a.m. with a formal, recorded greeting by former station manager Don Davis (about whom I'll talk more in a bit), then the National Anthem, after which I'd hit the news sounder and do the news, and then I'd play my first record. Our religious collection included a lot of stuff I wasn't too fond of, but also included a lot of truly beautiful music by Lawrence Welk's musicians, plus Tennessee Ernie Ford, Mahalia Jackson, Hank Williams, the Statler Brothers, Elvis Presley, and my favorite, Johnny Cash. My religious Grandma Elsa was elated that her grandson was hosting the show, and tuned in every Sunday morning to hear me.

At 7:30 a.m. I played KTOB's first pre-recorded, pre-paid religious program, *Brother Ed*, who was an old-style radio preacher with a long-drawn monotone that sounded as if he was a man with a higher pitched voice who was being played at a lower speed. While he went on and on at length, in the background was organ music that sounded like it came right out of a funeral parlor. The show ran for thirty minutes, and then it was back to news at 8, a little more music, and then another program called "Frank & Ernest," in which the announcers, Frank and Ernest, stated that "today again we will have a *frank and earnest* discussion of religious topics."

Christopher on KTOB on a Sunday morning in 1978.

We also featured a couple of local programs. One was hosted by the late Reverend Roland Bond of the Petaluma Christian Church, who was also a member of the Petaluma City Council, and a very nice man. The last program on the show was the fifteen minute long offering from the Baha'i congregation in Petaluma, which was more enjoyable for me because of their all-inclusive attitude and progressive world view, not to mention their fast-paced theme song, "Have you heard of Bahá'u'lláh? Have you heard of Bahá'u'lláh? I've heard the glad tidings and I will tell you of Bahá'u'lláh…"

ACCORDIONS, POLKAS, AND GREEN WINE

Following the religious program I would engineer ethnic shows, which, like the religious programs, were paid programs which solicited and ran their own advertising. Beginning each Sunday morning at 10:00 was a local German named Walter P. Jeltsch, an accordionist and the owner of a German delicatessen, who hosted "Music of the Old Country." It consisted of his German commentary, plus recorded music, as well as music performed by him on the accordion live in the studio, and occasionally performed by his band in our lobby. He was a very nice man who always had funny things to say to me in his thick German accent, and I looked forward to relinquishing the mic to him each week.

Walter's contract with the station ended, and in his place we broadcast a local Portuguese tailor from the Archipelago of the Azores, who also worked as a travel agent, entertainment agent, and promoter. His name was Carlos Medeiros, and he hosted a show he called "Recordando Amigos de Portugal." Carlos was also very nice to me, and seemed to talk a lot and laugh about me in Portuguese on his show, which was a little annoying.

I'd hear my name swimming in a sea of Portuguese, and I'd look up. He'd laugh, I'd laugh, and he'd say, "Do you speak Portuguese?" And I'd answer, "Only 'recordando amigos de Portugal'," and he'd laugh again. He frequently brought green wine and sweet bread from his wife's kitchen. Carlos is still offering tailoring services in Petaluma, and, last I saw him, didn't look a day older than he did back in the 1970s.

A "REAL, LIVE DISC JOCKEY"

Eventually program director Barry "Downtown" Brown, who was also the afternoon-drive announcer, gave me Saturday mornings, too, which was really exciting, because the program didn't talk about God, was all in English, and I got to play regular American Top 40 music. I still have a recording of my very first shift on that show, back in 1979, and I must confess I'm embarrassed to quote myself as saying, "Good morning, I'm Chris Linnell, and I'll be on the air every Saturday morning from now on from 6-10 a.m. I can't believe it...I'm a real, live disc jockey!" In fact, I have a lot of recordings and *air checks* of my broadcasts from the 1970s and 80s at KTOB and KSRO, and none of them feels very flattering for me to listen to today. But, I suppose that's a good thing...it means I've matured. In all modesty I must say, however, that most of my production work back then was excellent and still sounds pretty good today.

One of the important duties of air talent at small-town stations back in those days was to do production work. A lot of the jocks hated it, but I relished writing and producing commercials, and much preferred it to air work. I was inspired as a teenager on Guam by the LP recordings of Cheech & Chong, which were comprised of character skits and included custom music, sound effects, and character voices, and were very funny. My training ground for radio production work was the marionette show soundtracks I so elaborately produced for myself as a teenager in my bedroom recording studio on Guam. I have them digitalized now, and, while some of the early ones are a bit amateurish, the later ones, some of which I produced at night and on the weekends in the production studios of KTOB and KSRO in my spare time, were excellent, with perfectly edited music beds, realistic sound effects, and a wealth of surprisingly distinct character voices.

For a long time I was the Saturday night guy at KTOB. I worked from 6-10 p.m., playing Top 40, which included rock and roll and disco, and I took requests and dedications. My first date with my first wife, in fact, was picking her up at her parents' house west of town, and bringing her in to sit with me in the studio while I did my radio show. She loved it, and I felt proud. That's where Carrie met my buddy, Robert, the guy who got picked up with me by the Secret Service. In fact, Robert and I enjoyed interacting with each other on-air on Saturday nights at the end of my shift and the beginning of his.

We also gravitated toward separate ends of the musical spectrum, as the music changed from one shift to another. My time slot featured a lot more disco, and his a lot more rock. As such, I called myelf "Disco Crisco," and he was "Rockin' Rob." The friendly back-and-forth interchange and good-natured teasing sounded great to the listeners, and led to Robert starting his own mobile DJ service. And I had his-and-hers t-shirts made for myself and Carrie, saying "Disco Crisco" on mine and "Disco Crisco's Chick" on hers, which we wore to station promotions. Yeah, it sounds awfully corny today, but, at the time, it seemed pretty cool, and the listeners ate it up.

I then did a stint as mid-day announcer at KTOB, as well, which included hosting the famous "Petaluma Swap Shop," a twice-daily listener call-in show which was the audio version of newspapers' classified ads, and the precursor to the Internet's www.CraigsList.org. In the background we'd play the LP version of the "Suicide is Painless" theme from the television show $M*A*S*H$, or the long album version of Chuck Mangione's "Feels So Good," and then announce the rules: "Welcome to the Petaluma Swap Shop, broadcast at 10:05 a.m. and 1:05 p.m., where you can buy, sell, or trade almost anything. No firearms, no garage sales, no cars, but anything else is ok. Call us at 763-1505 from Petaluma, Rohnert Park, Cotati, and Penngrove, or 795-8061 from Santa Rosa. Let's get to the phones." Most of the announcers hated it, but I loved it. Swap Shop was a chance to interact with real people on the air. What I didn't like about being an air personality was talking to myself...it bored me. I'm an improv man...I like to talk to people. In fact, that was what led to my favorite job at KTOB.

My second important promotion was to weeknights on KTOB, which meant I was no longer a "weekender," or just doing fill-in, but a full-fledged member of the air staff. This was also exciting because I was doing the shift with a partner for the first time, a guy by the name of Al Cates, who was ten years older, and had a lot more experience in radio, and in life. Al had a great radio voice, and a fantastic sense of humor, and was able to do some great character voices, so we made a perfect team. We called our program "North By Nights," and management let us kind of do our own thing. We hosted local dances at the Kenilworth Recreation Center, as we were trying to engage Petaluma's teenagers. Therefore, we were also allowed to play more modern music than was aired during the day.

You see, KTOB was what was called a "middle of the road" station, offering local personality, news, and information for our small town. As such, our music throughout the broadcast day shifted in sound as each daypart's demographics changed. Our morning show started with Frank Sinatra, Blossom Dearie, Mel Torme, and Kenny Rankin. Mid-days we'd do Tom Jones and Barry Manilow. Afternoons we'd play Top 40, and in the evening we'd shift into more of a disco and R&B beat. Our late night show played hard rock. When I joined the station in 1978 the Morning Man from 5:30-10 a.m. was Ron Walters, who was a little bit country and a little bit jazz. In fact, he had a beautiful voice, was a gifted jazz singer, and was infamous for actually scatting along on mic with the jazz artists he played. Mid-days 10 a.m. to 2 p.m. was David Wesley Page (currently the morning-drive anchor on Newstalk KSRO), whose cool, calm demeanor and smooth jazz tunes were directed toward housewives, and Barry "Downtown" Brown was the afternoon-drive host from 2-6 p.m. with the witty barbs, big city delivery, and fast-paced music. Jeff Angel worked from 6-10 p.m. and took requests and dedications from the teenagers, and Steve Stone was the hard rock night jock from 10 p.m. to 2 a.m. who rocked the town until the bars closed.

THE BANJO MAN

Ron Walters had been on KTOB since 1963, and had become a bonafide institution in Petaluma, kind of like the Bill Soberanes of radio. Ron was hooked up with the business, political, non-profit, performing arts, school athletic, and agricultural communities, and talked about who-was-who and what-was-what around town. He did play-by-play remote broadcasts of local high school sports, played the banjo, and was a member of the local community chorus, the Petaluma Harmoneers and Harmonettes. Not only did they do choral programs, they produced musical comedy theater in town, with exceptionally professional results. Aside from listening to Ron on the radio, my first exposure to him was seeing him as the lead in Meredith Wilson's *The Music Man*. He was fantastic.

The 1962 motion picture version is a favorite of mine, and I thought Robert Preston owned the lead until I saw Ron doing it on stage at the Phoenix Theater in Petaluma. I was astounded that our little town could produce such an incredible show, with a huge cast, full costuming, elaborate sets, and a full orchestra. In fact, playwright Meredith Wilson attended the premiere in Petaluma and gave the cast and crew a resounding review. Ron was the star of the show, playing Professor Harold Hill as if the part had been written for him. KTOB's Jeff Angel played Iggie Wolfington on a par with Buddy Hackett in the movie. As I mentioned earlier, Jeff is still working in local theater today, in fact, in Indianapolis; visit: www.AngelBurlesque.com.

Petaluma's *The Music Man* was the first really professional theatrical production I had ever seen (and the only one I'd ever seen in which I wasn't the star or director), so I was excited that my new town was filled with so much talent, so many resources, and so much local support for the performing arts. The funniest part was that I had never actually *seen* Ron Walters before seeing him on stage, and when my father and I jogged past the radio station one morning shortly after I started working there, we saw the disc jockey through the front window behind the mic in the studio. My dad asked me, "Is that Ron Walters?" I said, "No, he must be off today…Ron's much taller, and he has a full head of hair." Well, as it turned out, Ron was 6'7", standing on a stage, and wearing a wig in *The Music Man.* In the front window at KTOB he was seated and sans toupee, so he seemed to me to be way too short and way too bald to be the star of the show at the Phoenix.

Ron is multi-talented. In addition to being a great broadcaster, singer, musician, and musical comedy actor, as well as the Rona Barrett of Petaluma on radio, he is also an incredible entertainer. Just as I impersonated Bill Soberanes, naturally I developed an impression of the very characteristic Ron Walters voice, as well, which tickled everybody but Ron, it seemed. Though he never said anything about it, he didn't seem to appreciate my Ron Walters impression as much as Soberanes appreciated my Soberanes. I hope today Ron recognizes that it comes from respect and admiration and not from derision.

Ron would do live remote broadcasts at frequent retail promotions and at the annual Sonoma-Marin Fair, playing the banjo and singing "Won't You Come Home, Bill Bailey" and other such ragtime and gay-nineties tunes. I was called upon to engineer his program in the studio while he broadcasted from the fair, which I felt was a high honor, though I subsequently realized I was chosen mainly because nobody else wanted to do it. One of those mornings was also almost the end of my new radio career.

While Ron talked and sang and played the banjo and interviewed the farmers and ranchers about their cows and pigs and sheep and goats, he had to throw it back to the studio for news and commercials, some of which had to be read live. During one of these cutaways, with Ron at the fairgrounds listening to me for his cue, I had to do live copy for the Green Thumb Nursery, an important KTOB sponsor. I read all about the soil and pots and grasses and bushes for sale, and then had to read about the flowers. I said, "And, the Green Thumb Nursery has roses and lillies and fuchias…" At the end of the ad I said, "And now it's time to send it back to Ron Walters, broadcasting live from the Sonoma-

Marin Fair." Ron picked it up on the air, but what I heard in my headphones was that he was also talking to me directly.

"Well, thanks a lot, Chris. One thing, though. The Green Thumb Nursery sells FUCHIAS, not 'fu-CHI-uhz!" Well, how's a teenaged boy supposed to know that?

Ron started a video production service, "Top of the Bay Images," specializing in videotaping school athletics, and he has become a recording artist in the past few years, too, recording a charming album on CD of banjo-accompanied tunes called, *Songs My Grandpa Taught Me.* Every old-time Petaluman fondly remembers Ron's signature daily sign-off: "This is Ron Walters, your almost-friendly hometown announcer, saying thanks a heap, and don't forget what I told you yesterday."

RESPECT YOUR ELDERS

Another member of the staff who was a big influence on me was Don Davis, who came from Hackensack, New Jersey and worked at San Francisco's KFRC 610AM in the 1940s hosting several programs (e.g., "Rinky Tinky Time," "Dusty Records," and "Flying Discs") back in the day when radio stations were allowed to broadcast at higher power and could be heard almost coast-to-coast. Getting his start in radio in 1934 in Vermont, Don once told me that his father was a Baptist preacher, and that he left the east coast and came to California to get as far away from home as possible.

Don told me that he was the man who in 1944 discovered a bright and talented 19-year-old big-band singer named Merv Griffin. Don hired him as a singer on *San Francisco Sketchbook*, a nationally syndicated program based at KFRC. Band leader Freddy Martin heard Merv on the show and hired him to tour with his orchestra for four years. Within a year Merv used his tour income to start Panda Records and produce the first album in the United States recorded on tape rather than vinyl, *Songs by Merv Griffin.*

In the early 1950s movie star Doris Day got Merv a screen test at Warner

Brothers and he was on his way to stardom, hosting a variety of television game shows, and guest hosting the *Tonight Show* between Jack Paar and Johnny Carson. From 1965-1986 he hosted *The Merv Griffin Show*, competing for afternoon talk and variety dominance against fellow big-band singers Mike Douglas and Dinah Shore and winning seven Emmy Awards.

In 1964 his wife Julann suggested a game show in which contestants would be given the answers instead of the questions, and Merv created *Jeopardy*, and in 1975 created and produced *Wheel of Fortune*, selling his production company to Columbia Pictures Television in 1986, but retaining ownership of his two game shows. Merv Griffin made a billion dollar fortune in broadcasting and real estate, but may have completely forgotten about the man who gave him his start, good old Don Davis at KTOB. And, as Paul Harvey would say, "now you know the *Rest of the Story*. Good day."

Don Davis was the venerable Old Man at KTOB when I joined the staff. He had been the station manager when the station was still KAFP, but by 1978 had been relegated to selling ads and dubbing national commercials from reel-to-reel tape onto *carts* (which were like 8-track tape cartridges, but without the rubber wheel inside, so that, rather than running continuously, they could be placed into the machines beforehand and be actuated at the touch of a button). Cart dubbing was the mindless drone chore that everyone in radio hated the most. Don did still have some fun at KTOB, though. He hosted his own show of big-band jazz on Sundays from 5-7 p.m. It started off, "Welcome to *Music of the Good Old Days* on KTOB, Petaluma. I'm your host, Donald Davis."

In his sixties Don was a little bitty guy of about 5'4", if memory serves, and looked to me almost like a cartoon character, with big glasses hanging off of big ears. The 1961 picture that follows reveals him to be a truly suave and handsome dude with wavy, greased-back hair and a pencil-thin mustache, but in his sixties Don's hair had gone gray, and every day he wore the same exact clothes to work: a purple velour three-piece suit. Actually, in the late 1970s it was a lot more fashionable than it may sound today.

KAFP became KTOB under station manager Don Davis.

Don had the most incredible radio voice for a little old man...deep and rich and intelligent, and he always incorporated a bit of an echo behind him in the studio that made him sound as if he was still up there on the stage introducing The Dorsey Brothers or Laurence Welk to a crowd of jitterbugging Zoot Suiters and WWII flyboys. His show was played on eight huge fifteen-minute carts which were only used otherwise for our religious programs on Sunday morning, and they were filled with the finest big-band and jazz, peppered with recordings of interviews he'd done in the 1930s and 40s with every big-band leader and crooner that ever recorded an album. His show was truly a wealth of radio history. Unfortunately, though I loved jazz and ragtime, I hadn't begun to truly appreciate big-band at the time, and, along with the rest of the younger jocks, I used to think old Don was kind of funny.

Mind you, he had a great sense of humor, was always nice to me, and always helpful, patiently showing me how to do things and telling me stories about the good old days before television when radio was still king. But he certainly didn't fit-in with the way the rest of us wanted to sound. He sounded like top-rated KFRC in the 1940s, and we all wanted to sound like top-rated KFRC in the 1970s, with its loud and bold and ballsy Top 40 jocks spewing forth time and temperature checks on the intros to rock songs by Chicago and Boston and Fleetwood Mack.

Don smoked a pipe, and while it seemed that everyone in those days smoked in the studio, only he smoked a pipe. His office reeked of pipe tobacco, as did his records and his carts and his suit. And, perhaps because he smoked that pipe constantly, he was horribly asthmatic, and we all took turns mimicking him behind his back: "This is Donald Davis...wheeeeez...with *Music of the Good Old Days*...wheeeez...on KTOB." One of Don's advertising accounts was the local Culligan soft water dealer, and Don did all their ads; "Hey, CULLIGAN MAN...wheeeez..." We thought it was so funny at the time. Today I am also an asthmatic (cigar) smoker who sounds almost as bad as Don did. Karma always gets you in the end.

At age sixty-seven Don suffered a heart attack in the office of his doctor and died. We all attended the funeral, and Ron Walters, who I remember frequently had loud spats with Don about this thing or that, stood up to give the eulogy, and began a long speech about how we all took *Good Old Don* for granted. He talked about how no one wanted to dub spots, "So who did it? Good old Don." Nobody wanted to handle certain accounts, "So who did it? Good old Don." I'm telling you, there wasn't a dry eye in the house when Ron left the podium, and I learned a valuable lesson about appreciating people when they're still here.

A few years later I was talking to a friend whose family lived right next to Don's little cottage out at 1030 Lohrman Lane in the rural area west of town. I asked her if he was ever married, and she said, "Oh, no...Don was gay." I said "WHAT? Don Davis was GAY?" She said that he lived in that little cottage with a younger Filipino man, and died with no children and no parents; just a sister in North Carolina. On top of the fact that he had to work to his dying day, and had to see his fame and success diminish until he was regarded more with derision than with respect by his younger co-workers in the business he helped create, he also had to lead a double life, hiding his beloved partner from even his co-workers.

It's a shame that radio will never be what it was, but it's good that some things in American society have changed. It's just a shame that it happened too late for…Good Old Don.

THE BIG TIME…IN LOCAL RADIO

One night on KTOB in 1981, I played Chris Rea's "Fool if you Think it's Over," and *back-announced* the song as I faded it out, whereupon I asked the listeners, "Do you think it's over? Fool." I then brought the music back up again for the REAL fade ending twenty seconds later. A few minutes after that, one of the station's studio lines lit up, and I answered it. "Hey, man, that was funny. You're good. Listen, I'm Scott Mitchell from KSRO in Santa Rosa. Do you wanna come up here and work with us?" Needless to say I was elated. (Scott, by the way, is back at KSRO today: www.HigherPowerHour.com)

I went up to KSRO 1350AM in Santa Rosa and was interviewed and hired by the program director, the late Jerry "Johnson" Ignacio. But a few days later, before I was scheduled to begin working, I got a call from Jerry Ignacio again. He apologized, and said that he didn't realize that I had a third-class FCC license; KSRO had a directional antennae which required operators with a first-class license. This was an insurmountable obstacle, unfortunately, because, while my third-class license required passing an exam, the first-class license certified an operator as having electronic engineering skills which I didn't have. Basically, it required a person who could build a radio station from scratch. That would take years of training and a lot more talent and interest in electronic engineering than I had.

I was horribly disappointed, to say the least, but I was glad that I was still working at KTOB, as I've never burned my bridges behind me. The bright side was that just a few months later the FCC changed its requirements and a third-class licensee *was* qualified to operate a directional antennae. I immediately called Jerry back, and he put me to work right away, and before long I was working full-time from 6 p.m. to midnight Sunday through Friday, with an hour of commercial production prior to my airshift, which was to begin at 7. This thirty-six hour week also left me with my Saturdays free, my Sunday mornings and afternoons free, and my weekdays free, so I could continue to work on marketing my entertainment services and attending college on weekdays, and perform clown shows on Saturday and Sunday afternoons, singing telegrams on Saturday night, plus pull KTOB weekend airshifts on Saturday and Sunday mornings.

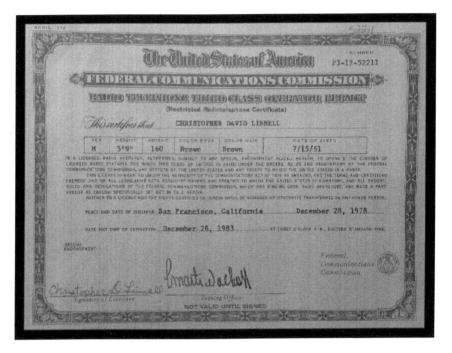

Christopher's second FCC license. Sometime prior to its expiration in 1983, the FCC changed the rules, and these licenses were made valid for life.

I worked at both stations for a while, until I was certain that KSRO was a sure thing, and then I finally left KTOB after four years and spent the next five years at KSRO, and at KREO (which our parent company, Finley Broadcasting, acquired in 1986), working as an air personality, commercial writer, announcer, and producer, and, eventually, and finally, as an account executive.

My job was created when the evening jock, Michael "Alexander" Cimarelli, was promoted to mid-days, between Jim "Shamus O'" Grady (1936-2013) in the mornings and Reg Lester (1943-2009) in the afternoons. When Mike was originally training me for my new shift, I noticed that he took a wooden awards plaque off the wall and placed it on his seat for his entire airshift, replacing it before leaving for the evening. I was puzzled by this, but didn't ask any questions, because I assumed he liked sitting higher or on a firmer surface.

On my first night I came in and was greeted by Reg Lester, who was a big, tall Anglo in his forties with a big, black, furry 'fro. He was Mr. Slick on the air, a local celebrity, who, like most jocks, brought in a stack of joke books and paraphernalia with him that he never actually used, except as a security blanket. As far as his personality was concerned, Reg outwardly seemed quite friendly, but over the course of five years I spent working with him, I found him to be a little insincere, kind of like a car salesman or a game show host.

At the beginning of his shift Reg was professionally dressed, if a bit 1970s Vegas in style (but, of course, in the early 1980s most people dressed that way). He usually wore expensive leather loafers, polyester dress slacks, a brightly colored patterned sport shirt, with the collar folded out over the collar on his polyester sport coat, and he wore a few gold chains. At station promotions he was famous for wearing his trademarked tacky yellow tuxedo.

Reg was a handsome fellow, and seemed gregarious enough, with a big-market feel about him. But he didn't look as natty and well-groomed at the end of his five-hour airshift, which was a stressful drive-time program, featuring live news, sports, weather, traffic, and feature reports, and, generally, an eighteen-minute-per-hour commercial load. This was the largest load allowed at the time by the FCC, which amounted to almost a third of each hour devoted to commercials. Most of the spots were primarily dubbed onto carts, although some were live copy. The cart load for each hour amounted to as many as three dozen, stacked and laid-out chronologically, into *spot sets*.

This required a lot of attention for the announcer, who had to pull in advance the commercials for the next hour, arrange them into an order that precluded competing sponsors being placed together into spot sets, and then stack them up so they were ready. Music was played on two turntables from 45s or LPs. Although in the five years I worked for KSRO engineers also installed CD players, and short-lived "digital audio tape" players, or *DATs,* introduced by Sony in 1987. They were supposed to be the new high-tech thing...they weren't.

The jock was kept busy cueing records, shifting and loading and unloading carts containing commercial spots, public service announcements (PSAs), and station sounders, plus preparing and pre-reading live commercial copy, answering listener and feature phone calls, and interacting with the news department. He did all this while watching the clock constantly and back-timing everything to make sure he stayed on schedule, made the required top- and bottom-of-the-hour station IDs ("KSRO, Santa Rosa"), and met the network news and feature feeds precisely on time. Anyone who thinks radio was easy in the days before computers was never in the studio during morning- or afternoon-drive. It was stressful and required an exceptional ability for concentration and multi-tasking. And you had to be funny and entertaining, to boot.

So at the end of his shift each afternoon, dapper, slick, and professional Reg Lester was a sweaty, harried mess. His black curly locks were dripping with sweat, his shirt was soaked and the shirt tales were hanging out of his trousers, his shoes were off, and he was exhausted. When he got up from his chair and relinquished the mic to me on my first evening, hauling his box of books and papers and his headphones, sport coat, and shoes, he staggered out of the studio and down the hall toward his desk in our joint announcer office, muttering his trademark off-mic phrase, "I be SWAMPED, brutha...I be swamped!"

Excited that this big, classy, 5,000 watt station was now mine for the first time for the next five hours, I plopped right down into the chair...which splashed. I suddenly had a sinking and nauseating realization that the reason Mike Alexander always put that wooden plaque on the chair when Reg left the room was *not* that he liked to sit higher on a firmer seat, but that it was the only way to keep his butt dry after Reg sat there sweating into the seat for the five hours from 2-7 p.m Monday through Friday each week. Well, I was definitely in the big-time now, and I had the sweaty butt with which to prove it!

KSRO IN SANTA ROSA

KSRO was a truly impressive radio station in those days, and a definite step above the two separate locations in which KTOB was housed while I was there. KSRO was located at 627 College Avenue on the northwest corner of the intersection with Humboldt Street in a newer Colonial-style building encased in red brick and surrounded by lush green ivy, with stately columns supporting a broad, white, wooden top. Centered above the door were the station's call letters prominently proclaimed in gold metal on the white wall above the dutch doors, and they were backlit with blue neon light after dark, and up above the building perennially flew the American flag, lit from below at night.

KSRO by day and night.

Inside was a classy reception office with matching couch, side chairs, and coffee table, and a wide brown desk for Doris, the pretty, petite, polite, middle-aged receptionist who looked like she was another one of Lawrence Welk's lovely Champagne Ladies.

On a side note, on my last day at KSRO, April 30, 1987, I had worked like a trooper through my full two weeks' notice, and I said goodbye to everyone else on staff. As I approached Doris' desk on my way out through the lobby, and after seeing and chatting with her on a seemingly friendly basis daily for a full five years, I said, "Well, Doris, it's been a pleasure working with you." And she responded, with grave and icy sincerity, "I never liked you." Ouch. That taught me two valuable lessons: 1) Always maintain a professional relationship with your co-workers, as Doris had, regardless of your actual feelings about them; and 2) Never assume anything about anyone until you leave the job. Thank you, Doris…those lessons have served me well in the decades since.

The KSRO building on the inside was divided into halves (but no have-*nots*; sorry…I couldn't resist a gratuitous pun). The east side of the building housed the bookkeeper, sales offices, coffee room, and the cluttered office of veteran morning man and account executive Jim Grady. In the center was the spacious office of general manager and vice president Frank McLaurin. It was a classy room, indeed, with a beautiful executive desk, credenza and side chairs, a couch, and a minibar, if I remember correctly.

Behind Frank's office, across the hall and against the north wall in the back of the building, was the conference room. The west side of the building was devoted to programming, production, and engineering, with myriad studios, all joined with huge, double-pane, soundproof windows. Each studio's walls were covered with white sound-absorbing tiles, and, while the motif may look a bit dated in pictures today, it all looked very professional, new, and fresh in the early 1980s, and, at the time, it was definitely the finest, classiest, best-designed broadcast building I had seen north of the Golden Gate.

The transmitter was located several miles away on Santa Rosa's old, abandoned, World War II-era U.S. Army Air Corps airfield, housed in a nuclear-safe bunker with extremely thick concrete walls. I only visited the transmitter site once, and it reminded me of the 1959 Burgess Meredith "Time Enough at Last" episode of Rod Serling's *Twilight Zone*, in which Meredith's character emerges from a bank vault to find that he's the only survivor of a nuclear holocaust.

I met Burgess Meredith once in the mid-1980s at a party in the Southern California home of my first wife's uncle, Motown Records vice president Guy Costa, who was the nephew of Don Costa, Frank Sinatra's arranger. Meredith was a friend of the family, and seemed like a very nice and humorous old gentleman, wheelchair-bound on the day we met, and accompanied by a caregiver. He was full of wit and wisdom and personality, though. He died of Alzhemier's disease in 1997 at age eighty-nine after an incredible performing arts career spanning six decades.

Back on College avenue, the first studio off the KSRO lobby to the left toward the west was an alternate air studio which could also be used for production purposes or for interviewing groups, such as sports teams or bands.

KSRO's master control room, Studio A.

Next was Studio A, the master control room, a huge space on the southwest corner of the building filled with a wide, round, Formica-topped custom desk bearing a pair of turntables on one side, and hundreds of cart bays on the other for all our commercials, PSAs, and sounders. In the center were the twin control boards, with round *pots* (potentiometers) and touch-sensitive keys, a high-tech touch I'd never seen before, which were slick and quiet, but which could also be all simultaneously and inadvertently activated by one touch of static electricity…in a studio carpeted wall-to-wall.

This was not a very bright idea. On numerous occasions the jock would rush into the studio from the bathroom as a song or commercial ended and touch a key without remembering to ground himself on a metal surface first, and the entire soundboard would spark, and every key would switch, wiping off the air whatever was on the air, and vice-versa. In the center was an electric analog clock, which our chief engineer perennially kept at precisely the right time, so that we could synch with our numerous periodic network feeds.

Christopher on the air at KSRO in June of 1982.

Above the clock were a couple of lava lamps pointing down, which provided excellent reading light for copy, but were extremely hot to the touch, and tended to add a few unneeded degrees to the already stuffy air in the studio. Those lamps were hanging from a huge console hanging on two stainless steel poles from the ceiling. The console contained our transmitter remote control and the Emergency Broadcast System alarm, which sometimes went off while the announcer was talking...an annoying circumstance, but a necessary one, as KSRO in those days was the lead EBS station in Sonoma County.

All in all, Studio A was quite impressive, and seemed to me to measure up to and exceed even most of the San Francisco stations' studios...it always looked to me like the bridge of a space ship. Up on the wall, visible from the lobby, was a white, three-by-four-foot needlepoint carpet bearing the groovy 1980s KSRO logo. From his seat the announcer could look directly into the auxiliary control studio (and the lobby beyond that), the master news studio, and the auxiliary news booth. Actually, the best part of working on the air at KSRO in the 1980s was that studio. Except for the office of the general manager, the conference room, and the engineer's garage containing the KSRO panel van, Studio A was the largest room in the building, and the on-air announcer felt that he was certainly in control.

The one glaring thing the room was missing was a window (pardon the pun) that actually looked outside. In fact, except for the lobby, there was actually not even one tiny window in the entire building! And that may be the main reason that in my five years there I felt so claustrophobic and, for all intents and purposes, decided to end my career as a radio personality. I hated that locked-up feeling. To this day I have resisted working indoors forty hours a week.

THE Q-TIP

The general manager was a real character, to be sure. Frank McLaurin (1923-2009) told me that as a young man he got his start in broadcasting as a page on *The Jack Benny Show*. In fact, Frank sounded *exactly* like Jack Benny to me, but was much more handsome. He and his wife of fifty-three years, Barbara, were fit and tanned, both with thick, beautiful heads of white hair (for that reason I learned that many on staff derisively referred to Frank behind his back as "The Q-tip"). Frank was very distinguished, always impeccably dressed, and gave the appearance of an old-style business gentleman. They lived in a spacious home on the grounds of Santa Rosa Golf & County Club, and always reminded me of Judge and Mrs. Smails, the characters played by Ted Knight and Lois Kibbee in the classic 1980 movie *Caddyshack*.

Staunch conservatives and pillars of the community, the McLaurins golfed and sunned and drank cocktails at fancy affairs. Frank was a true perfectionist, widely respected in his community and in the broadcasting industry, and an excellent executive, who demanded the best from his staff, but managed to be pleasant, personable, and humorous, albeit a bit paternalistic at times. I always liked and respected him, and he seemed to like me, too.

When I finally went to him in late 1986 to apply for an opening in sales, after more than four years in programming and production, Frank said, "We always wondered why you didn't apply for this job earlier." Flattered, I said, "Really? Why's that?" Frank said, "I like the way you walk." I was a bit startled at first, not exactly sure what that meant, but he went on to explain, "Have you ever seen Lester draggin' himself around here? You always walk fast, and forcefully, like you've got somewhere to go. I like that. You'll be good in sales." Well, I wasn't so sure about that. I was at a turning point in my career and in my life, and I was hoping that I was making the right decision.

Back in 1983, after a year of working full-time as the evening announcer, I was in seventh heaven. I was just twenty-one-years-old, with five years of experience in radio, currently working at the best station in the market, entertaining professionally, and working in television on the side; I was looking forward to a bright career in broadcasting. I had also recently become engaged to Carrie, and we were planning to buy a house at the time of our wedding, scheduled for March 31, 1984.

And then I got a call on my day off from Chris Turner, the new program director, and my new boss. Jerry Johnson had passed away, and Chris took over, and he seemed to me to be a rude, caustic, abrupt, sarcastic, conceited, jealous prima donna, and I didn't care much for him. He asked me to come in and see him. I thought I was in some kind of trouble...and I was right. Chris told me that KSRO, which was the oldest station in the Sonoma County market and had always been number one in the Arbitron ratings, had just fallen victim to a monumental change in the radio industry.

We had lost our position in the ratings to KZST 100FM, which had been on the air for several years with an adult-contemporary, elevator-music format typical of many FM stations at the time. To compete with KSRO and the other AM stations, KZST had developed an AM format, but in FM stereo. FM stations across the country were doing this, and with personality, news, information, and a much nicer stereo signal, the listeners here and across the country were switching their dials to FM and away from AM. As a result, KSRO, which had always before based its sales upon the Arbitron ratings book, would be changing gears in our sales strategy, focusing more on customer service and less on "the book."

Frank had decided to tighten the station's belt, and had just laid off the least senior employee, newsman Tim Ryan (who, as of this writing, has been a reporter with KCBS in San Francisco for years). As I was the second least senior employee, I would be laid off next. Ugh. Laid off. That was the first time that had ever happened to me. I was crushed…I felt powerless. To be fired for cause was one thing, but to be laid off because of something that was entirely out of my control; that was heat-breaking.

Chris took me into Frank's office, where the big boss sympathetically buried the situation in a lot of financial data that was all so much gobbledygook to me at the time. Frank offered me a very nice letter of recommendation, but Mike Alexander would be moved back into my position, and I was out. I asked if I could continue doing commercial production, and keep a weekend airshift, and Frank said that would be fine. I went home that night and told Carrie that our dream of buying a home may well have been dashed. As it turned out, we were able to afford a mobile home, which was better than renting, but a disappointment, nonetheless. Hold that thought…here's another series of asides.

SHAMUS AND MERLE AND HILARY AND SMOKEY BEAR

We recently lost morning man Jim Grady, and it was a sad thing. Shamus O'Grady was a true institution in Sonoma County, as KSRO's morning man for thirty-three years at the time I joined the station. He eventually lasted forty-four years at KSRO until 2004, at which point he was fed-up with the new owners, Maverick Media, and resigned to take weekend mornings at KZST.

A round fellow with a bulbous nose, Jim was the king of wisecracks and ad-libs. He was at his best chatting with people on the air, with his gravelly voice and corny remarks. I was lucky enough to be asked by Jim to do a lot of my celebrity impersonations as cut-in features on his show. Being a packrat, I saved every piece of copy I wrote, every creative ad I produced and voiced, and every bit I did on the Grady show.

Grady was honored at a memorial service on March 8, 2013, and hundreds turned out to remember the man with whom Sonoma County awakened each morning for five decades. In the crowd were many KSRO veterans, and I managed to get a picture with several of my former co-workers.

Jim's partner on the air was operations director Merle Ross, who had also been at the station for decades. Merle was teary-eyed in his moving tribute to Grady at the memorial service, and though he himself was over eighty years of age, he still looked exactly as he did when I first met him in 1981: handsome, distinguished, intelligent, and humorous, with a full head of white hair and a slim, trim physique. And that brings to mind a brief Hilary Bacas story, as well as two others.

KSRO veterans at the Jim Grady memorial on March 8, 2013; left to right: Larry Chiaroni, Christopher Linnell, Merle Ross, Tim Ryan, John Burgess, Sue McGuire-Chiaroni, David Wesley Page, Shauna Lorenzen, and Merle's daughter, **Santa Rosa Press Democrat** *reporter Randi Rossman.*

We had an excellent news director, Hilary Bacas, who was Merle's protégé, and a slim and attractive woman in her thirties. I made a terrible Barack Obama faux pas when I first met her, however (I'm referring to Obama's 2013 characterization of California's Kamala Harris as, "by far, the best looking attorney general"). Being a Groucho Marx fan, I recalled his line as Dr. Hugo Z. Hackenbush in the 1932 movie *Horse Feathers* when he met the beautiful young owner of the sanitarium, played by Thelma Todd. "Well, you're the prettiest owner of a sanatorium I've ever met," Dr. Hackenbush said, with a flirtatious look in his eye. So I said to Hilary, "You're the prettiest news director I've ever met." I judged by her reaction that she wasn't as familiar with Groucho quotes as I was, and that a new era was dawning in the parameters of workplace relationships…and I'd just breached them. I didn't do that again.

Back to Merle. One day Hilary brought her beloved German sheppard to work with her, so I figured that dogs were welcome. So one night I brought my west highland white terrier, Mandi McFergus, with me to work. And the next morning I got a very early call from Merle, who asked, "Chris, did you bring your dog here last night?" Puzzled, I said, "Yeah. How'd you know?" Merle stoically responded, "Because there was dog shit under my desk this morning." Oops! Sorry, Merle. He never mentioned it again, but I suspect he never forgot.

One night, close to my midnight sign-off, I was monitoring the police scanners in the news room and heard that there was a residential structure fire underway just outside of town. I took down the address and a few other notes, and, after signing off at midnight, jumped in my car with a notebook, tape recorder, and a microphone with one of those square KSRO 1350 NEWS signs affixed thereto. I was intent on getting the scoop and leaving the story and some *actualities* (recorded interviews with first responders) for Merle's morning newscast. I drove to the rural location and found a spacious ranch-style home fully engulfed in flames. I wandered around for a few minutes, taking notes, and then approached the fire captain and identified myself as a reporter from KSRO.

I asked him a few questions, recording his responses and diligently taking notes as best I could, and then queried, "Do you know who lives in this house?" He answered, "No, I don't, but the mailbox is right over there." I made my way to the end of the driveway and leaned in to see the name on the box in the flickering red glow: "ROSSMAN" it said. "Rossman? That's my BOSS, Merle Ross!" Just then I saw Merle emerging from the front door with the flames at his back. He was wet and dirty, and carrying a few singed miscellaneous personal effects. I just stared at him with my mouth open and the microphone inadvertently pointed in his direction, not knowing exactly what to say. Merle looked disgusted and said to me in the kindest tone he could muster, "Just leave a note for Hilary, Chris...she'll get the details in the morning."

I was shocked, embarrassed, and humiliated all at the same time. Merle ambled off before I could begin to apologize. To complicate matters, this was the holiday season, and Merle and Ann had their Christmas tree fully decorated in the house, and it burned along with everything else. Our staff Christmas party was just a few days off, and my co-workers came up with a rather beautiful idea. We were all to bring Christmas ornaments as gifts to Merle and Ann, to replace the family heirlooms they'd lost in the fire. But my co-workers had an equally ugly idea about presenting them to the Rossmans. As I was in the business of providing costumed impersonations, I was elected to make the presentation, costumed as none other than Smokey the Bear. Merle and Ann, class act that they are, took the rather daring gag in good humor.

THE MOST IMPORTANT LESSON IN BUSINESS

Back to the story of my lay-off. Asking Frank if I could stay on staff part-time doing production and as a weekend announcer at KSRO was the best decision I could have made. I was now a full-time entertainer and a part-time broadcaster, and I continued to work at the station through 1986. I always felt, however, that the managers of this station, and radio stations in general, were not paying attention to what was most important. I had noticed at both KTOB and KSRO that the sales staff seemed to be much better treated and were certainly much better paid than the programming and production staff, and I didn't understand why.

After all, programming was the product. The station was selling Jim Grady and Reg Lester, I thought, not a ratings book or a special deal. I always felt that the on-air staff was the most important thing at the station, and I couldn't understand why we were treated as second-class citizens. Reg and Jim and our venerable old operations director and morning news anchor, Merle Ross, always wore nice clothes to work; many days including even neckties. So did Mike Alexander. However, the other members of the air staff, news team, and production crew all wore casual, even sloppy clothes, and I didn't want to be one of the crowd.

Over the years I worked part-time in production, I usually wore nice clothes and a neck tie, and was teased relentlessly about it by my colleagues on the production and programming side of the building, as if I was some sort of ass-kissing turn-coat. Frankly, I didn't linger from one coffee break to another, trying to see how little I could get away with doing by the end of the day, as was the practice of some of my colleagues. I prided myself on the quality and speed of my work. I began to realize that if I ever wanted to be paid fairly for my work, make a decent income, and be treated with some level of respect, I would have to switch sides of the building.

When a sales position opened up (as they frequently did...the sales staff may have been better dressed and better paid, but the less senior account executives were flighty, and drifted in and out of our employ on a very regular basis), I jumped at it. I went home and told Carrie that I was going to apply for the open sales job, even though all my talent and interest and passion was in writing and producing the commercials, not selling them. I looked at Frank McLaurin and Merle Ross and general sales manager Gordon Lofgren and Jim Grady and local sales manager Jack Levar and account executive Sandi Lojko, and realized that they were all making near or in excess of six figures a year, drove nice cars, owned nice houses, and seemed to love their jobs just as much as I loved mine.

I had also recently been talking to stand-up comedians I met while working one night a week as a performer at a local radio station, which was also a restaurant and nightclub, called the Studio KAFE. These comics were from out of town, some of them were fairly well-known nationally, and new ones came in every week as headliners at the Studio KAFE. But what surprised me was that one of them, who was married and lived three hundred miles away in Bakersfield, told me he was earning just fifty bucks for his appearance that night, along with a free dinner and a bar tab, and that his deal there was typical of the deals he got as a stand-up comedian traveling the circuit full-time. I said, "How can you work that cheap day after day, especially with all that travel away from home?" He said, "Well, my current wife works…and one of these days I'm gonna get my big break and then it'll all pay off."

I did not want to waste my whole life on the road working for pennies when I had a wife and pets and a house in a town I loved. I decided that I would rather take a regular job at a small-market station and stay home with my wife and raise a family than travel around chasing after a dream. So on October 22, 1986, I put on my best suit and buried all my doubts and fears and headed into Frank's office and told him I wanted that open sales job. That's when Frank told me he didn't know why I hadn't asked for the job before, and that he liked the way I walked, and that he thought I'd be a great account executive.

On October 27 I called my friend and colleague, Scorby the Clown, and gave him all of my standing Crisco the Clown bookings. The next day I went clothes shopping and bought myself a new camel sport coat and some slacks and shirts and ties and socks and t-shirts. I also sold my prized pickup truck with the camper shell and carpeted insert (which I bought specifically for hauling my puppet stage), and bought a nice, conservative Chrysler LeBaron sedan. I wanted to look the part.

I was determined to devote myself to this new job. Jack Levar was my supervisor, and he took me out with him on sales calls in training. And that's when I learned why the sales staff was treated so well, and the programming and production staff was seemingly ignored, and it's when I truly learned how the business world in general really operates. Now it must be said that I didn't particularly care for Jack up to that point. I respected the fact that he seemingly sold more time than all the other sales people combined, but to those of us on the programming/production side of the building, he was obnoxious and pushy and would come barreling down the hallway into our office and start barking orders at us and shoving production orders in our in boxes and he never seemed satisfied with what we did.

But when I saw him with his clients in stores and offices and warehouses, I saw a completely different man. He was funny and sweet and smart and engaging, and his clients seemed to love and respect him. He was still kind of pushy and aggressive, but I came to realize that his clients expected that of him and respected him for it. I learned that in business, for good or for bad, sales are made based not so much upon the merits of the product but on the level of service and value offered.

Jack seemed rarely talked about the station's disc jockeys or the music or even the news and information. He talked about the ads and the demographics and the reach of the campaign and the deal he could make on it and the service he'd provide. And when his clients stalled by throwing up obstacles, saying they weren't ready, or they had to ask someone else, or they weren't sure if they had the money, Jack just kept on pushing and prodding and cajoling them…and one after another they relented, and when he walked out that door they were happy that he'd done it. It was the most amazing thing I'd ever seen…it was magic.

Try as I might, though, with my newfound vision and passion, I did not seem to have the same kind of magic with my clients as Jack had with his. Jack and Gordon and Frank were very supportive, and our frequent sales meetings were geared to pump us up and fill us with fresh ideas and renew our passion for our product and our industry, but I never seemed to catch on. Jack came in every day at 6 a.m., and rarely left before 6 p.m., and I figured that I just wasn't working hard enough. I wanted so badly to be good that I started getting up at 4:00 every morning, arriving at 6 a.m., and staying until Jack had already gone.

I wrote all of my clients' ads myself, and produced and voiced them myself, too.

I worked my ass off for six months, and was still barely making my monthly *draw* (an amount advanced to a sales person against commission expected to be earned later in the month). I was gaining weight, suffering from heartburn and asthma, and when I came home from work in the evening I'd sit on the couch and eat my dinner in front of the television and then fall asleep right there. I was absolutely miserable for the first time in five years at KSRO and for the first time in nine years in radio. On April 16, 1987 I finally gave up. I dragged myself into Gordon's office and told him that I couldn't take it anymore, and gave him two weeks' notice that I would be resigning on April 30. He and Frank and Jack all tried to talk me out of it, and they were very polite about it, but they were not understanding at all. I was letting them down...they still all felt that I should stick with it and I'd be a success, but I'd had all I could stand. It just wasn't the fun that I got into radio to have.

I continued to do freelance production work and remote broadcasts for KSRO for some time thereafter, but I should have taken a weekend airshift to just stay on the payroll. That was my biggest mistake. I went home to Carrie and told her, "Well, I'm a professional entertainer again." It was tough for a couple of months, but before long I was busy entertaining and doing freelance contract commercial production on KSRO and KREO and all the other Sonoma County radio stations of the day through 1997, including KZST, KPLS, KVRE, KMGG, KXFX, and KRP-Q105.

BACK TO THE TOP OF THE BAY

In 1993 I got a call from a familiar voice. It was Dan "Phillips" Hess, who worked at KTOB prior to the date on which I started there. In fact, it was his resignation from the station that trickled-down to my being hired. Dan worked as the mid-day host under the name Dan Phillips, and I remember the other jocks and co-owner and general manager Bob Lipman and bookkeeper Phyllis Hart all talking about how "Dan Phillips did this," and "Dan Phillips did that." I knew that Dan Phillips was the pro at the station, and that KTOB would never be the same without him. Well, Dan Phillips/Hess was now part owner of the station with the previous co-owner with Lipman, Dave Devoto (who was also Bill Soberanes' partner in the World's Wristwrestling Association), and they had rescued the station from the clutches of bankruptcy and the FCC and poor management decisions by several intervening owners.

Or maybe it was just the change in the small town radio industry. When I joined KTOB in 1978 we had five full-time air personalities, a two person news department, four full-time account executives, a chief engineer, a general manager, a bookkeeper, and a *traffic* person (who did not report about the flow of cars around town, but worked off-air, manually creating the program logs in the days prior to computers), plus at least a half-dozen weekenders and good old Don Davis (who also did some sales).

The station was alive and well and making a profit in a town with a population base of under forty-thousand people. But within just eighteen years our population was closer to fifty-thousand, and the station had succumbed with fewer than a half-dozen on staff, all of whom were either owners or management. Things changed. Small town radio stations were dying (along with Sonoma County's KFTY TV50, and our local newspapers which are now downsized, under-staffed, and corporate-owned).

Dan and Dave were able to get ahold of the station again because Dave was smart enough to maintain ownership of KTOB's single most important commodity base: the transmitter's equipment, tower, building, and real estate. Dave brought in as a partner Dan, who was a radio engineer with a first-class FCC license, and who had made a big success of an ad agency he created in the meantime, and together they planned to rebuild the station from scratch. I was very excited, even though the plan was to automate programming with computers at first, with just a live morning announcer and news veteran George McManus.

It was Lesson Time for Christopher again, as I made a ridiculous error at a lunch meeting with Dave and Dan. When they first told me that they were planning to hire a morning announcer, I immediately blurted out, "Wow! Fantastic! Is Ron (Walters) available?" They both looked at me as though my fly had been open, and then laughed and told me that they were considering hiring *me* for the job.

The lesson here, again: in business think about yourself first, stupid. Dan needed my help in production, and eventually they hired me as the station's morning-drive announcer from 6-9 a.m. Monday through Friday.

It didn't last very long, however. By the fall of 1995 Dave and Dan had to cut us two live announcers and automate KTOB's entire broadcast day, and then eventually, and sadly, they sold it to Korean investors. Today it broadcasts programming produced out of town, in Spanish, specifically for the Latino community. That's wonderful for them, but it's a terrible loss for Petaluma in general, which no longer has a locally owned and operated community radio station broadcasting in English. I still feel as though this might be at least partially my own fault. Originally Dave and Dan had asked me to also do sales, but I steadfastly refused, having learned my lesson seven years earlier at KSRO.

In 1996 I worked for Stan Marvin as an air personality at KMGG "Magic" 99.7FM, and simultaneously as an air personality, commercial writer & producer, fill-in news anchor, and default public service director for KRPQ "Q105" at 104.9FM. The last regular radio work I did was to volunteer as co-host of a weekly talk show on public radio on KRCB 91.1FM in Rohnert Park from 2002-2003.

ACTING IN LOCAL COMMERCIALS

In January of 1983 I received a call from Ron Satter and Judith Martens, who were looking to hire a clown for their son's birthday party. They were television producers at Santa Rosa's KFTY TV50. They were also doing an ad for a client named "The Window Doctor." While they had a gray haired, respectable, Marcus Welby-type to play the lead role, they wanted to depict a homeowner who was humorously suffering through domestic life with leaky windows, and decided that Crisco the Clown was perfect for the role. The poor clown was depicted shivering in his living room, wearing mittens and a scarf, bemoaning the fact that he had leaky windows in the depth of winter. The Window Doctor came to his rescue, installing modern double-pane windows.

After this job for KFTY there were many more, acting as spokesman in a series of ads for Transco Transmissions, and for Niles Buick, and for the Quality Inn. On June 2, 1988, I did a commercial for a Japanese sushi restaurant called Musashi, but I don't like fish, and I had told them that I'd take the job, but I absolutely wasn't about to eat sushi. I did end up eating some cucumber slices surrounded by white rice and wrapped in sea weed, but no fish!

I had the most fun, however, doing commercials for Kassin-Shubel Chevy-Olds, a car dealership in the little Russian River wine country town of Healdsburg. Each month they hired me to portray a different seasonal character: in January I was a lone football fan bundled up in the stands; in February I played a cupid in an incredibly embarrassing outfit advertising "a sweetheart of a deal"; in March I played a leprechaun in an outfit that made me appear as though I had jumped right off a box of Lucky Charms cereal; and in May the pièce de résistance was my performance, in full drag, as Gus Shubel's MOTHER, using the voice and mannerisms of Jean Stapleton's Edith Bunker of the television show *All in the Family*.

The copywriter/director/producer on most of these was a lovely lady by the name of Theresa Champagne, who remains my friend to this day. I had a big crush on her, and she thought I was funny, so we had the perfect working relationship. She also produced a number of live remote broadcasts in which I served as host from shopping centers, the Sonoma and Marin County fairs, and several home improvement shows. These were live spots run during a pair of movies. Each time there was a commercial break, the station would cut to me on location, and I'd be found doing something kooky or bizarre at different booths, games, attractions, or contests, such as playing blocks with kids in an interactive toy booth, lounging disrobed in beds, easy chairs, and showers, and demonstrating various patented household giummicks, such as the Zyliss Swiss kitchen tool, mimicking the style of a cheesy fair exhibit hall hawker.

Once at the Sonoma County Fair we had planned to have me demonstrate a basketball hoop game in the carnival, and in rehearsals while the movie was playing I missed the shot time after time. We thought it would be funny if that happened on camera, seemingly as an accident. When we went live, though, I actually shot the basketball directly through the hoop on the first try, and, trying desperately to maintain my composure, I said, "And we'll be back for more fun at the Sonoma County Fair after these important messages," and then, when the *cut* signal was given I exploded into laughter and amazement. Theresa was kind enough to save me the out-take, which I have to this day.

LIVE FROM THE STUDIO KAFE

In 1987 I was hired by a couple of local entrepreneurs, John Duran and Jon Gilbert, who had opened a brand new business in downtown Santa Rosa that was rather unique: a restaurant and bar that was also a cable FM radio station called the Studio KAFE 96.1FM. The KAFE's literature described the place as "a stylish 'soft tech' bar, nightclub, cable radio station, and restaurant serving freshly prepared lunches, dinners, appetizers, and a Late-Nite/After-Theatre Menu. The KAFE features LIVE 'Radio Cabaret' broadcasting, comedy, jazz, classic rock & roll, and dancing." Their star attraction was KREO 92.9FM air personality Steve Jaxon, who became a co-worker of mine in 1987 when KSRO's parent company, Finley Broadcasting, purchased KREO in the nearby Russian River Wine Country town of Healdsburg.

The Studio KAFE featured "delicious food for the gourmet listener," including beef, pork, chicken, pasta, and seafood, in entrees bearing movie- and music-themed names, such as Adam's Rib, Judgment at Hamburg, and The Mousse That Roared, and at the top of the menu was Steve's own signature, five-topping pizza, "The Jaxon Five." The entertainment line-up included traditional stand-up comedy on Monday (featuring such up-and-comers as Chris Titus, Rob Schneider, Dana Gould, and Sam Guttman), and The Blair Hardman Jazz Party on Tuesdays (Blair Hardman, at www.BlairHardman.com, is not only a fine musician, by the way, he has a dry, quick wit and was Jaxon's morning show co-host for a while, and he is also the talented voice artist and production wizard of www.ZoneRecording.com in the tiny town of Cotati, home of the annual Accordion Festival at www.CotatiFest.com).

Music and comedy continued at the KAFE on Thursdays and Saturdays, Celebrity DJ Night on Fridays featured local celebrities and weekly host Glenn Mitchell of KREO, and music, comedy, and talk were combined on The Steve Jaxon Show every Wednesday. I was hired as a regular featured performer for that show at a ridiculously low weekly rate that was augmented by free food, open- and close-billing as Christopher & Co. Celebrity Impersonations, and periodic :60 commercials about my entertainment services which I produced and which aired on KAFE's daily radio schedule.

On various occasions in sketch comedy in 1987 and 1988 I portrayed such original characters as a Cajun chef, the "Dolly Llama," a lunatic toy inspector, and the drunken denizen of a cheesy Las Vegas-style "drum bar," plus I did a variety of fully-costumed celebrity impersonations on the show in skits and in my own segments, including Clark Gable, Rodney Dangerfield, William F. Buckley, Phil Donahue, Dana Carvey's The Church Lady of *Saturday Night Live*, Jackie Gleason's Sheriff Buford T. Justice of *Smokey and the Bandit*, Carroll O'Connor's Archie Bunker of *All in the Family*, and Johnny Carson's Mighty Carson Arts Player characters Art Fern and Floyd R. Turbo from *The Tonight Show*.

I had a ball working on the show, but I remember one terrible night, too. Late the night before I had made some Sloppy Joes at home in my new crock pot, and my wife told me, "Make sure to put that stuff in the refrigerator before you go to bed." Well, being *a guy*, that advisory from my wife fell on deaf ears. I left it in the crock pot, and then next afternoon dished up a sizable portion for myself before heading off for my gig at the Studio KAFE. By the time I arrived at the job and got into whatever costume I was to be wearing first that night, I was starting to feel a very strange gurgling deep down inside.

As my cue approached the growling turned into an aching, and then sharp, steady pain, and I was beginning to feel a bit queasy and nauseous. I did my first act, during which I recognized that something awful was imminent, but I plodded on, in character, resistant to the tell-tale signs my abdomen was giving me. As the crowd laughed and applauded I made a hasty retreat for the back door, which was closer than the restroom. I got into the back gravel parking lot and absolutely exploded, fortunately from the top, not the bottom. After emptying the entire contents of my stomach and that damned crock pot, I wiped my mouth, rushed back to my dressing room, changed into my next character, and then headed back to the stage. After completing that act I played a return engagement in the parking lot.

More lessons learned in my show business career: 1) Never leave the food in the crock pot overnight; 2) Listen to your wife when she tells you something; 3) Never eat a new homemade recipe within the twenty-four hours prior to a public performance, and 4) When your contract includes free food, don't eat at home. Fortunately I had already learned Rule Number One in show business: the show must go on. As has happened many times I was ill in my four decades of entertaining, I performed like a trooper on stage without my colleagues, clients, or audience being "any the wiser," as Stan Laurel would have said.

THE BIG TIME...IN ACTING

In June of 1986 I decided that I should try to obtain an agent in San Francisco and begin to audition for national television commercials and voice work, so I picked up a copy of the 1980 book *Acting in Television Commercials for fun and profit* by veteran commercial actor Squire Fridell (illustrated by Barry Geller), published by Harmony Books of New York. It provided me with simple, step-by-step instructions about how to obtain an agent and begin working in commercials. I followed his directions to the letter, and was roundly rejected by every agent in town, except one, Roman Fedorczuk of L'Agence Models & Talent, who took me on as a client.

On March 17, 1995, by the way, I became truly discouraged when I ran into Squire at an audition. I fawned over him in an embarrassing fashion, telling him how much I appreciated the help his book had given me. And then I got the job and he didn't, and I realized that this business would be rough. Squire had been in over three thousand commercials and had even written a book on the subject, and he was still out there bustin' his hump, losing jobs to younger actors such as me. I figured that I should not expect to make a lifelong pursuit out of commercial auditions.

The reason that Squire was at that San Francisco audition, by the way, is that he and his commercial actor wife, Suzy, packed up and left Los Angeles in 1986, and bought some twenty-six acres in Sonoma's Wine Country. Today they are the proud proprietors of GlenLyon Vineyards and Winery in Glen Ellen, California (www.GlenLyonWinery.com). Squire is the winemaker, and he and Suzy plant, raise, harvest, and crush the grapes, and age, bottle, and market the wine, and they even have on-site a well-appointed cottage for rent by the night.

As I mentioned earlier, veteran news anchor Wanda Ramey got me an appointment on August 26, 1986, with her San Francisco agent, Joan Spangler of LOOK Talent (one of the agents who had originally rejected me when Roman Fedorczuk accepted me two months earlier), and before long I was auditioning for SAG and AFTRA union productions with both agents and with some very high-profile performers, all of whom pretend to make a better living than I do. The list includes Greg Proops and Mike McShane of *Who's Line is it, Anyway?*, actor Wayne Knight of *Seinfeld, Basic Instinct, Jurassic Park,* and *The Exes,* and voice artists Thom Sharp, Joe Paulino (www.4Joe.com), Denny Delk (www.DDelk.com), and fellow KTOB alumnus Tom McGraw.

Tom, in particular, is definitely *not* pretending to make a living, it appears; he is now CEO of First National Bank of Northern California (and, according to an article in the February 4, 2011 edition of the San Francisco Business Times, "McGraw's family owns about 5 percent of the $714 million bank."). In his spare time he serves as chairman of the board of the Pomeroy Recreation & Rehabilitation Center for the developmentally disabled. His modest website mentions none of this, however; just his incredible acting and voice credits: www.TomMcGraw.com. When we worked together at KTOB in the late 1970s, Tom was earning minimum wage ($2.65/hour back then) for his four-hour shift from 10 a.m. to 2 p.m. following mine on Saturdays, and commuting from Pacifica to do it. Somehow he managed to improve a bit more than I did.

Now back to *my* illustrious career. On one of my first union productions I learned a very valuable lesson about working in the big time when I tried to do what I had always done as an appreciated courtesy for the over-worked and under-paid crews in television productions in the Sonoma County market: namely, help with carrying the equipment. It was before dawn on the set, and I was standing around with nothing to do while waiting for my wardrobe and makeup appointment.

I saw crew members lugging equipment that had been off-loaded from a truck and was sitting on the ground, so I picked up a couple of pieces of equipment and followed the crew to the set. One of the guys ahead of me dropped his load, turned around, saw me, and just about jumped out of his skin. "What the hell are you doing? You're *talent*, aren't you?" ("Talent" is the condescendingly sarcastic term for actors used in the industry.) I said, "Yeah...I was just helping." He responded curtly, "Well, that's *my* equipment and *my* job. Stick to what you know...standing around and looking pretty." Rude awakening, but a lesson learned in the fast-paced world of professional filmmaking.

And I am so good at looking pretty, after all. (Ahem.)

THE MODEL ACTOR

Speaking of looking pretty, when a woman says she worked as a model, society tends to think she's stupid, shallow, conceited, and bulimic. But when a *man* says he's worked as a model, society isn't quite as kind. And when I say that *I* worked as a model, people always laugh, because, let's face it, while I did look kinda' cute in diapers, and fifty years later the kids all seem to like my shaved head, Santa beard, handlebar mustache, cigar-smoking', *kilt-weain' dude* look, I've never been in the same *Handsome League* with Clark Gable, Cary Grant, Sean Connery, Mel Gibson, or Justin Bieber. (Justin Bieber?)

But that doesn't mean that I did not work as a model. You see, modeling is not just about handsome and beautiful and sexy…they need far more *real people* in modeling than they need beautiful people. And Roman at L'Agence and Joan at LOOK did, indeed, book modeling jobs for me. They were fun, they were easy, and they were lucrative…eventually.

On Thursday, May 26, 1988 I posed at a construction site in San Francisco as a construction foreman for U.S. Sprint. I grossed $700, my agent took her 20% off the top, and then didn't mail me a check for my $560 until December 29. Maybe the client paid her late, or maybe they paid her right after the job…I'll never know. Models have no union; there's no one to restrict agents to 10%, or to ensure that payment is made in a timely fashion. The work is fast, easy, and lucrative, but there is some risk.

In the June 21, 1992, edition of Image Magazine I was featured in a Macy's photo spread in bed…with my daughter. They were doing a dads-as-kids-and-vice-versa theme, and I was the daddy cuddled up in bed in P.J.s with a teddy bear as my eight-year-old daughter sat in mommy clothes on the edge of the bed reading me a story. During the June 1994 Congressional campaign I was featured, again as the husband and father type, in an anti-Doug Bosco mailer for Congressman Dan Hamburg's reelection campaign. Apparently he was targeting the wrong guy…he lost to the man who lost the seat to Bosco in 1990, Frank D. Riggs. Two months later, on August 8, I was the disgruntled airline passenger in a half-page ad for Blue Shield on page B6A of the *Wall Street Journal.* And in the March 2006 "Special Gardening Issue" of *Martha Stewart LIVING* magazine I was the nursery owner husband in an ad for the United States Postal Service.

As I said, modeling isn't just about looking pretty. Sometimes there's actually acting involved. In 2001 my modeling went online as I portrayed "The Caring Banker" who appeared full-screen with a misty, sensitive expression on the www.Impact.Schwab.com website of Charles Schwab. This was the modeling job I'm most proud of, as the photographer told me in great detail the expression he sought: a sweet, understanding, sensitive banker who would listen to his clients. With a little focus I was able to give him exactly what he'd asked for. We were both very happy with the result, as was the client.

Christopher as "The Caring Banker" for Charles Schwab in 2001.

And, by the way, as I also said, modeling can be lucrative. The pay for that job was $800, less 20% for my agent, so I netted $640. I did what's called a "go-see" modeling audition two days before, and the job itself, at 3 p.m. on February 16, took only forty minutes. Plus I had another job in San Francisco that morning, from 6:30-8:30 a.m. at KYLD "Wild" 94.9FM. They needed a Frank Sinatra during their morning show. I charged them $350.

I took a two hour nap in the van between jobs (as I worked late in my home office the night before, didn't sleep, and drove in to San Francisco at 4 a.m.), and then I dropped in to visit casting director Nancy Hayes. After the modeling job I hurried back up to Petaluma because I had another job that evening from 7:30-10:30 p.m. at the U.S. Coast Guard Training Center at Two Rock just west of town, which meant that I earned another $420. I performed at the "Rocks & Shoals Club" for several years, thanks to Avis Linnins, the manager, who was a very loyal client. All told, it was a $1410 day. Sometimes pretending to make a living actually worked quite well. If only that happened on a regular basis...

ACTING IN INDUSTRIAL FILMS

I started working on industrial films (which is a misnomer, as they were actually shot not on film but on videotape under the AFTRA contract), and they were kind of a drag, because they required memorizing dozens of pages of boring dialogue (a skill not necessary for actors in the production of thirty-second television commercials and movie extra work), and working on camera, under hot lights, and in character for hours on end, as opposed to the shoot-for-a-half-hour-and-wait-for-four-more work ethic in commercials, network television programs, and movies.

The worst part of industrial films, however, is that most actors work for simple scale and receive no residuals and little credit. My AFTRA membership covered this work on videotape, and it was what commercial and movie actors did when they were hard-up for cash. I only worked in four industrials that I can recall, two for Bank of America (1988 and 1989), one for Del Monte in 1988, and one for Viacom in 1989, always typecast as either the young husband / father or the yuppie salesman.

ACTING IN NATIONAL COMMERCIALS

Commercials, on the other hand, were normally only thirty seconds long, required little memorization of dialogue, and could be extremely lucrative even for a scale actor under the SAG film contract, because you received compensation based upon the number of times the ad aired and the number of people who would supposedly see it; therefore, if your ad aired during the

Superbowl, the Oscars, or the Olympics, or for more than a few weeks, a couple of days of work could amount to tens of thousands of dollars in residuals. And even extras with non-speaking roles could be upgraded to the status of *principal* if the director thought that your face should be prominent or that you'd be good doing a few lines. In fact, generally speaking, if your face was recognizable in the finished commercial, your status would likely be upgraded after the shoot and the checks would start rolling in.

I worked background for many national television commercials, but only five as a principal. I did an ad for MCI in 1990, pitching a "personal 800 service," that played repeatedly for months on TBS. On a Pontiac shoot in the late 1980s the perfectionist director said "Perfect," after the first take, but added, "let's do one more for safety." Hours later he finally called it a day...after the *eightieth* take...ugh.

I was a businessman in an ad for Ariel Communications in the early 1990s, a great job that required neither the customary audition, call-back, nor wardrobe call. They called me on a Saturday morning and said, "Your resume says you play golf. Are you available today?" I rushed down to San Francisco and spent several hours simply playing golf for the camera at the beautiful Lincoln Park Golf Course in San Francisco. The commercial played in Latin America for years, and resulted in thousands in residuals. The best part was the fact that the job pushed me over the $5000/year earnings threshold for free health and dental insurance through SAG, for me and my wife, and it lasted for two years.

The funniest commercial I did was for Roy Rogers Family Restaurants in 1992. In that ad, the narrator said "Roy Rogers is back, and to celebrate we created a new sandwich...something different. So we sent our man to the strangest, most exotic place we could think of: San Francisco. Introducing Roy Roger's new Sourdough Grillers..."

As the narrator talked about strange and exotic San Francisco, I was shown in iconic San Francisco settings, stumbling through roller-skating Buddhist monks, staring at a beautiful girl in a dress made of ivy, and watching a businessman play simultaneously with multiple paddleballs. The narrator continued, describing the sandwich, and concluded, "...with toasted sourdough bread, just like in San Francisco. Hey, where better to find great flavor than a place where even the people are flaky?" The last image is of a family of three hippies literally hugging a tree.

Although this ad did not air in the Bay Area, word of it reached the "Left Coast," resulting in quite a bit of controversy. San Francisco Mayor Frank Jordan and others complained that the sponsor was making fun of the "freaks" featured in San Francisco, such as the bald and bearded leathermen supposedly intimidating yours truly on a cable car, as depicted in the picture that follows. The irony was that I actually was (or would become) a roller-skating, bald, bearded leatherman and tree-hugger, yet I was playing the *normal* "Man from Roy Rogers" in the ad.

A further irony lay in the fact that fifteen years after the picture below was taken, I would be driving those motorized cable cars every day...in a kilt. But that's in the next chapter.

*Christopher as "The Man From Roy Rogers" being accosted
on a cable car by "typical" San Francisco "freaks."*

ACTING IN NETWORK TELEVISION PROGRAMS

As far as network television shows were concerned, most based in California were and are shot in Los Angeles, of course, and while some of my actor colleagues actually would drive to L.A. to audition, I did not, and there were far fewer national network television shows shot here in the Bay Area. Actually, from the time I joined SAG in 1989, fourteen have been shot in San Francisco, but only two of those lasted longer than one season, namely *Midnight Caller* from 1988-1991, and the CBS television crime drama *Nash Bridges*, shot in San Francisco from 1996-2001, starring Don Johnson and Cheech Marin.

Most of my actor colleagues were elated about the projects, of course, especially *Nash Bridges*, which lasted two years longer than *Midnight Caller* and shot twice as many episodes. Many of my colleagues worked repeatedly in those 122 episodes as extras, but I was busy entertaining and working other jobs and was unavailable for auditions most of the time it was being shot. I was actually hired to entertain the crew one day, but Don and Cheech were nowhere to be seen. And I did work as an actor, too, but on just one single, solitary episode, #97: "Hard Cell," in 2000. I played Ralph, the cold-storage manager who found a naked woman's body in the deep freeze (Don and Cheech weren't in that scene, so I didn't see them then, either, unfortunately).

The freezer in which my scene was shot was in the old, abandoned Letterman Army Hospital in San Francisco's Presidio, and was not functional, so I didn't get any *cold pay*. In fact, I was bundled up for the part in extremely warm clothes and the makeup crew had to constantly wipe away and cover up all my sweat. Hey, I had it easy...the poor girl playing the corpse didn't need the pale blue makeup they smeared all over her; after laying supposedly dead and completely naked on the floor all afternoon she was frozen solid. Furthermore, she was presumably just an extra working for scale; but, as I had a speaking role I was given my own trailer dressing room and received residual checks for years.

As a matter of fact, I was amazed just two days prior to this writing to receive another residual check for that *Nash Bridges* shoot I did on March 3, 2000. The cable TV reuse fee was issued on December 31, 2012, but it supposedly wasn't received by SAG-AFTRA (which recently merged into one union, by the way) until February 26, and wasn't mailed, supposedly, until May 23. I didn't receive it until June 11, almost thirteen years after the shoot, and almost six months after it was supposed to be paid. The amount? I grossed $20.44. My net after withholding was $11.60. Hey, I said that I was pretending to make a living, remember?

Funny thing happened on the set of that shoot that taught me another valuable lesson about the business. My character was to be interviewed by detectives Harvey Leek and Evan Cortez, played by Jeff Perry and Jaimé P. Gomez, respectively. Now, I had never watched the show and was not familiar with those two actors, and those facts became suddenly and blatantly obvious to them. While we were waiting in our spots for shooting to begin, I jealously remembered how many of my colleagues had gotten multiple roles on the shows in the years it was shot in San Francisco, and I conversationally asked Perry, "So, have you guys been working a lot on this show?" He looked at me dumb-founded, as he and Gomez were co-stars, billed right after Johnson and Marin. Perry shot Gomez a look, and then sarcastically replied, "Yeah…almost every week." It wasn't until I actually watched my episode in reruns on television months later that I realized my pathetic ignorance. The lesson learned: always research the project before walking onto the set.

ACTING IN MOVIES

As I mentioned, San Francisco had only fourteen television shows actually shot in town after I joined SAG (which covered television shows shot on film) in 1989, but we did have more than our fair share of movies. In fact, according to the San Francisco Film Commission, there were 143 shot after I joined SAG in 1989…and I only worked on eight, three of which the SFFC doesn't count because they were shot outside of San Francisco. Again, I was busy entertaining and working other jobs when most of them were shot. Many of my colleagues worked many days each on scores of these movies.

Unlike commercials, movie shoots were less likely to pay residuals, which were typically reserved for the main characters and the well-known actors, most of whom were cast in Southern California even if the project was to be shot in San Francisco. Furthermore, movie shoots didn't pay as well as commercials for a day's work, but could be lucrative nonetheless even for extras because, unlike commercials, movies took months to shoot, rather than days, so getting hired as an extra on a movie could amount to a month or two of employment, working up to six days a week and twelve hours a day before shooting was completed.

Extras could also appear in multiple scenes. With overtime, missed or late meal or break penalties, and hazard pay (for night-time shoots, rain, smoke, or even cold weather), an extra's gross for a movie shoot could easily amount in the thousands of dollars. I worked on eight movies, always as an extra, and was always glad to get the work. The lone exception was my speaking role in *Carrier* in 2004, but that was an independent film with little exposure and poor distribution, and it was produced under a SAG deferred pay independent film contract, which meant that the actors are only paid if the movie is sold into a distribution contract, which *Carrier* never was. So I was a volunteer.

In 1993 I worked as an extra in a television movie shot in Oakland entitled *Firestorm: 72 Hours in Oakland*, and I worked as an extra on *Mrs. Doubtfire*, starring Robin Williams, Sally Fields, and Pierce Brosnan. In fact, my old canine companion, Cuthbert the Cocker, also worked on that movie (playing Frisbee with me on the lawn at the Richmond Marina), and actually received his own paycheck for his efforts. In 1994 I worked as an entertainer on the Walt Disney movie *Angels in the Outfield* with Danny Glover, Tony Danza, Christopher Lloyd, Adrien Brody, and Matthew McConaughey. I was hired specifically to entertain the hundreds of background extras playing spectators, who were sitting in the hot sun all day while the crew set up each shot in the Oakland Coliseum.

In 1994 agent Joan Spangler booked me on the Fruitopia tour, and my acting career stalled. When I was offered the tour there was one item on the contract that was objectionable. I called her and asked her to negotiate a better early-cancellation clause with the Fruitopia people because I had several lucrative summer fairs booked that I'd have to cancel, and if they cancelled the tour early, I wanted to be fairly compensated. It was the only time I actually asked Joan to negotiate a contract for me in all the years she represented me. When I didn't hear back from her I called her up and said, "What did they say?" Joan answered, matter-of-factly, "They said no."

Great. Swell. Thanks a lot, Joan. I took the job, cancelled my fairs, and, as it turned out, they cancelled our halfway through.

In addition to Fruitopia, I was busy entertaining, working in local radio, and constructing a website for my business, so I didn't do many auditions. As far as my agents were concerned, L'Agence had gone out of business, and LOOK eventually dropped me due to inactivity. See, originally, when I was already with Roman, Joan pitched herself to me by saying that she was "the best agent in the city," and that Roman was a modeling agent who was new to acting and voice work. She told me that she could get me more work. But these agents really just sit on you and tell you to promote *yourself* and then they collect commissions on the actors who become successful on their own. The ones who don't they drop. But I didn't realize that then. I was too busy pretending to make a living as an entertainer.

By the way, the way I learned that I'd been dropped by LOOK was a very nice *form letter*...not addressed to me, personally, but nonetheless personally signed by Joan Spangler. Gee...thanks a lot, Joan.

Casting agents began calling me directly after a while, including Beau Bonneau, Nina Henninger, and Nancy Hayes, from whom I'd obtained most of the really good jobs over the years. In 2000 I did *Nash Bridges*, and in 2004 I worked as an extra and shared scenes with Samuel L. Jackson, Andy Garcia, and Angelina Jolie in *Twisted* (in one scene actually appearing quite clearly onscreen for a second as a police detective, following behind Jolie, flashing my badge to security as I entered the police station). That same year I had the speaking role in *Carrier* which I mentioned earlier, and worked as an extra, playing a chestnut vendor, on *Memoirs of a Geisha*, though I believe my scene was cut from the movie (as it's not in the DVD edition I bought). I also worked in 2005 for several days and in several scenes on *Pursuit of Happyness* with Will Smith, and my last movie role was playing a gun-toting thug on *Valley of the Heart's Delight* with Pete Postlethwaite and Bruce McGill in 2006. It was not a well-known movie, but it was a period piece set in San Jose, California, in 1933, and I got to take part in my only on-screen shoot-out.

TONGUE LASHING

I mentioned the independent film, *Carrier* a couple of times, and, while it was a lot of fun, is was also yet another opportunity to learn yet another lesson on set. Written, produced, and directed by Paul Didier-Mogg, it was a science fiction movie in which the *USS Hornet* aircraft carrier in Alameda played the central role. The role I played was that of a smarmy high school teacher who wooed and then turned-off a female colleague in his apartment. The scene required some kissing and necking and petting, and it was the first time I had ever been asked to do that.

Mind you, several years earlier, in the late 1980s during my first marriage, I had worked on an industrial film for Bank of America, and was required to look into the eyes of my on-screen wife and tell her sincerely that I loved her. It's "pretending to make a living," right? It was acting. A guy who could do on and off-stage all the stuff I could do should certainly be able to handle that, right? Strangely, I found it very difficult. Acting about any other subject was easy, but pretending to love someone other than my wife...those feelings were difficult to muster. I managed it, but I don't know how convincing I looked.

So, here I was again, perhaps fifteen years later, in a similar setting, being asked this time to kiss a girl on screen. Hollywood actors do it all the time...and much more. But rather than be excited by this prospect, I was scared stiff (no pun intended). Based upon the fact that I'd had the earlier trouble just saying "I love you" to an actress, I decided that I would not stumble this time. I tried to trudge forward, dutifully, with the petting and necking and, finally, with the kissing, and I felt that the first take wasn't as tough as I thought it would be…in fact, it was kind of fun. I had kissed a lot of women, but I was married or dating them all. The last time I kissed a woman that I wasn't at least dating was in junior high school when we played "Spin the Bottle."

Director Paul and the rest of the crew were preparing to do another take, and I was kind of looking forward to it, myself. However, my pretty colleague had a slight critique for my performance. She leaned in toward me and whispered, "Next time, please don't use your tongue."

Oh…okay. Note to self: keep thy tongue in thy mouth.

Christopher the actor in his twenties.

Christopher the actor in his thirties.

10 - On the Road with Christopher

As I said earlier, the 9/11 terrorist attacks in 2001 pretty much destroyed my corporate comedy business. But I was actually ahead of the curve without even knowing it, thanks to one of my loyal entertainment agents, Thomas Schoenberger, who is himself an extremely talented "polymath, composer, historian, entrepreneur, event designer, inventor, and writer" (www.ThomasSchoenberger.com). As I said, Thomas had booked me for scores of big, lucrative events at wineries in Napa and Sonoma, and he kept trying to tell me to learn about wine, although I always resisted.

I've never been much of a drinker. I like strawberry margaritas when I'm eating at a Mexican restaurant, I'll drink a small glass of champagne on celebratory occasions, and I might occasionally have half a beer to be social with friends while shooting pool or singing karaoke, or while sitting and smokin' a stogy and reading on the patio on a very hot day. I have also for the past few years been taking my "medicine" most every night before bed: a single shot of whiskey to clean out my arteries (hey, don't trust *me*; Google it).

I had no interest in wine, and no affection for wine snobbery, frankly. I'm a daily cigar smoker, but I don't like cigar snobs, either. Booze, cigars, food, and women are the same to me in this respect: the expensive stuff rarely seems as enticing as the cheap stuff. But Thomas insisted that I was living and operating my entertainment business in Wine Country, and, as such, I simply must learn to distinguish a chardonnay from a burgundy, and sparkling wine from distilled brandy. Thomas also insisted that I should start doing tours. "You could do the whole tour dressed as W.C. Fields or Groucho Marx. It would be great! There'd be no competition!" Well, he was right about that, I felt…who would want to be stuck in a tour bus being driven by a costumed impersonator? I knew better than to stay in character with a group as one character for an entire day. Originally I pooh-poohed the idea, and told him to just keep booking me for walkaround.

I did want a regular income and benefits, though, and I ran into an old acquaintance in San Francisco one day. Chuck Lambert is a sergeant for the San Francisco Police Department, and I saw him standing on a street corner one day with a card table helping an SFPD recruiting team. Chuck said, "Why don't YOU apply? We offer great benefits and job security." Well, I couldn't argue with that. The starting pay (during free academy training) was annually about the most I'd ever made in a year, and, according to Chuck, the requirements weren't too stiff. Furthermore, my late maternal grandfather would have been proud...his first career was as a California Highway Patrolman. So I applied. Aced the written test, aced the physical agility exam, and breezed through the oral board, as well. But my background package was inches thick, what with my advanced age, dozens of past jobs, and thousands of individual clients. My fellow applicants were mostly kids in their twenties who'd had one or two high school or college jobs before getting into the military or attending the police academy.

I went through the process with the SFPD twice, but my daunting background investigation was not initiated either time. So I applied to the City of Novato and the City of Oakland, as well, both of whom also offered a salaried academy scholarship and a better rate of pay than the SFPD. Novato called me and the lieutenant told me that I'd just turned in the highest score ever on their written exam, but, subsequently, the oral board apparently felt I hadn't done enough community service. (Note to self: when a police oral board asks you why you want the job, say "I like to help people," NOT "I'm looking for a steady job with good benefits.")

I had passed Oakland's written exam and had just been offered an oral review when I saw a banner on the roof of a limousine company right here in Petaluma: "Tour Guides: $48,000/year and UP!" I thought this sounded easier and more fun, and with a similar salary, so I called my dad and asked him what he thought. "Well, nobody shoots at tour guides," he said matter-of-factly. My mind was made up. Thomas had been harping on me for years to look into doing tours, so I applied for the job. A couple of weeks later I was using my entertainment skills in a brand new way: as a tour guide. And I loved it. For the most part.

That Petaluma company, which shall remain nameless, was a sleazy outfit that was actually paying minimum wage. "The real money in this job is in the tips," they coily responded when I asked them how minimum wage added up to the amount on the sign on the roof. The worst part was that they told their customers that the "gratuity is included." Sadly, this tactic is still the industry standard today.

Anyway, I was working for them on September 11, 2001. I was asleep in the morning, and was having a bizarre dream about flaming people falling out of windows. I opened my eyes and realized that my dream was actually happening. My alarm clock turned on my television set to the news in those days, and there on the screen was the image of flaming people falling from the World Trade Center. I called in to work to ask if my run was still on, as the television was reporting that all air travel in the U.S. had come to a screeching halt. The ops manager said, "Yeah, we're telling everyone to come in as usual, and we'll see what happens." I showered and dressed and raced down to the yard, prepped my stretch limo, and then headed for SFO to pick up my clients.

The freeways were absolutely and eerily vacant, but there was a backup of livery vehicles ahead of me on the overpass to the San Francisco International Airport. The SFPD was on-site, turning us all away, saying that there were no inbound flights that day. I headed back to San Francisco and detoured through the financial district to see for myself if there were any cars there…and there was nothing. It was absolutely dead. There were no vehicles, no pedestrians, no workers, no homeless people…no *no one*.

Back at the barn the drivers were all huddled around the television (which reminded me of the sad day in 1986 when I stood with my co-workers in the KSRO newsroom and watched the Space Shuttle *Challenger* explode), and I realized that this horrible tragedy would not only end all my entertainment work for the foreseeable future, it would also be the end of livery work, as well.

Fortunately that was not the case, as wine tours continued, and I worked for a number of companies, always trying to work two jobs, as usual, just in case I got fired or laid off. This was a practice I adopted back in 1982 after I was laid off by KSRO. It explains why I've had so many jobs in my life, *and* why I've never collected unemployment insurance.

Through the early 2000s I drove stretch limousines, vans, and minibusses through every county of the Bay Area, hosting parties and weddings and nightclub runs and quinceañeras and wine tours just about everywhere. I did wine tours in Napa, Sonoma, the Russian River, and Healdsburg's Dry Creek and Alexander Valleys, and, more enjoyably, I also did history tours of Yosemite, Muir Woods, and San Francisco, and this is where I really shined. I had studied history in college, and had considered teaching, so doing history tours of my beloved San Francisco was perfect for me.

CABLE CAR CHRISTOPHER

In 2007 and 2008 I was doing tours for the local KOA Kampground in Petaluma, a great job with nice people…a family-owned franchise with a great reputation company-wide. The best part was that for the first time in a long time, my commute was only about ten minutes long. The first season I drove commuter vans filled with a dozen RVers visiting from across the country and around the world. Every morning in the summer we left from KOA in rural Petaluma and headed down to San Francisco for an excellent all-day tour. In 2008 the tour was done in a much roomier and more comfortable minibus that could hold up to twenty-two passengers.

On the way south through Marin county I told them about the Spanish and Mexican history of California. Once in San Francisco I let them out to walk across the Golden Gate Bridge, took them to the Sutro Bath ruins, Ocean Beach, Golden Gate Park, the Haight Ashbury, City Hall, and let them take a cable car ride up and over Nob Hill and into the financial district. They got a nice long lunch break at Fisherman's Wharf, I narrated a walk-through of Chinatown in which we visited the famous Fortune Cookie Factory, and then I took them up to the rich people's houses in Pacific Heights and finally to historic old Fort Point. As we drove back across the bridge I served them Ghirardelli Chocolate and played a karaoke version of "I Left My Heart in San Francisco," leading them in song as Tony Bennett as we bid farewell to the City by the Bay. We'd usually get stuck in commute traffic in Marin, so I'd send back my list of celebrity voices and take requests all the way back to Petaluma. It was a truly fantastic tour and a fun day.

One day at Fort Point I saw one of those motorized cable cars that were all over town, and started talking to the driver. It looked like a lot of fun, so I checked out the company, interviewed with owner Christine Gridley-Bennett, and secured a position as Cable Car Guide. The company, which was housed on one of the historic piers on San Francisco's Embarcadero, had a fascinating history.

Arnold Gridley was Christine's recently departed father. He was somewhat of an institution in the city, and a real old-style San Francisco character. His ancestor, George W. Gridley, was a sheep rancher who came east during the Gold Rush, and settled in Butte County in California's lush Central Valley, founding the town of Gridley, and establishing what would become a 960 acre ranch.

Arnold Stirewalt Gridley was born in San Francisco's Marina District in 1912, and made his living as a rice farmer in Gridley, a saloon owner and realtor in San Francisco, the landlord of a number of the city's old Tenderloin District residential hotels, and as sort of an entrepreneur of classic vehicles. He purchased at a 1990 auction the old *San Leandro* and *Fresno* ferry boats used by Southern Pacific Railroad and the Key Transit System from the 1920s-1950s, hoping to restore them and convert them into office space or charter boats or floating museums. But his most interesting purchase was at an auction back in 1958 at which he bought thirteen of the San Francisco Municipal Railway's classic, historic, original cable cars. He had their cable car chassis removed, and had box truck chassis and motors installed, and used them as tour busses, the first ever such innovation. He also manufactured new motorized cable cars, using sold oak and brass and the original plans which he obtained with the cars in the auction. At the peak of his company's success he had the world's largest fleet of sixty motorized cable cars offering daily city tours year-round, and he chartered the vehicles for parties, weddings, promotions, parades, as well as for movie, television, and commercial shoots.

Gridley's motorized cable cars were used in Superbowl and World Series victory parades, the annual Pride Parade, the famous Rice-A-Roni commercials ("Rice-A-Roni, DING-DING, the San Francisco treat"), and lots of television shows, including *The Streets of San Francisco*, *Midnight Caller*, *Nash Bridges*, *The Bachelor*, *Real Housewives*, *Hells Kitchen*, and *Good Morning America*.

Plus the cable cars were movie stars, appearing prominently in *A View to a Kill*, Roger Moore's last James Bond movie (and the only movie in which James Bond was featured riding in a San Francisco cable car, namely Gridley's beloved old number 22, an original 1904 San Francisco Cable Car which Gridley converted in 1958), and *The Rock* starring Sean Connery and Nicholas Cage, plus *The Hulk*, *Pal Joey* with Frank Sinatra and Kim Novak, *The Heartbreak Kid* with Ben Stiller, and *Four Christmases* with Reese Witherspoon and Vince

Vaughn.

I drove a charter one day to the San Francisco Giants' beautiful new ballpark on the Embarcadero with panoramic views of the Bay Bridge and the East Bay.   I was to meet the promotions crew of a major motion picture completing production.   They weren't shooting the movie in San Francisco, mind you, just promoting it in our city.   It was the 2009 action movie *12 Rounds* starring bodybuilder, professional wrestler, and budding movie star John Cena.   They had charted our motorized cable car because a climactic scene in the movie took place on a trolley car in New Orleans, so they wanted John to be interviewed on a trolley car when they promoted the movie in San Francisco.   While I didn't get to actually drive him anywhere, he was nice enough to pose with me for the picture below.

Christopher with wrestler, bodybuilder, and actor John Cena.

I loved driving the cable cars.   Numbers 44 and 25 were my regular cars, but I frequently drove historic old number 22, the James Bond car, manufactured in 1904.   With their brass bars and brass bells and gold-trimmed red paint, they were certainly the most interesting vehicles on the road, and attracted so much tourist attention and so many pictures, that I figured we could stop driving tours and just charge for photographs and we'd make more money. But there's nothing really as exciting as having twenty-eight passengers on board an open-air car when you're going up and down San Francisco's hills or driving across the Golden Gate Bridge.

MY SAN FRANCISCO TOUR

My tour started at Fisherman's Wharf, and I would greet each passenger individually before we departed, making them feel as though they were a part of the show. I'd find out where they were from, and play around with them a little bit with improv, puns, and physical comedy, putting them into a good mood before we hit the road. We'd be off on our two-hour tour through Fisherman's Wharf, past historic Aquatic Park, and onto Lombard Street, which is Highway 101 through the north end of San Francisco, where there are no freeways. As we passed the exclusive Marina District, I'd tell my passengers all about the 1915 Panama-Pacific Exposition, celebrating the construction of the Panama Canal. The expo was the reason the city filled-in this riparian habitat with debris from the 1906 earthquake and fire, making a quagmire of quicksand during the 1989 Loma Prieta Earthquake, during which liquefaction caused buildings to collapse into a raging inferno that consumed one entire block of the neighborhood.

We'd pass by the brand new Letterman Digital Arts Center, named for the historic Letterman Army Hospital which preceded it on that spot, headquarters of George Lucas' high-tech Lucasfilm movie studio, housing Industrial Light and Magic and LucasArts. Then we'd pause for pictures of the jewel of the Pan-Pacific Expo, the reconstructed Palace of Fine Arts, and then wind our way into the historic San Francisco Presidio, founded by the Spanish as a military outpost in 1776, and the longest continuously operated military base in the United States when it was decommissioned by President Bill Clinton in 1994. We'd drive along scenic Crissy Field, where in the 1920s and 30s Colonel Henry H. "Hap" Arnold pioneered military air strategies that would help in his development of the U.S. Army Air Corps during World War II, and, eventually, the U.S. Air Force.

We'd pause at the Military Intelligence Service Language School, where during World War II, and in complete secrecy, forty-two Japanese-American soldiers in the U.S. Army would learn to translate Japanese military communications, and interrogate captured Japanese soldiers in battle zones, all while the Nisei soldiers' own families may well have been imprisoned in American internment camps in the dessert. On the tour I also pointed out the building in which the commanding general of the Western Defense Command, Lt. General John L. DeWitt, made the controversial recommendation for the internment of 120,000 American citizens of Japanese ancestry (signed by President Franklin D. Roosevelt as Executive Order 9066).

I'd show my passengers the beautiful and sad Presidio Pet Cemetery, where military families would bury their deceased pets, and the stables and barracks of the famed Buffalo Soldiers Ninth and Tenth Cavalry Regiments, the African-American cavalrymen who escorted President Teddy Roosevelt through San Francisco during his 1903 visit, and who rode on horseback each summer from The Presidio to Yosemite and Sequoia National Parks to serve as the first U.S. Park Rangers.

We'd then head down to the San Francisco base of the Golden Gate Bridge to Fort Point, which is a brick fort with seven-foot-thick walls constructed by the U.S. Army between 1853 and 1861, initially to defend the Gold Country, but by the time of completion tasked to protect the San Francisco Bay from attack during the Civil War by the Confederates. It was built on the site on which the Spanish had constructed the Castillo de San Juaquin in 1794, to protect the Golden Gate specifically from the ambitious British and Russians, who were just as hungry for territory as the Spanish.

The Spanish fort was made of adobe brick, and was armed with a dozen brass cannon. The U.S. Army blasted the cliff away and built Fort Point of granite and red brick, featuring three tiers of *casemates* (vaulted rooms housing cannon), and a *barbette* tier on the roof with additional guns and a sod covering to absorb the impact of enemy cannon fire. At its peak five hundred men manned 102 smooth-bore cannon (although the fort was designed for 141 cannon) and made San Francisco Bay the best defended body of water in the world...for at least a few weeks. After two hundred men spent eight years building the state-of-the-art fort, rifled barrel cannon made it obsolete as soon as it opened for business.

We'd take a break at the fort, for the restrooms and to take photographs of the spectacular views of the Golden Gate Bridge and the bay, and then, if we had time, I would typically lead my guests inside and give them an abbreviated tour of the courtyard and the powder magazine.

Cable Car Christopher at Fort Point with good old #25.

At that point the highlight of the tour was just around the corner, as we'd curl back up through the trees, past Pilots' Row, the houses in which the married officer pilots of Crissy Field formerly lived, and then up and around and across the Golden Gate Bridge. A very large minority of our passengers were from abroad, and many of them were visiting for the first time. For them, this was the highlight of their entire visit to San Francisco: riding across the Golden Gate Bridge on a cable car!

The weather at The Gate is usually cold and windy, even on sunny days. The only really warm days we got on the bridge were from August through October, but the rest of the year it was usually foggy, cold, and windy as hell...especially on an open-air cable car. My passengers would huddle together under blankets we provided and brave the conditions as best they could in a spirit of adventure. In the rain we also distributed disposable plastic ponchos, but everyone got thoroughly soaked anyway. After the first winter I had learned my lesson; I purchased a rather expensive head-to-toe Gor-Tex rain suit and a waterproof hat, and was the only *dry* driver at the company in inclement weather.

Our tours went out every day; in sunshine, blind fog, 45 mph winds, and driving rain. Almost everyone from outside of the Bay Area was surprised by how cold it is crossing the gate 245 feet above the water at 45 mph, but I loved the cold weather. I'm too old and too heavy and too hairy to be comfortable working in extreme heat. I thought I was gonna die working in ninety-degree temperatures every day in the Napa Valley. San Francisco's natural air-conditioning suited me just fine. I mean, you can always dress up, but you can only dress down so far...at least while you're working. In nice weather I wore a kilt, but I got tired of middle-aged married women peeking and grabbing as I climbed into my seat (yeah, you'd be surprised...it happened all the time). And the kilt was a definite liability on the windy cliff on the Marin side of the bridge, because that's where we headed next.

The Marin Headlands have several spectacular parking spots with absolutely incredible views of the bridge. I loved driving my passengers up the snake-like two-lane road, rattling off history to misdirect them. You see, as far as I'm concerned, if you can't scare the passengers a little, you're not truly showing them a good time. This would be the first of several spots at which I would use a bit of misdirection to make my passengers think they were about to die. The trick was in timing my remarks based upon the flow of traffic. Frequently my favorite parking spots would be filled, so I'd have to improvise a turn-around, or a stall, or just fill with historical information until a car got out of the way. But I could usually manage to get my guests thinking about something else at exactly the moment when I'd gun the engine across the road and head into the parking space.

What my passengers never realized is how far the front wheels were behind the front seat, under the trolley. See, the passengers all felt the front of the trolley was as far as we could go. But I knew that I was clear for eighteen inches up from the ground and for a good three feet behind the front window. In other words, as I distracted them with mind-numbing historical data or anecdotes, I'd be gunning the front of the trolley right over the curb and to the edge of the 300-foot cliff. To accentuate the surprise, I'd loudly ring the bell and shout on the mic, "Oh, my god, THE BRAKES ARE OUT! THE BRAKES ARE OUT!"

With my passengers screaming bloody murder, the passersby and photo bugs nearby would see that the wheels were well behind the curb, even though the front of the trolley *appeared* from the inside to be practically dangling over the edge of the cliff. Hey, anytime you can get your passengers to scream and onlookers to laugh (or vice-versa), you are offering an entertaining tour, to be sure.

We'd disembark on all but the foggiest days, and my passengers would have a chance to take some incredible pictures of themselves in front of the gorgeous Golden Gate Bridge. I'd usually take most of the pictures myself, because most people can't take a well-composed shot, and I wanted my bridge and my city and my trolley and my tour to shine in their memories. My favorite, trademark gag was my cliff shots with the passengers. Invariably one of my passengers would ask to pose with me in a picture, and I'd say, "do you want to take an *Adventure*

Shot?" Considering their heart rates were just now returning to normal from my last hair-raising stunt, some were a bit reluctant to do anything that I considered *an adventure.*

I'd usually find one or more hearty souls to join me, though, and I'd take them to the edge of the cliff. Well, this was not actually the *edge* of a *cliff.* It was a slight rise in the ground with the Golden Gate Bridge looming in the background, and, from the lens of a camera held near the ground, the effect was that we were falling off the cliff. We'd lay down on the ground with our feet pointing toward the bridge and our heads toward the camera. We'd extend our arms in front of us and grab the rocky soil in front of us, and then I'd encourage them to look horrified and scream bloody murder! As they did this, I'd take one hand and grab the back of their jackets or shirts, as if I was pulling them to safety. This always made for a great shot, and then every other formerly timid soul on the trolley would want to also pose for *The Adventure Shot.*

**Cable Car Christopher helping Rebecca and Alan Quinn
to survive "The Adventure Shot."**

After driving back across the bridge to San Francisco's Presidio, I'd take them to Langdon Court, overlooking the Golden Gate, and show them some of the concrete gun bunkers at Battery Godfrey that were part of the coastal defense of the harbor from the Civil War through WWII, and tell them about the several nearby Nike Nuclear Missile bases which took over the task as part of the doctrine known as Mutually Assured Destruction during the Cold War.

We'd drive by the glorious Pacific Coast WWII War Memorial, the spacious home of General Frederick Funston, who commanded the fighting of the San Francisco Fire of 1906 and housed thousands of city residents on the Presidio in the months thereafter, and past the Golden Gate Club, formerly the non-commissioned officer's club, which has hosted historic treaty signings, important corporate meetings, fancy fundraisers, and myriad weddings.

We'd then enter the Main Post, which is a broad, open expanse surrounded by historic buildings, including the Spanish officer's club, with adobe walls constructed in the 1790s, and the Montgomery Street barracks, aka Infantry Row, the nation's first brick barracks, which were constructed in the 1890s after the Indian Wars and housed our troops through World War II. One of those buildings was converted into the fascinating Walt Disney Family Museum during the time I was doing daily tours (www.WaltDisney.org).

Also at the Main Post is the old powder magazine, and the site of the home of General John "Black Jack" Pershing, which burned to the ground while he was chasing Francisco "Pancho" Villa across the Texas / Mexico border. The fire claimed the lives of his wife, Frances, and their three daughters, Helen, Ann, and little Mary Margaret; only the general's 6-year-old son, Warren, survived.

We'd then head out the Presidio gate and up an extremely steep block of Pacific Avenue (a 13% grade, to be precise), on which I'd pretend as though the cable car was not going to make it to the top, to the horror/delight of the passengers. We were now in Pacific Heights, one of the three most expensive places in which to live in San Francisco, and our cable car would slowly pass the

Lyon Street "Billionaires' Steps" down to the security-camera-bedecked roof of the seventeen-million-dollar home of the former San Francisco mayor, U.S. Senator Diane Feinstein, one block below at the west end of Vallejo Street. We'd drive along the "Gold Coast" stretch of Broadway Street (also known as "Billionaires' Row") from Lyon Street at the edge of the Presidio, past Baker Street and the crazy zig-zag driveway for 2798 Broadway Street (which actually goes down what should be down Broderick Street), and then to Divisidero Street.

Along the way we passed the stately six-million-dollar home of composer Gordon Getty (www.GordonGetty.com) and his wife, Ann, at 2880 Broadway Street, the living room of which was fictitiously spoiled by a famously grisly murder in the 1992 Michael Douglas / Sharon Stone thriller *Basic Instinct*. The Gettys have hosted the likes of Presidents Barack Obama and Bill Clinton, Spain's King Juan Carlos and Queen Sofía, England's Princess Margaret, opera stars Plácido Domingo and Luciano Pavarotti, and ballet dancer Rudolf Nureyev. The Gettys and their staff and doggies would sometimes be outside, and would always smile and wave at our cable car as we drove by.

A couple of doors down is 2850 Broadway Street, the seven-million-dollar, high-tech, silver box house of Oracle CEO Larry Ellison and his then-wife, Melanie Craft, featuring spooky liquid crystal "smart windows" that go from transparent to opaque right before your eyes, accented with white and green nighttime laser lights. On two separate occasions I saw Steve Jobs coming out of Larry's house, in his trademark big ol' blue jeans and black long-sleeve turtleneck t-shirt, and both times got him to wave at my passengers.

Across the street in an eighteen million dollar home at 2835 Broadway Street live Oracle heiress Nicola Miner and her husband, writer Robert Mailer Anderson, who, when I'd ring my trolley bell, would sometimes activate their six-foot-tall *and well-hung* garage-top kinetic sculpture robot, "Goliath" by artist Nemo Gould. They were also nice people who would always smile and wave when they were outside.

*No, this is **not** Steve Jobs, but Nemo Gould's anatomically-correct
(and rather well-endowed) robot, Goliath, above the garage of
Robert Mailer Anderson and Nicola Miner at 2835 Broadway Street.*

The intersection of Broadway and Divisidero in San Francisco is one of those spots where even the locals pause to take a look around. It's the top of the hill, with dramatic downhills to the north and the east. So steep, in fact, that we would frequently find semi-tractor-trailer rigs stuck on the crest of the hill. It's almost hard to fathom until you see it, but professional truck drivers from outside the Bay Area would use G.P.S., or Thomas Brothers or A.A.A. maps, which would make the neighborhood seem so simple: rectangular blocks in all directions with right angles at each intersection. With no local knowledge it's not hard to understand how a professional truck driver could get himself and his rig into a lot of trouble. Especially if he's paying more attention to the map than to the elevation.

On a regular basis, truckers would find themselves stuck in a residential neighborhood surrounded by breathtaking drops on all sides, and no way out except to back up ten or fifteen blocks, which you just can't do when you're hauling a trailer with a Peterbilt. As a result, they'd try making a ninety degree turn down a grade that's so steep that the front props on the trailer grind themselves into the pavement and lift the back of the tractor off the ground.

The Atlas Towing Company in San Francisco used to provide all our towing services, because at seven tons and more than thirty feet in length, our cable cars necessitated a big-rig tow; and with a fleet of sixty vintage cars from fifty- to one-hundred-years-old, we got towed a lot. One night my cable car died at the intersection of Broadway and Van Ness, and the wait was extraordinarily long. When he finally arrived, the tow man apologized and said that when he got the call he was hoisting one such errant trucker off the crest of that aforementioned intersection. Mind you, I had seen that happen to another truck just six hours before that very afternoon! I asked him just how many times a month they had to do that, and he told me they had to help at least two truckers a month on average from just that one intersection at Broadway and Divisidero.

The Teamsters' Quandry.

So, we were at the top of that intersection, 328 feet above sea level, but because our eastbound approach was nearly level, as was Divisidero to the south, my passengers didn't really notice as we approached that we were teetering at the top of a very tall hill. Heading eastbound the view to your left, to the north, is absolutely amazing. The hill is so steep, it appears as if the ground simply disappears. You can see the bay and Angel Island and Alcatraz and Marin County in the distance, but you can't see anything but rooftops within a mile, because it's all three hundred feet below you.

When we reached this intersection, I would stop, wait for cross traffic, and then roll into the intersection and physically point to the left and verbally tell everyone, "Take a look at this incredible view to the left . . ." At this point, as they ooo'ed and awe'd at an 18% grade, I would slide through the intersection, jam it into first gear, and then gun it at the top of the hill to the east, and the cable car would literally drop beneath my passengers' butts as we went straight down a 15% grade that is almost as steep as the one I had told them to look at. They would scream and laugh, and, while in first gear we weren't going faster than 10 mph, the engine was working so hard that it was louder than usual, and with me ringing the bell and shouting over the microphone, "IT'S THE BRAKES AGAIN; THE BRAKES ARE OUT," my passengers were getting another adrenaline rush.

When they regained their composure, I'd point out the six-million-dollar home at 2640 Broadway Street of then Speaker of the House, Nancy Pelosi. You know, it's funny, we're used to seeing images in the media of liberal protestors outside the homes and offices of conservative politicians, but on various occasions middle-aged female members of Code Pink were encamped outside Pelosi's home, and when she came out one morning, boy, was she was angry! She must have thought, "How dare they protest outside MY house? I'm a Democrat...and a woman!" Looked great for my passengers, though. What a photo opp! Liberal protest at Nancy Pelosi's house. Who wouldn't want a few shots of that in their vacation album?

So, down the hill we'd head, and wind our way around a bit, past Danielle Steele's house and the *Mrs. Doubtfire* house, and eventually the cable car tour would cross Van Ness. I would tell my guests about how in 1906 General Frederick Funston ordered a full city block on either side of this broad avenue dynamited to keep the great fire from burning across town. The plan, along with a soft drizzle and a shift in the wind, succeeded at stopping the fire, but all those regular G.I.s were usin' dynamite, with which they had no training, and almost caused as much damage as if the fire had been left to its own devices.

I'd also point out old St. Brigid Roman Catholic Church, which survived the 1906 earthquake and fire (and Gen. Funston's dynamite), but suffered damage in the 1989 Loma Prieta Earthquake and needed seven million dollars in repairs and maintenance. The archdiocese, deep in financial need due to settlements in the Catholic priest sex abuse scandal, decided to cash-out, despite the desperate pleas of parishioners, and the real-estate-hungry Academy of Art University snatched it up and was giving classes inside.

At this point there were two different directions I used to take, depending on the time of day and traffic. One route was south on Van Ness to California Street, and then east up and over Nob Hill. But my original route continued straight into the Broadway tunnel, which connected the Western Addition to the Financial District, and which, on an open-air cable car in broad daylight, was relatively dark and spooky.

Except for the clanging and echoing of our brass bell, the tunnel could also have been boring, because there was nothing for my passengers to look at; so, with the cable car speakers bouncing the sound off of the tunnel's concrete walls and ceiling, I would ring the bell as we entered and then sing an accelerated and abbreviated version of the spooky, haunting Gene Wilder boat song from the original 1971 movie *Willy Wonka and the Chocolate Factory*:

> Round the world and home again
> That's the sailor's way
> Faster faster, faster faster
>
> There's no earthly way of knowing
> Which direction we are going

There's no knowing where we're rowing
Or which way the river's flowing

Is it raining, is it snowing
Is a hurricane a-blowing

Not a speck of light is showing
So the danger must be growing
Are the fires of Hell a-glowing?
Is the grisly reaper mowing?

Yes, the danger must be growing
For the rowers keep on rowing
And they're certainly not showing
Any signs that they are slowing

At the conclusion I'd cackle as Margaret Hamilton's witch from *The Wizard of Oz*, "E-he-he-he! I'll get you, Dorothy, and your little dog, too! E-he-he-he!" As we exited my cackling echoed through the tunnel with the clang of the bell.

Funny thing happened in that tunnel one day. Funny for the passengers, that is, and scary for me. A young newlywed couple was sitting in the front right corner at my two o'clock (as the two to four front passengers actually sat ahead of the driver in the cable car). They seemed to be having a good time, but when we got into the tunnel, the girl suddenly screamed bloody murder. "MY RING, MY RING...I LOST MY RING!" Her wedding ring had apparently slipped right off her finger and down to the running board below, and was bouncing along as we drove through the tunnel.

Now, I couldn't stop in the tunnel. The speed limit is 35 mph, and that's what I always drive in there, but cars in the left hand lane always seem to think this is a Lady Diana / paparazzi tunnel, and they punch it and whiz by much, much faster. There was also on the right a raised concrete sidewalk with a steel railing about the same height as the top brass bar on our cable car, and only a few feet away. Without a word the valiant young groom jumped clean over the brass bar, down onto the running board, scooped up the ring (with the steel railing on the sidewalk literally inches from his back), and then back over the brass bar and into his seat. As he slipped the ring back on her finger, the crowd on the trolley cheered . . .and my heart was beating almost out of my chest.

After the tunnel we'd head south along Stockton Street through Chinatown, where I'd point out the humor of the many misspelled shop signs, monstrous throngs of people, and live fish, dead birds, and roasted mammals floating, hanging, and turning in the store windows, and then we went through the Stockton Tunnel to Union Square, where my passengers would marvel at the famous department stores, exclusive shops, and racy billboards. Lots of history there, too, what with the historic St Francis Hotel that survived the 1906 earthquake and fire, and the 1901 Admiral Dewey Monument, topped by a nine-foot-tall statue of the young, beautiful "Big Alma" de Bretteville Spreckels, the real-life six-foot-tall "Great Grandmother of San Francisco" and descendant of Napoleon Bonaparte, who posed for the Robert Ingersoll Aitken statue as a starving young nude model before she met her "Sugar Daddy," Adolph B. Spreckels, the sugar baron.

Then it was up through the Chinatown gate and along historic Grant Street, and west on California Street, up three blocks and a 14% grade to the top of Nob Hill at 324 feet above the bay, to see the truly decadent Flood Mansion, survivor of the Great 1906 Earthquake, since 1889 the home of the exclusive and ultra-conservative Pacific-Union Club, and the last-remaining home of the era of the Big Four railroad barons, Stanford, Crocker, Hopkins, and Huntington.

To the west is incredible Grace Cathedral with its 24-carat-gold Lorenzo Ghiberti doors (replicas, actually, since 1990), forty-four bell carillon, labrynths, and *Bullitt* and *Family Plot* movie credits, plus the spectacularly artistic Veterans' Memorial Auditorium. Also on Nob Hill are two world-famous hotels: the Mark Hopkins with its sky-scraping "Top of the Mark" nightclub, and the Fairmont, where Sean Connery threw the FBI agent off the penthouse balcony in the movie *The Rock*, and where Tony Bennett first sang "I Left My Heart in San Francisco."

The Flood Mansion and the Fairmont Hotel were the only two buildings on Nob Nill to survive the 1906 earthquake, although they were both gutted by the fire and rebuilt. Across Sacramento Street from the Fairmont is the apartment building that was the residence of Kim Novak's character in the 1958 Alfred Hitchcock thriller, *Vertigo*, starring Jimmy Stewart as the SFPD detective-turned-stalker on psychological disability.

My favorite part of Nob Hill, though, was once again misdirecting my passengers' attention down a couple of very steep streets. On my alternate route we'd head south on Mason Street, and at 308 feet above sea level I would point to the east on my left and say, "Look at that incredible view down California Street through Chinatown and to the Financial District."

On my original route we'd be heading north on Mason, and I'd point to the east, on my right, down Sacramento Street. In both cases I drove us off a much steeper cliff; the grade down from Nob Hill to the next block north at Clay is a 15% drop (49.2 feet down in 1/10 of a mile). You remember cartoon cars going off a cliff, and how the characters' hats would linger in the air as they dropped? That's how it felt. The screams could be heard for blocks.

We'd drop two blocks down an 18% grade on Mason Street to the Cable Car Barn and Museum, where the cable cars *that are still attached to the ground* are powered. You can step in the door and for free watch the monstrous gears spinning those steel cables all over San Francisco at precisely 9.5 mph. We'd then cut over through North Beach, where Francis Ford Coppola's restaurant, Jack Kerouac's Alley, and Carol Doda's boobs are legendary landmarks, and where Washington Square played host to cinema history time and time again.

Across from Washington Square Park is Saints Peter & Paul Church, known as The Italian Cathedral of the West, where Joe DiMaggio had his wedding photos taken with Marilyn Monroe, and where his funeral was held, as well. It's also where Cecil B. DeMille shot one scene of *The Ten Commandments* in 1923, Dirty Harry Callahan shot a scumbag in Dirty Harry I (*Dirty Harry*, 1971) and prevented a self-immolation in Dirty Harry V (*The Dead Pool*, 1988), and where Whoopi Goldberg played a hip R&B nun in *Sister Act 2: Back in the Habit* in 1993.

An hour later I'd do another two-hour tour, and then after another hour I'd do it all over again. It was fun, it was lucrative, but it was repetitive. And on the best days the traffic was awful, but on the worst days it was unbearable.

RIDE THE DUCKS

If Arnold Stirewalt Gridley was the father of the motorized cable cars, Christine Gridley was their sister. She managed the company when her father passed away, but her dad was the one with the real passion for the business. One day she received an offer she couldn't refuse from Herschend Family Entertainment of Norcross, Georgia, outside of Atlanta. Founded near Branson, Missouri in 1950, HFE owns, operates, and manages twenty-six themed entertainment properties across ten states, including Dolly Parton's Dixie Stampede, Dollywood, and Splash Country, plus Silver Dollar City, and Ride the Ducks in Branson, Philadelphia, Stone Mountain, Newport, and San Francisco.

Duck Guide Captain Chrome and Truck Duck 5.

Ride the Ducks started in Branson in 1977 and now carries over a million guests annually in their ninety vehicles, as the nation's largest amphibious tour vehicle manufacturer and operator. They started with World War II DUKW amphibious vehicles converted to tour busses, and then went on to manufacture their own longer ducks using milk truck chassis. The tours are patterned after the atmosphere aboard Disneyland's Jungle Cruise, and include some marginal history in a duck soup of quacky jokes, silly puns, loud music, and passenger quacking with plastic, patented "quackers" given to all.

As I'd been driving livery vehicles and doing tours since 2001, I was ready for a new challenge when the Duck People took over. I loved my cable car tour, but doing three daily two-hour tours four days a week in heavy traffic was getting repetitive, and I didn't want to get burned-out. I thought the ducks looked like a great way to stay fresh in my tour guide skills without retiring from cable car duties. The Duck People seemed nice enough...a little TOO nice, in fact. There was something kind of sugary-sweet, Lawrence Welk / Mr. Rogers about them, but I couldn't figure out what it was...until the orientation.

They got us all into a meeting room one day on board the historic 1927 ferry boat *Santa Rosa* on Pier 3. The room was equipped with bagels and donuts and juice and coffee. There were about a dozen of us, and a motley crew we were. Three of the drivers were over sixty-five years of age. Experience, yes, but they were older than my parents.

Henry Schaeffer was the lead driver. He was over seventy-years-old, but trim, fit, and handsome; a Summer-of-Love hippie who nonetheless today looks like a respectable grandpa, and had been doing cable car tours for Gridley since 1969. Henry had weathered decades of heavy traffic, political protests, police actions, myriad natural disasters, shootings, bombings, and some equally trying workplace upheavals, including a situation in which a number of his fellow drivers tried to organize and pursue collective bargaining. Old Arnold Gridley fired them all; and later faced a judge and had to re-hire them and pay some stiff fines. Henry Schaeffer managed to ride this storm for decades, and had become one of San Francisco's best respected tour guides among his many professional peers.

Also on staff were a number of felons who were paying their debts to society and had found their way to our company because Christine Gridley liked to hire staff from the Delancey Street Foundation, an excellent San Francisco non-profit offering residential rehabilitation services and vocational training for all felons except sex offenders. The forty-year-old organization used the labor of its own resident clients in 1989-91 to build a beautiful, modern, 370,000 square-foot complex of buildings on the Embarcadero near the San Francisco Giants' ballpark. Delancey Street houses a restaurant, café, catering company, bookstore, auto maintenance facility, and moving company, in addition to apartment space for five hundred clients.

While Delancey Street started in San Francisco in 1971, it has since expanded to include Los Angeles, New Mexico, North Carolina, and New York. The average Delancey client has a history that includes sixteen years of substance abuse, four prison sentences, gang membership, no skills, functional illiteracy, and no job held longer than six months. They sign their futures over to Delancey president and CEO Mimi Silbert, and are literally in the program's custody 24/7, working in the program's businesses, learning trades, and living on the premises, leaving only on business, until the completion of their original sentences. If they can't get with the program, or if they commit or threaten to commit any act of violence, or use any controlled substance, it's back to prison.

These people are in the program for from two to four years, and all earn high school GEDs, and can even earn bachelor of arts degrees. Each client also acquires marketable job skills, and may choose three of the following fields: food services, construction, auto maintenance, bookkeeping, printing, advertising, retail sales, and, of course, truck and livery driving. And, while our Delancey employees were, generally, diligent, motivated, and friendly, they did certainly give our crew a collective "worldly" appearance that no doubt put-off the Duck People a bit.

Our ops manager under the Gridleys was Charles Palm, who was one of the best bosses I ever had in my life. He continued a while under the Duck People, but did, certainly, have kind of a wordly feel about him. HFE figured that he wasn't "corporate" enough to continue...big mistake on their part. Last I saw him he was still driving cable cars for the company, though. The new general manager of our franchise was Cory Roebuck, who was an up-and-coming HFE executive with Bay Area roots and, at the time, a decade of experience in theme park management. He was a bright, personable, energetic young fellow about whom I can't say enough nice things; he's the other greatest boss I ever had in my life. Cory was a former police officer, and an Emergency Medical Technician, and is as of this writing the general manager of HFE's Silver Dollar City in Branson Missouri. Cory's boss, Chris Herschend, vice chairman of the board of HFE and the majority owner and president of Ride the Ducks, was also a very nice man. But in personality he reminded me a bit of Jerry Mathers of *Leave it to Beaver*, about whom I spoke earlier.

Back to the infamous orientation. You see, as the Herschend Family Entertainment orientation commenced, we were told that HFE was a company that operated based upon "Christian values and ethics." The presentation included a video which featured the all-male management team hugging and holding hands and praying. In fact, the praying and preaching and proselytizing went on at some length...an uncomfortable length for most of us. After all, this was not a church service; this was our workplace. These people just bought our company and were now our employers. Besides, this was San Francisco, the land of the free and the home of the independent-minded, progressive, rebellious, and politically correct.

My stomach was in my throat, because I loved my job, but this firm's religious views had no pertinence to my job. Fortunately, I didn't have to be the first to speak. As soon as the video closed, Henry Schaeffer launched into a tirade, telling the Duck People in no uncertain terms that they had no right to come here and buy our company and then try to shove their spiritual philosophies down our throats, especially in San Francisco. Next in seniority was the second to chime in, Dan "The Man" Callahan, a crusty old Irishman and veteran tour guide, who, like Henry, never took shit from anyone in his life. Dan said, "I'm not a Christian; I'm an artist," and went on to tell them they had no right to show such an offensive video during a compulsory employee orientation. The third speaker was another old coot who was third in seniority, and then I took my turn.

I told them directly that showing us this video created a hostile working environment that was a veiled effort to collude us into accepting their religion to keep our jobs. I told them that we would take legal action if that video was ever shown again, and that if any retribution was enacted upon any of us every newspaper, radio, and television reporter in the country would be getting our story. Furthermore, I said something to the effect of, "I know you guys feel that because you're Christians, you're right, and there's no reason for anyone to object, but please try to see this from our perspective. You come to our town and buy our company and own our jobs. You imply that you expect us to adopt your 'Christian values and ethics' in order to keep our jobs. Imagine that OUR company came to Branson, Missouri, and bought YOU. And then we showed a video in which all the men kissed each other and said, 'We are a queer-based San Francisco company with queer values and ethics.' Do you feel that gnawing in your stomach right now as I say this? That is exactly how we all feel right now. That is a hostile work environment. You can not come to San Francisco in 2008 and show us this video. It's not legal, it's not professional, and it will not be tolerated."

Both Cory and Chris fell all over themselves apologizing and telling us that in no respect did they mean that we had to adopt their religion. They said that this was a new video, and they didn't know all that praying was in it, and they assured us that it would never be shown again. I was satisfied with their response, whether it was sincere or not. But a number of my co-workers were not. Several of the drivers stood right up and told the Duck People that they refused to work for a company that attempted to proselytize them right at the orientation, and then they walked right out.

I went home that day and told my husband that I was probably going to lose this job. Even if they didn't just flat-out fire me right off the bat, they certainly would not be tolerant of my improvised jokes and independent and irreverent manner. But Chris Herschend took my tour and gave me a great review, telling me that he'd never met another tour guide with a better recall of facts and a more fun and enthusiastic delivery. Although Cory told me that he did ask him, "Do we really need to point out the Fisherman's Wharf Hooter's restaurant on our tour?" I lasted two more years at the company, having a wonderful time in my cable cars and ducks, and was actually awarded the "Quacktastic" award as the best employee at the end of their first year owning the company. In fact, that brings to mind a whole other story.

DAVE AND CHRIS HEAD EAST

Ride the Ducks offered me, as "Quacktastic" award winner for 2008, a trip for two to any one of the company's franchises. I was encouraged by management to visit the company headquarters in Branson, but I didn't care as much about duck tours, amusement parks, and country music as I did about history. I decided that if I went to Philadelphia or Boston, I could make side-trips to other big cities and make the most out of what may be my only chance to see New England...all expenses paid, anyway.

Now, my dad was a member of a fantastic drill team during his time at Santa Rosa High School. They were called The Campions, and they were national champions in the 1950s. That was the only time my dad had ever been east of Colorado. My one trip to Detroit on the Fruitopia Tour in the summer of 1994 with my second wife was as far east as I'd been in the United States. My husband didn't want to take the time off of work, so I asked the Old Man if he'd like to see The Big Apple and the White House, and he said he was game. After checking maps and logistics, I chose Philadelphia as our destination, and our travel arrangements were made by HFE. My dad and I packed, and, on the appointed day, I picked him up at his house and we were off to see the wizard!

I talked at some length about my dad earlier, but I didn't say too much about his personality. He's one of the nicest, friendliest, funniest guys you'd ever wanna meet. I don't mean funny as in pestering you with jokes about "a priest, a minister, and a rabbi," and I don't mean funny as in twisting every single word around and making a stupid pun out of every sentence. I mean he's the kind of guy who can laugh about almost anything. Nothing's sacred, nothing humiliates him, nothing is too far beneath him or too far above him, nothing is too old or too new, or inappropriate. He'll laugh about almost anything almost any time. That much, at least, we have in common. I certainly have been scolded by my mother, grandmother, sister, teachers, girlfriends and girl friends alike (in fact, by all women in general), for being inappropriate, childish, base, crude, loud, indelicate, nasty, brash, obnoxious, and generally a dirty little boy. Mind you, those women all laughed at me, too, but they are women; so, by definition, they have to draw very dark lines around what they can and what they can't laugh about. That's the rule, right?

My dad is where I picked up the stubbing-the-toe gag into every door, wall, furniture leg, and dropped object, and the hitting-the-head gag into every door jam, window, wall, and major appliance. He got this Laurel & Hardy, Three Stooges, Kramden & Norton crap from the movies, and television, and *his* old man, and all of his older brothers. It's kind of the family heritage. So...you put these two guys on an airplane together, and busses and trains, and what's gonna happen? It's a wonder the T.S.A. didn't haul us away. And it's a good thing we didn't bring "The Wives," because there were no dirty looks when we stubbed our toes and hit our heads and flirted with the ticket gal, and the T.S.A. ladies, and the flight attendants, etcetera. In short--we had a wonderful time.

I had also been a professional tour guide and bus driver long enough to know that you don't rent a car in a strange city and set out on your own unless you've got ample time to explore. We had just one day each in Philadelphia,

Manhattan, and D.C., so we took bus tours and crammed in as much of each city as was humanly possible. And we saw it all. Well, almost. In New York we didn't get to the Statue of Liberty, but we saw it from the Empire State Building, and we took the subway and walked across the Brooklyn Bridge. In D.C. we didn't see the Smithsonian or the Lincoln Memorial or the Pentagon, but we saw everything else of importance, including President Obama flying right off the White House south lawn and over our heads in Marine One (along with its decoy in the "presidential shell game," as the Secret Service refers to this misdirection which is their standard operating procedure). And in the evening after our Philly Duck tour, while my tired dad watched a Philadelphia Eagles game on the television in the hotel room (live from their stadium that we could also see from our window), I took a self-guided walking tour of the City of Brotherly Love.

Christopher and David Linnell ravaging the East Coast
under the watchful eye of the U.S. Secret Service.

THE SONOMA VALLEY WINE TROLLEY

So in 2010 I took five months off to write my screenplay, and when I was done I took a job delivering packages for FedEx Home and Ground. That job was a ball. I got great exercise and didn't have to be funny and talking all day. I drove around Wine Country every day in comfortable clothes petting dogs and cats and horses and goats and catching people in towels coming out of the shower. With no passengers on board I could listen to music and smoke my cigars and fart and sing and swear to my heart's content.

I delivered packages to my ex-wife and school friends and former clients and to Tommy Smothers and Joe Montana. I loved that job...except for the hours. 7 a.m. to 7 or 8 p.m., sometimes later; once 'til after 11 p.m. No overtime, no health insurance, no sick days. I worked through high fever and back pain, in the heat and the cold and the rain and the snow. The company treats their contractors as bitches, and the contractors treat their drivers as slaves. In the fall of 2013 I'll be back at it again, but with a contractor who makes sure I finish at a reasonable hour.

Wine tours meant less freedom, but more money. So in 2011 I worked for a Napa limousine company, but I truly missed my cable cars. I spent two years working for FIDM, the Fashion Institute of Design and Merchandising in San Francisco at www.FIDM.edu, speaking in local high schools on a variety of topics relating to FIDM majors and prepared within the framework of the California State Curriculum for Education. As is the case with FedEx, each job I choose allows me to drive around and meet new people every day.

One day I was looking through job listings on Craig's List, and I saw an ad that piqued my interest. Somebody was hiring trolley drivers...in SONOMA! This was less than a half-hour from my home, with no daily commute traffic; a far cry from the monster commute to and from San Francisco during rush hour morning and evening. I was so excited that I couldn't see straight. I thought I'd never get to drive a motorized cable car again unless I moved to San Francisco, which was never gonna happen. I mean, I love San Francisco, but, let's face it: I love the MOON, but I wouldn't wanna live there, either!

JOHNSON CAT CLOWDER

Here's a very long story with a very happy ending. For the first few months of my work as a tour guide aboard the Sonoma Valley Wine Trolley, I made daily visits to historic Buena Vista winery. You see, my wine tours were at least as much about history as they were about wine. After having done wine tours for several years throughout Napa, Sonoma, the Russian River and Healdsburg's Dry Creek and Alexander Valleys, I had a firm foundation in wine history when I started doing San Francisco history tours aboard my beloved motorized cable cars in 2007. When I learned in 2011 that there was a wine trolley in Sonoma, I jumped at the chance to do a tour that combined history and wine, on a motorized cable car, and just twenty miles away from my home.

Cable Car Christopher and the Sonoma Valley Wine Trolley.

One of our daily winery stops was Buena Vista Winery, ground zero for the history of wine in Northern California. Founded in 1857 by Hungarian entrepreneur "Count" Agoston Haraszthy, Buena Vista was, in the fall of 2010, a bucolic spot nestled next to a babbling brook in a heavily wooded canyon next to Bartholomew Park. After recent renovations by Jean-Charles Boisset, who purchased the place in June of 2010, it is today a more barren, but more historically accurate and quite architecturally and artistically beautiful place.

Jean-Charles runs a large family company (www.BoissetFamilyEstates.com) founded by his father, Jean-Claude, who was one of the few French winemakers who truly loved California wines. I was on hand one day when Jean-Charles told the story of his parents bringing him and his sister to Buena Vista when they were kids. While their parents tasted the wine, Jean-Charles and his sister explored the old caves, dug by hand into the hillside by Haraszthy's Chinese workers. Jean-Charles regaled his sister with stories of cowboys and Indians, and told her, "One day you and I will come here...and make wine." Buying the property was that childhood dream finally fulfilled.

Photographs prove that Buena Vista was, indeed, a much more barren spot in 1857, when purchased by Haraszthy, who had been looking across the United States for the perfect place to grow wine grapes. He had first attempted to make wine in Wisconsin, where he founded the village of Széptaj, later known as Haraszthy or Haraszthyville, and today called Sauk City. But the short, cool summer and long, cold winter were not the right environment for wine grapes. He moved the family west with the Gold Rush, and tried to make a go of vineyards in San Diego where he became the town's first marshal and the county sheriff, but the climate was far too warm and dry for wine grapes. After serving a brief stint as a state assemblyman, he moved the family to San Francisco, where he became the first U.S. assayer at the San Francisco Mint. He once again attempted growing wine vines near the Mission San Francisco de Asís (known today as Mission Dolores) and near what is now the Crystal Springs Reservoir on the San Francisco peninsula. Too foggy there, however.

When he finally made his way up to the town of Sonoma, Haraszthy finally found what he was looking for: dry, hot, sunny afternoons, and cool, humid, foggy mornings. The soil was loaded with minerals, and the land was wide open and perfect for vineyards. Haraszthy befriended Sonoma's founder, "General" Mariano Guadalupe Vallejo, who was also the town's preeminent winemaker at the time.

Vallejo was the comandante general of Mexican California at San Francisco's Presidio when he was ordered to push the northern frontier farther to Sonoma, and was ordered by his government to secularize the town's Franciscan mission in 1834. Vallejo turned the sanctuary into a winery, using indigenous grapes found in the valley by Padre Jose Altamira in June of 1823, when Altamira first arrived in the valley and founded the northernmost mission in the twenty-one mission chain along California's El Camino Real.

Haraszthy wasn't happy with "Mission Grapes," as they were then known, however. He wanted real European character for his wine. Other vintners were using European Zinfandel grapes, but Haraszthy wanted diversity. The California Viticultural Society published a nineteen-page report written in 1858 by Haraszthy about European varietals and winemaking techniques which was entitled, "Report on Grapes and Wine of California." It was well-received by vintners up and down the state, and he was appointed commissioner by the governor of California to return to Europe and learn as much as he could to help boost the California wine industry.

Haraszthy made the trip in 1861, accumulated one hundred thousand cuttings of over three hundred varieties of wine, brought them back all the way around the horn, and in 1862 returned to Sonoma and began planting them at Buena Vista, and distributing them throughout the state of California. It is for this reason that Count Agoston Haraszthy is to this day regarded as the "Father of California Viticulture."

However, the state of California failed to follow through with financial support it promised for his work, and with rising debt Haraszthy found difficulty keeping his head above water at Buena Vista. In 1863 San Francisco banker William Ralston fronted a group of investors, called the Buena Vista Viticultural Society, who infused the winery with the capital that Haraszthy needed.

But the vines were turning brown, as they had become infested with the minuscule phylloxera bug by 1866 (which the well-intentioned count had likely brought unknowingly on his vines from Europe), and Haraszthy, who had been accused several times before of chicanery, found that his newfound backers had lost confidence in him, accusing him of recklessly mismanaging Buena Vista. They forced him off the property, and he moved his family to a rum plantation he had purchased in Nicaragua, and disappeared the following year, supposedly falling victim to the crocodile denizens of a river on his new jungle farm.

One of the directors of The Buena Vista Viticulture Society was San Francisco businessman Robert C. Johnson, and it was in 1879 that Johnson and his wife, Kate Birdsall Johnson, bought Buena Vista, and in the following year built a monstrous Gothic Victorian "castle" on the property in which to live with their adopted and disabled daughter, Rosalind. In addition to being very rich, the Johnsons were considered rather eccentric. They weren't interested in making wine, they loved the environment, they loved animals, and they used the old stone winery buildings as stables for their horses and donkeys. And Kate had all these cats; Persians and Angoras. Hoards of cats, in fact.

In October of 1888 Kate received an urgent cablegram from her husband, who was on a business trip in Paris. He indicated that he was extremely ill. She rushed to France to be at his side, and was with him when he died the following March, leaving her in his will half of his estate, including the castle.

Kate returned home to Sonoma, and, the following year, their daughter, Rosalind, died of tuberculosis. All alone in the castle, except for servants and her pets, Kate was undoubtedly quite lonely. To "amuse" the cats, she also kept parrots and cockatoos, and even housed on the property donkeys, which she had obtained from Jerusalem. She asserted that they were the actual descendants of Christ's ass (or, perhaps I should say, the ass that bore Christ).

Kate heard about a 35-year-old Austrian artist named Carl Kahler who had recently arrived in San Francisco from Melbourne, Australia, where he had been commissioned to paint pictures of racing yachts. He also had developed an international reputation for his oil paintings of race horses...and cats. Kate was intrigued, and sent for young Kahler, who was famous, but poor, and was traveling around the world in search of rich patrons, such as Kate.

He arrived at the castle in Sonoma to find some forty-two cats occupying one entire floor of the mansion. Kate commissioned Kahler to paint a portrait of her cats, which was completed in 1891, at a price of $5,000. At 6' x 8.5' the oil painting is huge, but sold subsequent to Kate's death in 1893 for as little as $500. It was last offered for sale in 2002, however, for from $450,000-750,000 by art expert, auctioneer, and cat fancier Kaja Veilleux of www.ThomastonAuction.com in Thomaston, Maine. The title of the painting was inspired by a phrase commonly used by Robert Johnson prior to his death to describe his wife's cats: "My Wife's Lovers."

Kate Johnson would today likely be considered a cat *hoarder* fit for reality television, but she had a home in which she could easily accommodate and properly care for several dozen Persian and Angora cats. Local legend had it that Kate hoarded as many as two hundred cats, but, according to F. Turner Reuter, Jr., author of *Animal and Sporting Artists in America* (2008), "at the time of her death (she) had thirty-two cats and may have had as many as forty-six at one point." Reuter wrote about Carl Kahler, who was living in San Francisco from 1890-93 while he worked on this portrait. In fact, the portrait was for sale in a San Francisco art studio when the 1906 earthquake and subsequent fire occurred, and it was one of the few paintings to miraculously survive the disasters.

As for the cats, Kate had stipulated in her own will that the castle and a full third of her estate should pass, upon her death (which occurred in 1893), to the local Roman Catholic archdiocese to be used as a home for disadvantaged women. But she also bequeathed twenty thousand dollars to a distant relative to use to care for the cats in perpetuity. The relative certainly took care of the cash, but the cats may have been left to care for themselves.

The church let the property sit untouched until 1920, at which point it was sold to the state of California, which used the so-called Johnson Castle as the "State Farm for Delinquent Women," namely prostitutes, drug addicts, con artists, and petty thieves. One of the "wayward women" supposedly torched the mansion in 1927. It burned to the ground, and the Johnson cats were forced to live in the wild on the property as a feral clowder.

Now, you must be wondering through this long story what the connection is to Cable Car Christopher. Well, as I said, I used to visit Buena Vista Winery four days a week when I was hosting tours aboard the Sonoma Valley Wine Trolley. There was a fat, furry, black, feral Angora cat on the property who would come out occasionally and stretch in the afternoon sun. Staff members told me there had been dozens in years past, but somebody had trapped and neutered them all, and, through attrition, and occasional adoptions, the dozens had diminished to just this one, whom they'd aptly named, "Fluffy."

Some days Fluffy just sat on a stony ledge far out of reach, arrogantly looking down in condescending feline fashion at the passing crowd of tourists and staffers. But other days she'd saunter by the parking lot and meow at me, and, after a period of weeks, allow me to pet her and pick her up. Fluffy weighed in at a good twenty pounds, as the female staff of the winery would set out food occasionally; and, of course, Fluffy had the place to herself.

She could dine on nature's grand buffet without any feline competition. She slept in the wine caves, drank from the creek, ate birds and mice and gophers and squirrels, and viewed the goings-on at Buena Vista Winery and Bartholomew Park as if it was her own personal reality TV show.

Fluffy had a clipped left ear, indicating, as staff had told me, that at some point someone had captured the poor dear and engaged a veterinarian to humanely render her incapable of procreation. Fluffy was fickle, but she loved getting stroked, and I was the only one who regularly gave her this kind of close, personal attention. You see, she had a bit of a reputation.

Fluffy Birdsall Johnson

She would take only so much stroking before she'd suddenly erupt into a temper tantrum of growls and hisses and claws and teeth. In fact, the winery's new owner, Jean-Charles Boisset, was gunning for her, supposedly because a female guest had bent down to pet Fluffy one day, and she almost took the poor woman's arm off. In my fifty-plus years I've never lived without a cat in my house, so I knew better than to kick her and cuss at her when she got touchy in this manner. This is just a cat's way of setting boundaries. I held onto her and continued to talk to her and stroke her, and she realized that there was at least one human being who was tenacious enough to keep on with the lovin'.

Fluffy and I became quite friendly, and she would come out to greet me almost every day. I often told the staff that one day I should take her home to live with me and my husband and our cat and dogs. When the winery's renovation began, with heavy equipment and dozens of workers tearing up all the infrastructure of the place day after day, staff members came to me and said, "Jean-Charles said we have to get Fluffy off the property. Will you please take her home?" And I did.

So, Fluffy Birdsall Johnson is the last surviving feral member of the historic Johnson Cat Clowder, the founding members of which are depicted in Carl Kahler's 1891 painting "My Wife's Lovers." Their descendents lived ferally for multiple generations on the former Buena Vista Ranch and Bartholomew Park, and the last feral descendent to still live on the ranch is alive and well today, living at my house with my dogs and cat in Petaluma since January 16, 2012.

So, Kaja Veilleux…when do I get the painting?

"My Wife's Lovers" by Carl Kahler, 1891

CONCLUSION

I started out intending to just tell a you few stories and show you a few pictures, but I ended up giving you a pretty comprehensive look at what I've been doing for the past four decades. Thanks for hanging on 'til the end. I hope that you had a few laughs, and I hope that you picked up a few ideas.

I'm hoping that promoting this book will spur renewed interest in my entertainment services, and will create an audience for whatever I decide to write next. One thing is almost certain...the next project will be fiction, to avoid doing so much research. I thought that this book would be easy because I could write it from memory, but I didn't want to rely on my memory for dates and facts, so I did a lot of checking of things on the Internet and in my files. I actually thought that the only research I'd be doing would be confined to looking through my old booking sheets trying to find interesting stories. But what I found was that the stories just flowed...it was all the fact-checking that slowed me up.

If I had these four decades to do over again, I would have done some things differently. Obviously all the stupid mistakes that were the funny parts herein I would avoid, but that's how you gain knowledge and experience, by making mistakes. I would have accepted the offer of the Berman Family syndicate back in the late 1980s when they wanted to "back me," and I would have cancelled the singing telegram in Petaluma that kept me from performing for the executives at Harrah's Lake Tahoe when I was asked. Live and learn.

What I would not have changed was choosing to stay small and unknown in Petaluma instead of moving to Los Angeles and taking a chance on fame and fortune. I've always said that money is great, but fame sucks. In fact, in the last sentence of yet another feature article about my business in the September 6, 1994, edition of the *Petaluma Argus-Courier*, reporter Will Hart quoted me as saying, "I would like to be rich, but not famous." I was always happier being home with one of my spouses than out on the road, alone, in a motel.

The so-called Green Guru, Gene Karpinski, of the League of Conservation Voters, in the documentary about consumer advocate Ralph Nader, *An Unreasonable Man* by Henriette Mantel, says he once asked Nader why Nader had no personal life, and said that Nader "gave me a line I'll never forget: 'Gene, there are two kinds of people in this world, the hard-core and the spouse-corps. You gotta decide which side you're on.'"

Well, as much as I enjoy my work, I am definitely a member of the Spouse Corps. I love being married (all three times), I love Petaluma, and I wouldn't want to live anywhere else.

So, if you liked the book, please tell you friends. Mind you, don't lend it to them...tell them to buy a copy for themselves...it's worth the money. (Hey, I'm trying to make a living here, you know?) And please let me know if I can be of service to you, either as an entertainer, as a tour guide, or as a guest speaker at your next service club meeting or community gathering. I'd be happy to come to speak for your group...just buy a few copies of my book for your members. Call me at 707-762-2596 or e-mail me at: ChristopherLinnell@HireAStar.net.

Thanks so much for your time. Perhaps one day I can buy your book and you can tell me all about your journey in life, too.

THE END

APPENDIX

My mother gave me my first Crisco the Clown business card for my fifteenth birthday. Each year thereafter I would update my promotional materials. Beginning in 1982 when I started offering celebrity impersonations professionally, I had to print a list of celebrities I offered. Each year as the list of celebrities grew, so did the list of programs I offered.

For the first couple of years I printed everything on my huge old Royfax copier. But each year the printed materials became more complex, elaborate, and detailed, and I had to invest in professional printing. To minimize expenses I did all the design, writing, layout, paste-up, and much or most of the photography, artwork, and typesetting myself. The last few annual revisions each cost me about a thousand dollars.

When clients expressed a preference for materials via fax as opposed to postal mail in the early 1990s, I bought a computer and learned desktop publishing, moving the information from my brochures and into dozens of 8.5 x 11" sheets, which I would custom collate for each prospect inquiry, based on the individual services in which I perceived that client to have interest. Eventually my desktop publishing became web publishing, and all of my promotional materials were moved onto my website at www.HireAStar.net.

What follows is an archive of my promotional materials over the decades. Featured first is the single-sided, canary yellow flyer which bore the very first list of my celebrity voices; this flyer became a series of thirteen consecutive brochures between 1982-2001. Following that first sheet are the third, fifth, seventh, eighth, ninth, twelfth, and fourteenth revisions in chronological order. The fourteenth includes rates which I set on November 14, 1997. My rates have not changed since then, and are still current at the time of the publication of the first edition of this book.

STARGRAM is a Celebrity Impersonation Singing Telegram Service featuring the Redwood Empire's largest selection of celebrities, politicians, stars, and personalities, including:

EDITH & ARCHIE BUNKER
W.C. FIELDS and/or MAE WEST...$50 both
INSPECTOR CLOUSEAU
LT. COLUMBO
JIMMY CAGNEY
THE GODFATHER
GEORGE BURNS as GOD
RICHARD BURTON as KING ARTHUR
JOHN WAYNE
JIMMY STEWART
GROUCHO MARX
JOHNNY CASH
JOHNNY CARSON
RODNEY DANGERFIELD
LOUIS ARMSTRONG
CHEECH & CHONG...$50 both
JOHN F. KENNEDY
HARRY TRUMAN
STEVE MARTIN
CLINT EASTWOOD as DIRTY HARRY
SHERRIFF BUFORD T. JUSTICE
SAMMY DAVIS JR.
ADOLF HITLER
COLONEL KLINK
DEAN MARTIN
THE UNKNOWN COMIC
CLARK GABLE

FATHER GUIDO SARDUCCI
RALPH CRAMDON
HUMPREY BOGART
MR. ROGERS
BENNY HILL
TRUMAN CAPOTE   BING CROSBY
HOWARD COSELL   JOAN RIVERS
ELMER FUDD   RAY JOHNSON

MASKED IMPERSONATIONS

GEORGE WASHINGTON
RONALD REAGAN
RICHARD NIXON
JIMMY CARTER
GERALD FORD
THE AYATOLLAH KHOMENI
FIDEL CASTRO
YASSIR ARAFAT
IDI AMIN
DARTH VADER
LAUREL & HARDY...$50 both
POPEYE
BIG BIRD...$60 (includes costume rental)

OTHERS

CAPTAIN MUDD
EILEEN BRENNAN look-a-like...$45
CLASSICAL TELEGRAMS by Mary Tosler...$40

ALL FEES $30, except as marked
INCLUDES copies of the original lyrics
   and cartoon of celebrity featured
STUDIO recorded tape of telegram and
   background of celebrity...$10 extra
PAYMENT on performance in check or cash
   (POPICOC)

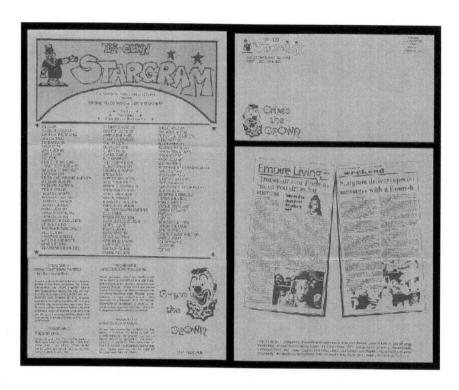

Christopher & Co.

WHO IS CHRISTOPHER?

This Is Christopher!

The Voices

CELEBRITY IMPERSONATIONS. . .

"LIFE OF THE PARTY"™ PACKAGE. . .

CHRISTOPHER & CO. LIVE

MASTER OF CEREMONIES. . .

SINGING TELEGRAMS. . .

THE CELEBRITY IMPERSONATION GAME SHOW. . .

CHRISTOPHER & CO. For KIDS. . .

CELEBRITY SQUARES for KIDS

The Fine Print

Who is CHRISTOPHER?

TALL TEX SHORT MEX SHOOT OUT

STILT WALKING, ETC. . .

Christopher & Co.

Christopher & Co.
celebrity impersonations

160 CELEBRITY VOICES
70 FULLY-COSTUMED
IMPERSONATIONS

"UH, who is this CHRISTOPHER?"

This is CHRISTOPHER!

Christopher Linnell is a professional entertainer who specializes in the celebrity impersonations he has developed over the course of 25 years, currently including over 150 celebrity voices, and more than 75 fully-costumed impersonations. He launched his career at age 13, began working in radio at age 15, and performed in his first television commercial at age 19. Since 1993 Christopher has performed in hundreds of radio and television commercials locally, regionally and nationally, and has performed live improv-comedy in venues throughout 14 of the United States and the island territory of Guam.

Parties

STARGRAM

'Life of the Party' ... Package

Stiltwalking

Stage Acts

CHRISTOPHER & CO.
LIVE!

The PRESS Conference

Walkaround

Game Shows

Celebrity Squares

CELEBRITY CLUE

Audio & Video

STEALS on TAPE

Christopher's Celebrity Impersonations

Rates for your
in the city of: San Francisco

Celebrity Impersonations: $ 240

STARGRAM Singing Telegram: $ 180

Christopher & Co. LIVE: $ 210

"Life of the Party"™ Package: $ 200

Christopher's BALLADGRAM: $ 270

The PRESS Conference: $ 270

CELEBRITY SQUARES™: $ 280

CELEBRITY CLUE™: $ 290

"You Bet Your Life"™: $ 290

Stiltwalking/Walkaround/Characters:
$ 360 ... for up to 2 hours
$ 75 ... /hour thereafter

Day-Rate: $ 1380 /day or $ 1080 /day

Consultation/Travel/Wait time: $ 60 /hour

Christopher Linnell
Christopher & Co. Celebrity Impersonations

PO Box 2127
Petaluma CA 94953-2127

707 763 3436

Christopher.Linnell@Hotmail.net
www.BreAST.net

These are the caricatures I drew back in the early 1980s of the celebrities and characterizations that I offered in my STARGRAM^{SM} Singing Telegram program. These dressed-up the lyric sheets that I handed to my honorees and clients, as well as my early brochures. As computers improved and I obtained Internet access, I began using actual pictures of the celebrities.

Left to right, top to bottom: Rodney Dangerfield, W.C. Fields, Inspector Clouseau, Darth Vader (in his underwear; Luke Skywalker stole his suit), Humphrey Bogart, Ronald Reagan, Johnny Cash, The Unknown Comic, W.C. Fields, Steve Martin, Cheech Marin, Rodney Dangerfield, Groucho Marx, Mr. Rogers, Yosemite Sam, Edith Bunker, James Cagney, Ronald Reagan, Sheriff Buford T. Justice, Johnny Carson's Floyd R. Turbo--American, Richard M. Nixon, Jack Benny, Inspector Clouseau, The Godfather, Frank Sinatra, Crisco the Clown, Carl Sagan, and, of course, the most important and most frequent celebrity I impersonated, Lt. Columbo.

On the following pages is a sampling of pictures of myself as different celebrities, in some cases accompanied by pictures of the celebrities themselves.

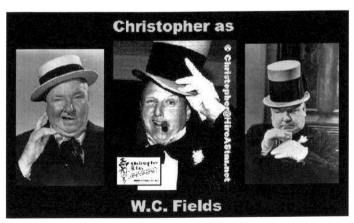

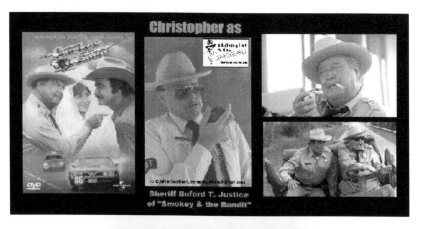

Christopher as
Sheriff Buford T. Justice
of "Smokey & the Bandit"

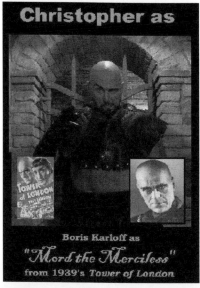

Christopher as

Boris Karloff as
"Mord the Merciless"
from 1939's Tower of London

Christopher as

Laurel & Hardy

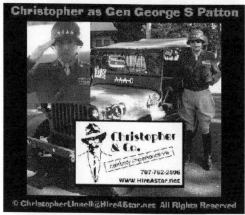

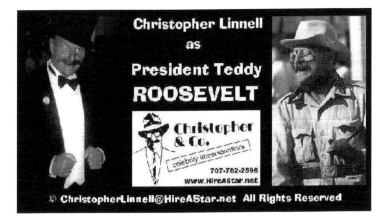

Finally is my current list of celebrity voices available on request for Christopher & Co. LIVE, the Life of the Party^{SM} Package, and Celebrity Squares^{SM} Game Show programs. Below is my advertising, on the back of the list, which was an excellent marketing tool, obviously, as everyone in the audience got a copy to take home. On the next page is the list itself. This is the most recent edition in a series of lists, updated over the decades every time a few new voices were added. Note that these are not *all* of my celebrity voices (omitted are many of the singers that are not offered for the above acts), just the celebrities that are most appropriate for my request acts.

MASON ADAMS
JIM BACKUS
BARNEY THE DINOSAUR
BENNY & ROCHESTER
BERGEN & McCARTHY
SGT. BILKO & COL. HALL
HUMPHREY BOGART
MARLON BRANDO
WILLIAM F. BUCKLEY
AL BUNDY
ARCHIE & EDITH BUNKER
GEORGE BURNS
RAYMOND BURR
RICHARD BURTON
PRES. GEORGE BUSH
JAMES CAGNEY
TRUMAN CAPOTE
JOHNNY CARSON
CHEECH & CHONG
THE CHURCH LADY
WINSTON CHURCHILL
ANDREW DICE CLAY
PRES. BILL CLINTON
INSPECTOR CLOUSEAU
LT. COLUMBO
HANS CONREID
BILL COSBY
HOWARD COSELL
WALTER CRONKITE
BING CROSBY
SCATMAN CROTHERS
RODNEY DANGERFIELD
SENATOR BOB DOLE
SAM DONALDSON
CLINT EASTWOOD
CHRIS FARLEY
W.C. FIELDS
AL FRANKEN
STAN FREEBURG
PAUL FREES
SGT. JOE FRIDAY
ELMER FUDD
ALAN FUNT
CLARK GABLE
GOOFY
RUTH GORDON
GILBERT GOTTFRIED
REV. BILLY GRAHAM

SYDNEY GREENSTREET
FORREST GUMP
BUDDY HACKETT
PAUL HARVEY
GABBY HAYES
KATHARINE HEPBURN
PEE WEE HERMAN
HOGAN'S HEROES
(Klink, Burkhalter,
Hawkschtedder, Schultz)
GEOFFREY HOLDER
THE HONEYMOONERS
(Ralph & Ed)
JOUN HOUSEMAN
JOHN HOUSTON
JULIO INGLESIAS
REV. JESSE JACKSON
MS. GERALDINE JONES
JAMES EARL JONES
SHERIFF B. T. JUSTICE

BORIS KARLOFF
CASEY KASEM
THE KENNEDYS
KERMIT THE FROG
CAPT. JAMES T. KIRK
DR. HENRY KISSINGER
BURT LANCASTER
LAUREL & HARDY
FLOYD LAWSON
ROBIN LEACH
SHELDON LEONARD
AL LEWIS
RUSH LIMBAUGH
PETER LORRE
BELA LUGOSI
GROUCHO MARX
JACKIE MASON
JAMES MASON
BILL MOEN
BILL MOYERS

FRANK NELSON
JACK NICHOLSON
PRES. RICHARD NIXON
GARY OWENS
ANDROGYNOUS PAT
GENERAL PATTON
H. ROSS PEROT
REGIS PHILBIN
EARL PITTS
POPEYE
WILLIAM POWELL
THE RAINMAN
THURL RAVENSCROFT
PRES. RONALD REAGAN
HARRY REASONER
RICKY RICARDO
JOAN RIVERS
EDWARD G. ROBINSON
ROCKY & BULLWINKLE
ANDY ROONEY
PRES. F. D. ROOSEVELT
CARL SAGAN
ARNOLD SCHWRZNGGR
LONG JON SILVER
RICHARD SIMMONS
SNAGGLE PUSS
SYLVESTER STALLONE
BEN STEIN
JACKIE STEWART
JIMMY STEWART
ED SULLIVAN
REV. JIMMY SWAGGART
SYLVESTER THE CAT
TERRRY THOMAS
TONTO
CHRISTOPHER WALKEN
JOHN WAYNE
DR. RUTH WESTHEIMER
JESSE WHITE
ROBIN WILLIAMS
WALTER WINCHELL
THE WIZARD OF OZ
(Scarecrow, TinMan,
Lion, Wizard)
WOLFMAN JACK
ED WYNN
MARTIN YAN
GEORGE ZIMMER

Made in the USA
San Bernardino, CA
10 August 2014